THE GHOSTS WE KNOW

SEAN KAREMAKER

D0885600

© Sean Karemaker, 2016

Library and Archives Canada Cataloguing in Publication

Karemaker, Sean, 1983-, author, illustrator
      The ghosts We Know/ Sean Karemaker.

ISBN 978-1-77262-003-0 (paperback)

    1. Graphic novels. 1. Title

PN6733.K37G46 2016   741.5'971 C2016-900437-6

First Edition
Printed in Gatineau, Quebec by Gauvin

Conundrum Press
Wolfville, Nova Scotia, Canada
www.conundrumpress.com

Conundrum Press acknowledges the financial support of the Canada
Council for the Arts and the government of Canada through the Canada
Book Fund toward its publishing activities.

Canada Council   Conseil des Arts
for the Arts   du Canada

THE GHOSTS WE KNOW

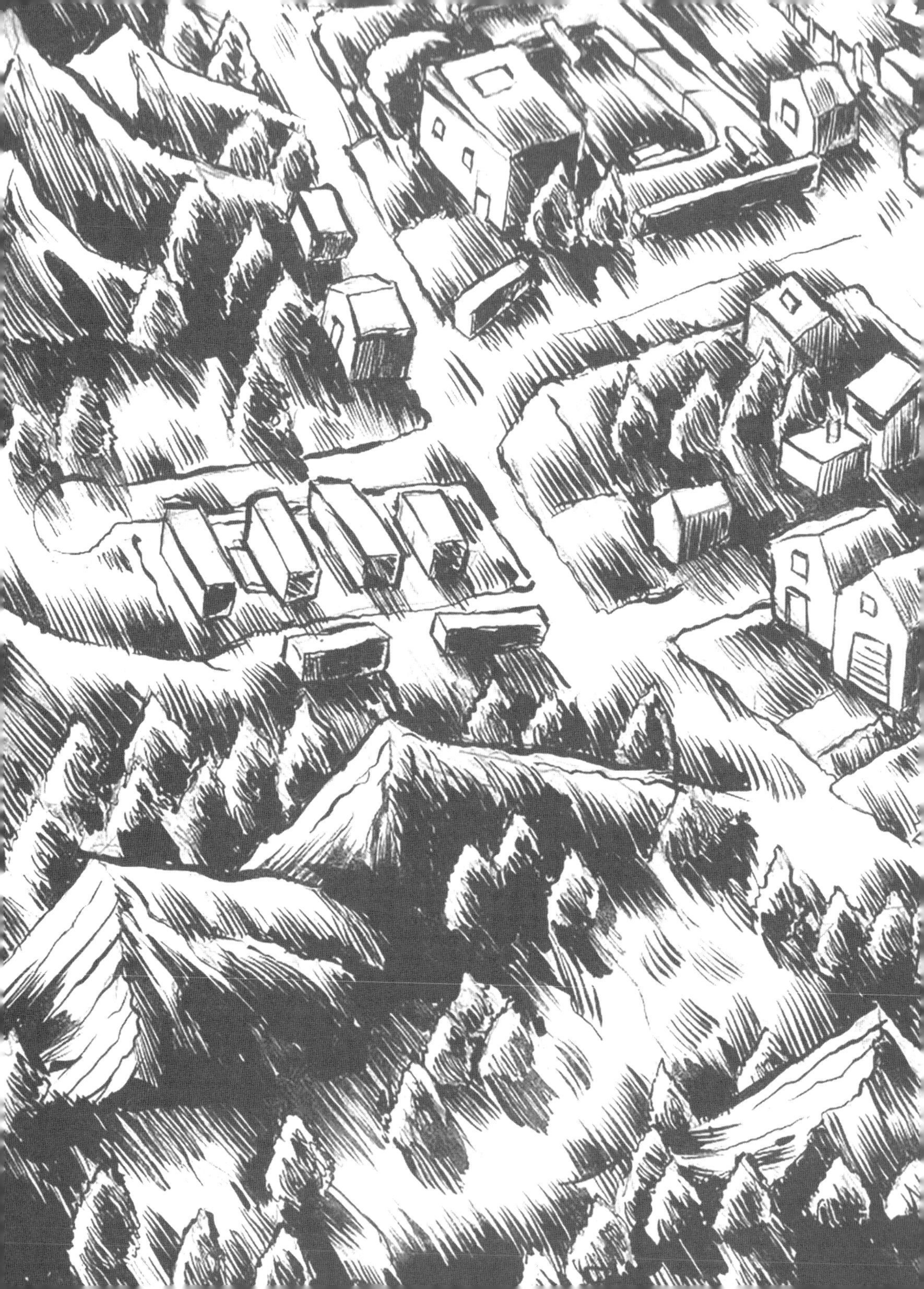

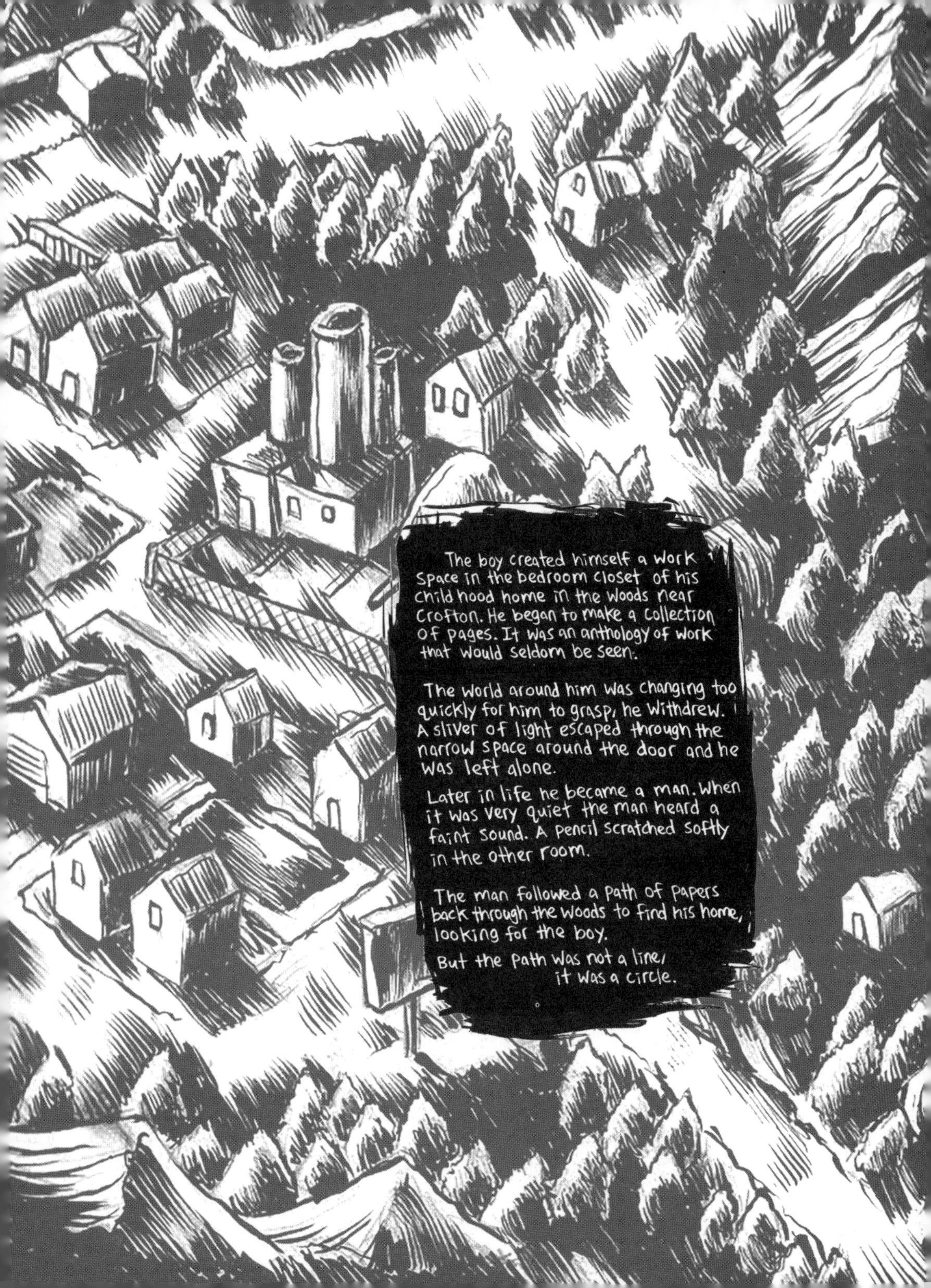
The boy created himself a work space in the bedroom closet of his childhood home in the woods near Crofton. He began to make a collection of pages. It was an anthology of work that would seldom be seen.
The world around him was changing too quickly for him to grasp, he withdrew. A sliver of light escaped through the narrow space around the door and he was left alone.
Later in life he became a man. When it was very quiet the man heard a faint sound. A pencil scratched softly in the other room.
The man followed a path of papers back through the woods to find his home, looking for the boy.
But the path was not a line,
it was a circle.

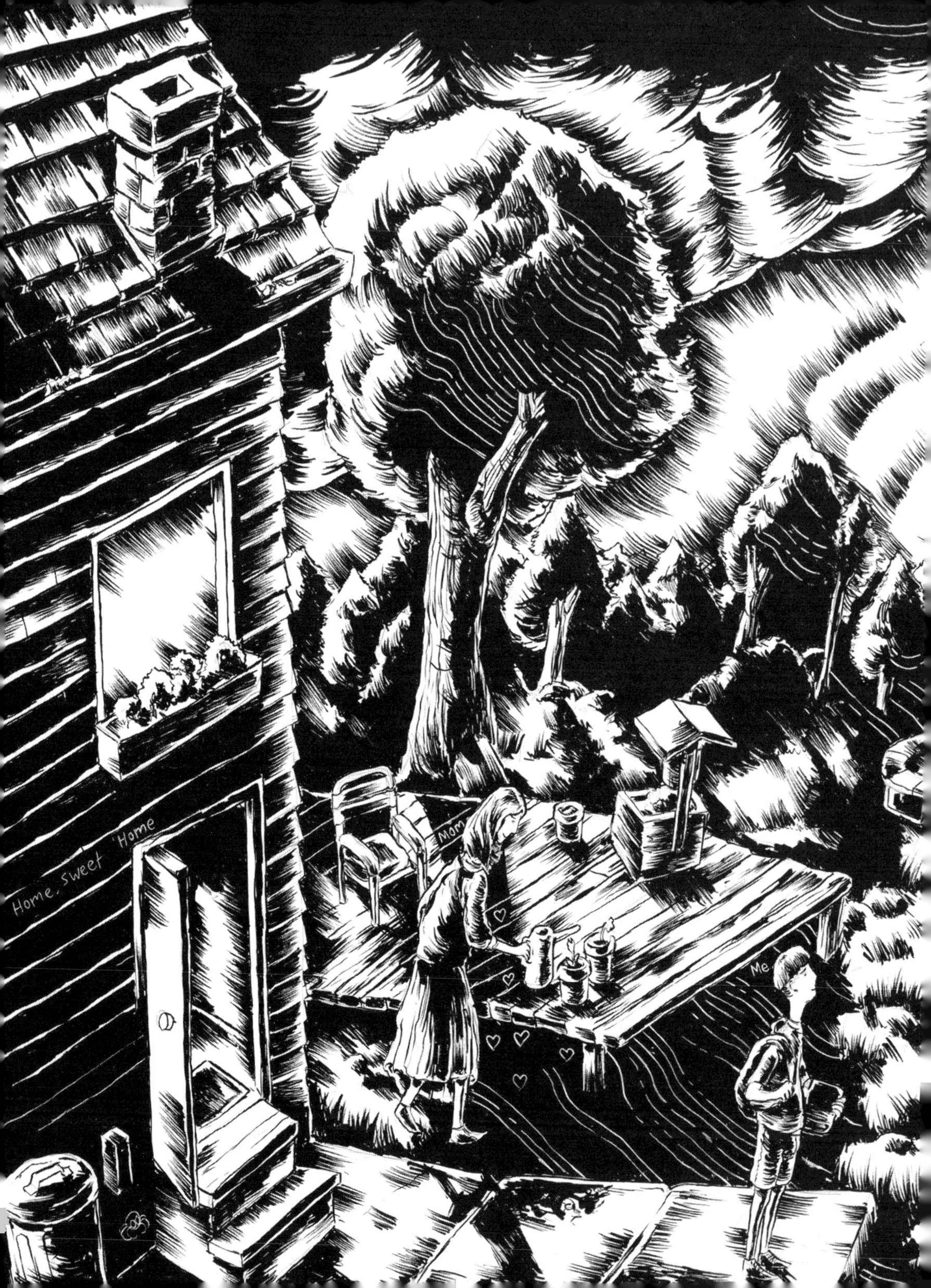
Home, sweet Home
Mom
Me

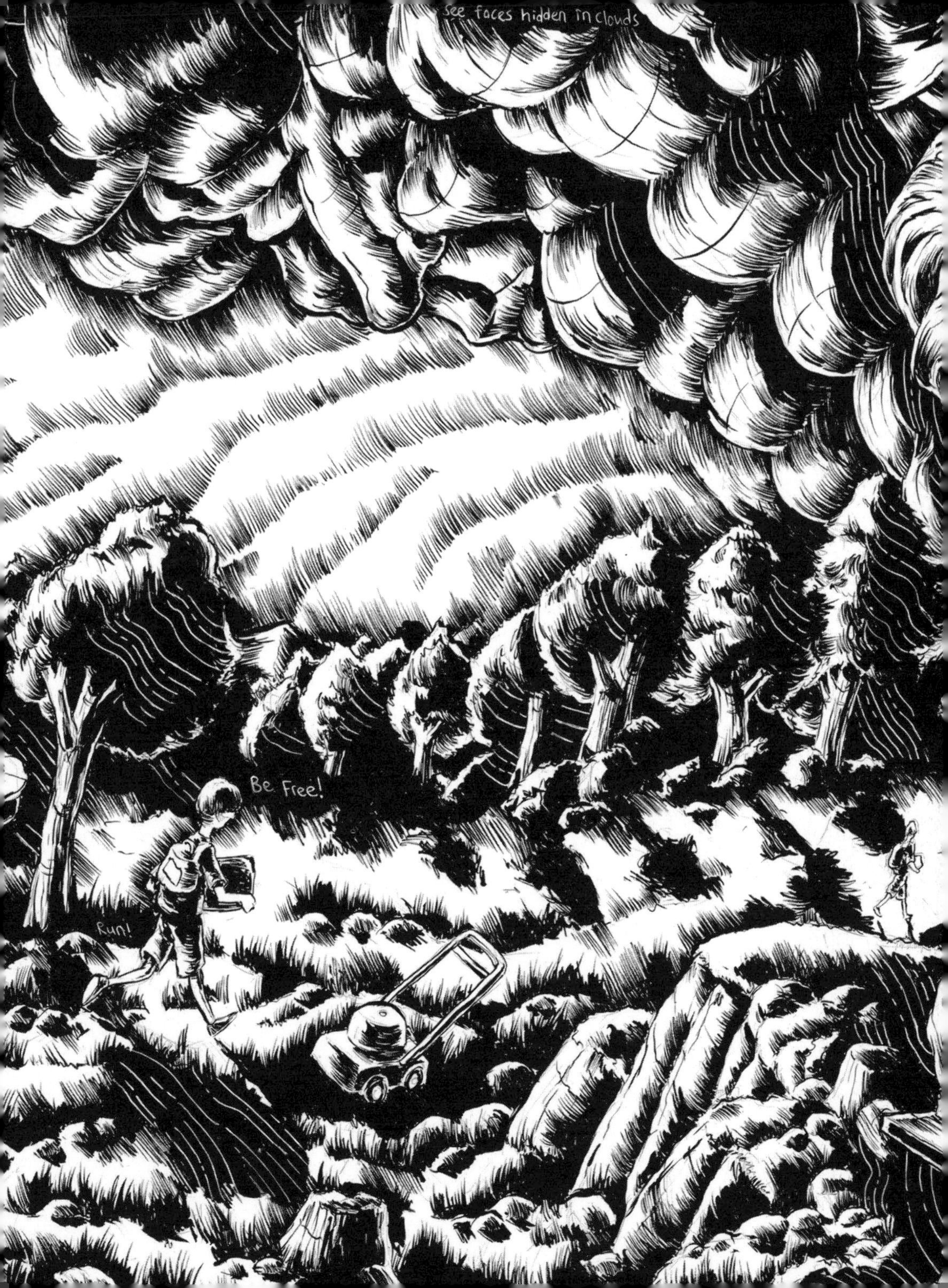
see faces hidden in clouds
Be Free!
Run!

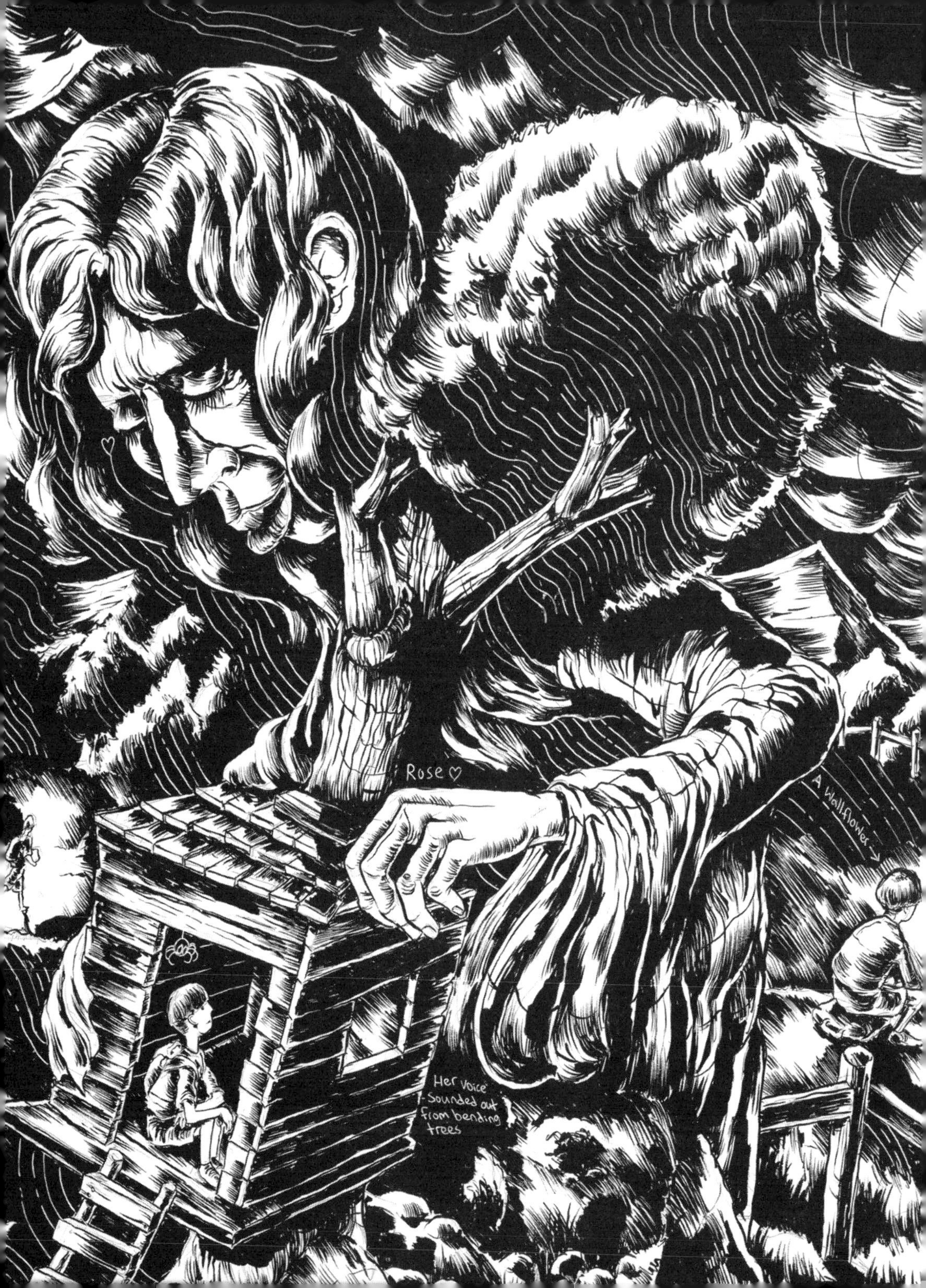
Rose ♡
A Wallflower →
Her voice sounded out from bending trees

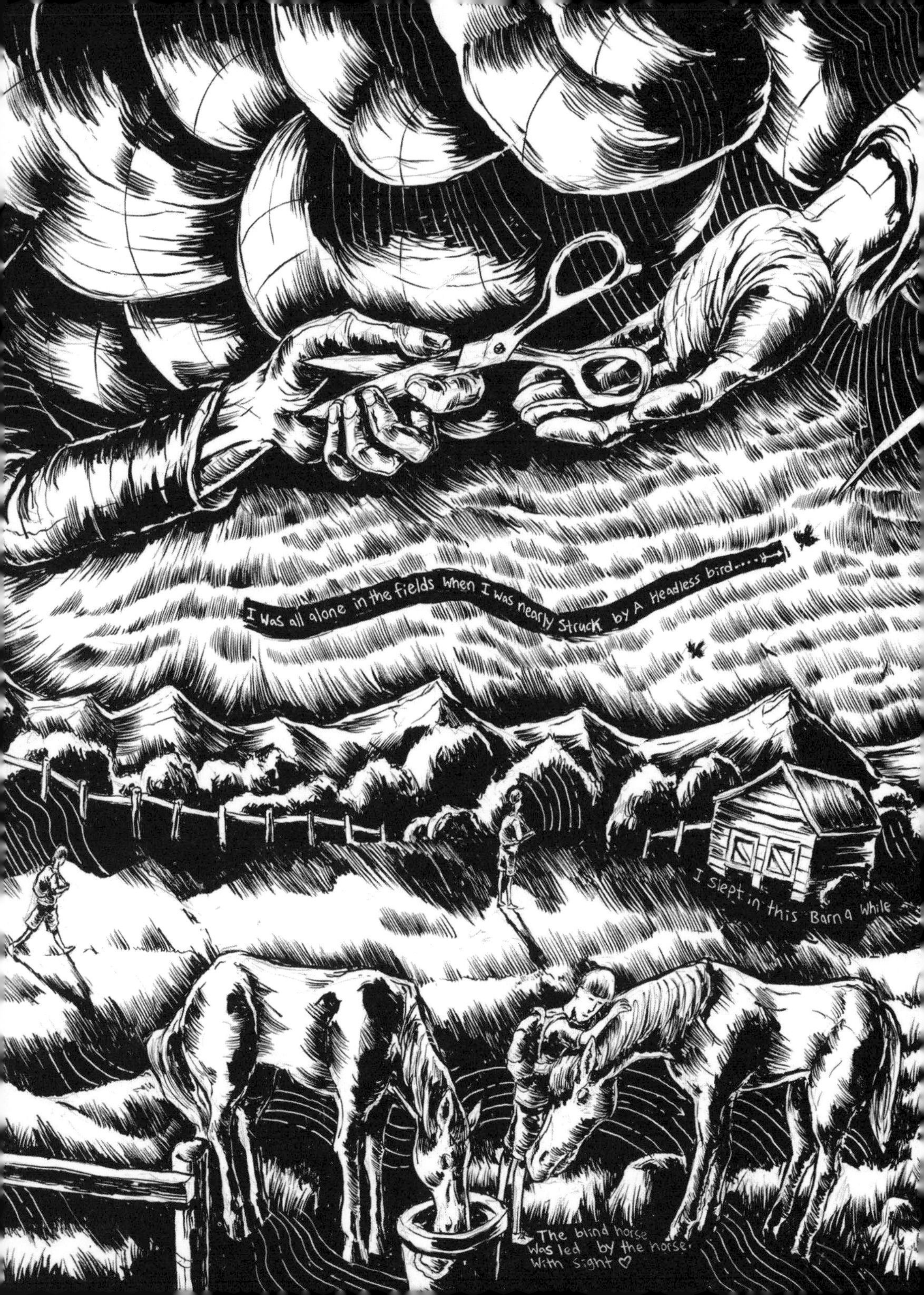
I was all alone in the fields when I was nearly struck by A Headless bird
I slept in this Barn a while
The blind horse
Was led by the horse
With sight ♡

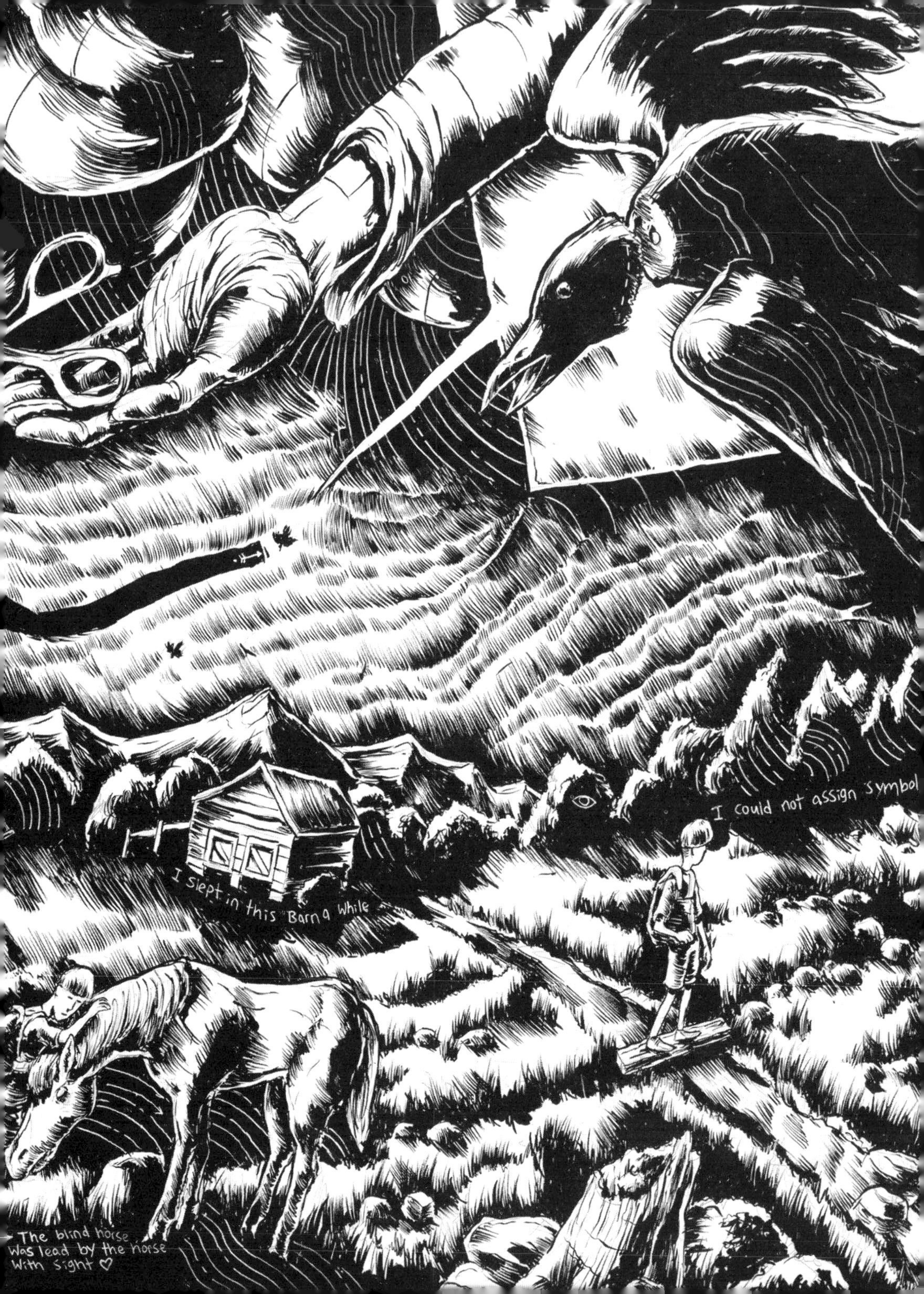
I could not assign Symbol
I slept in this Barn a While
The blind horse
Was lead by the horse
With Sight ♡

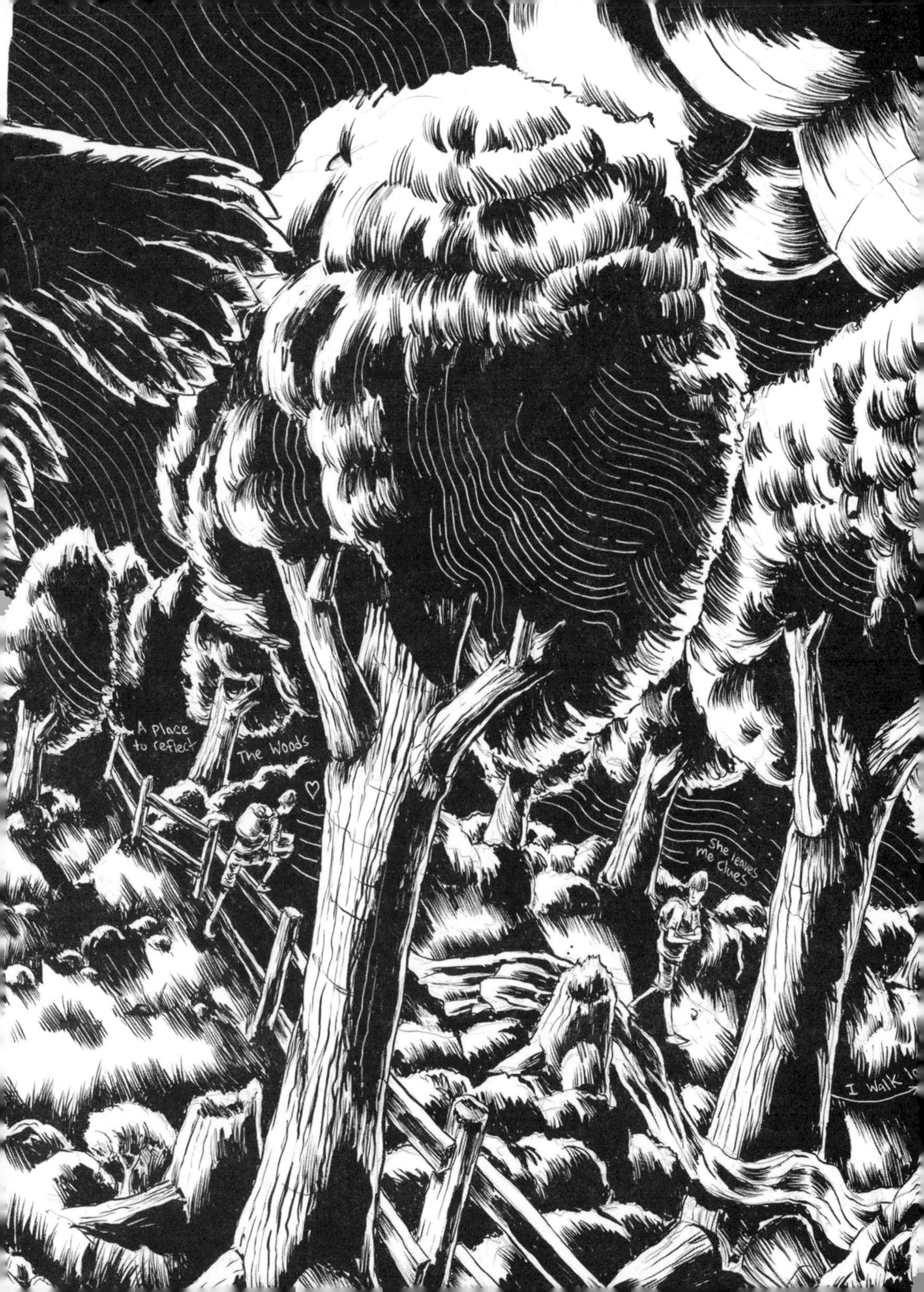
A place to reflect
The Woods
She leaves me clues
I walk

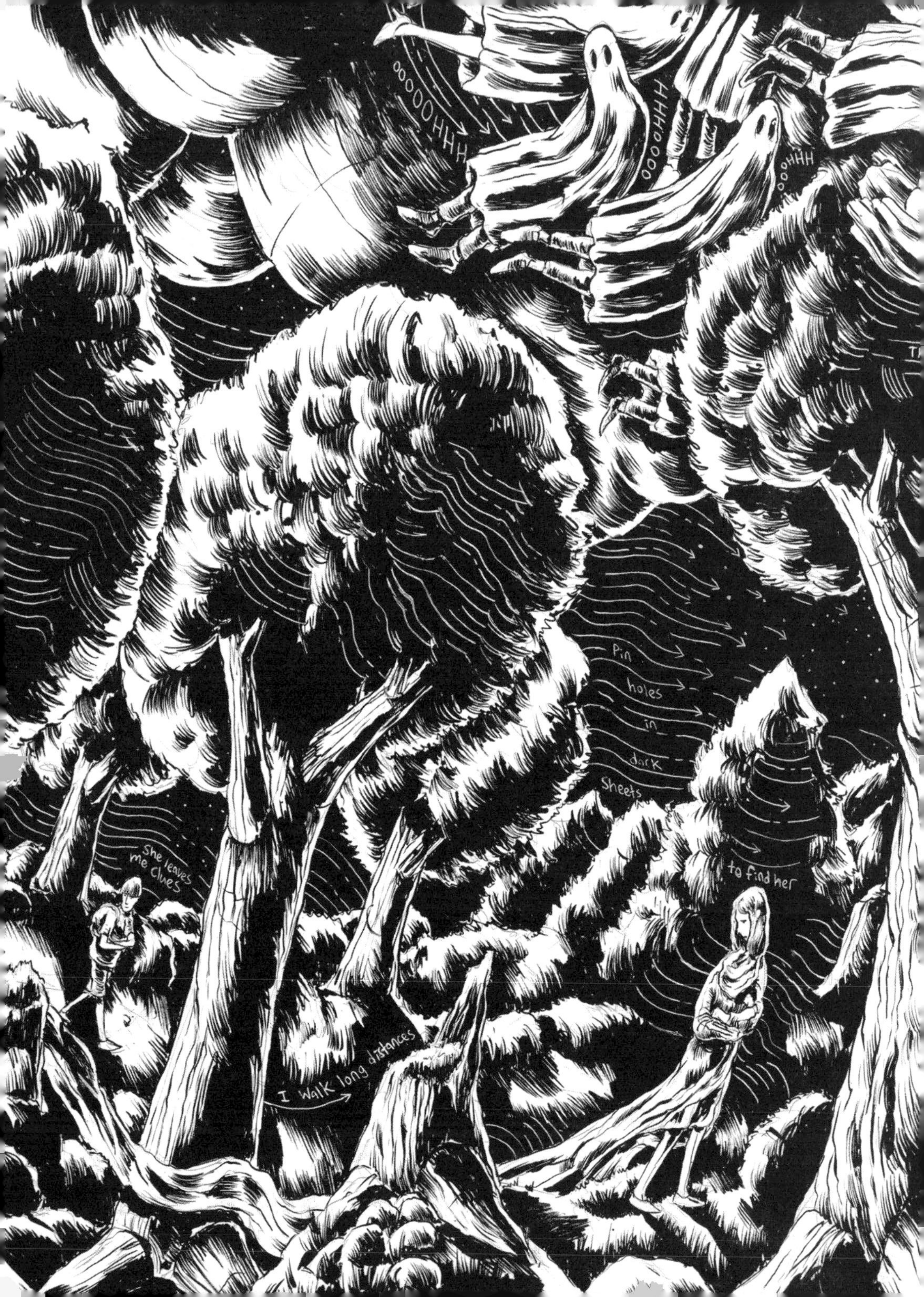

ooooOOOOHHHH
ooooOOHHHH
oooHHH
Pin holes in dark sheets
She leaves me clues
to find her
I walk long distances

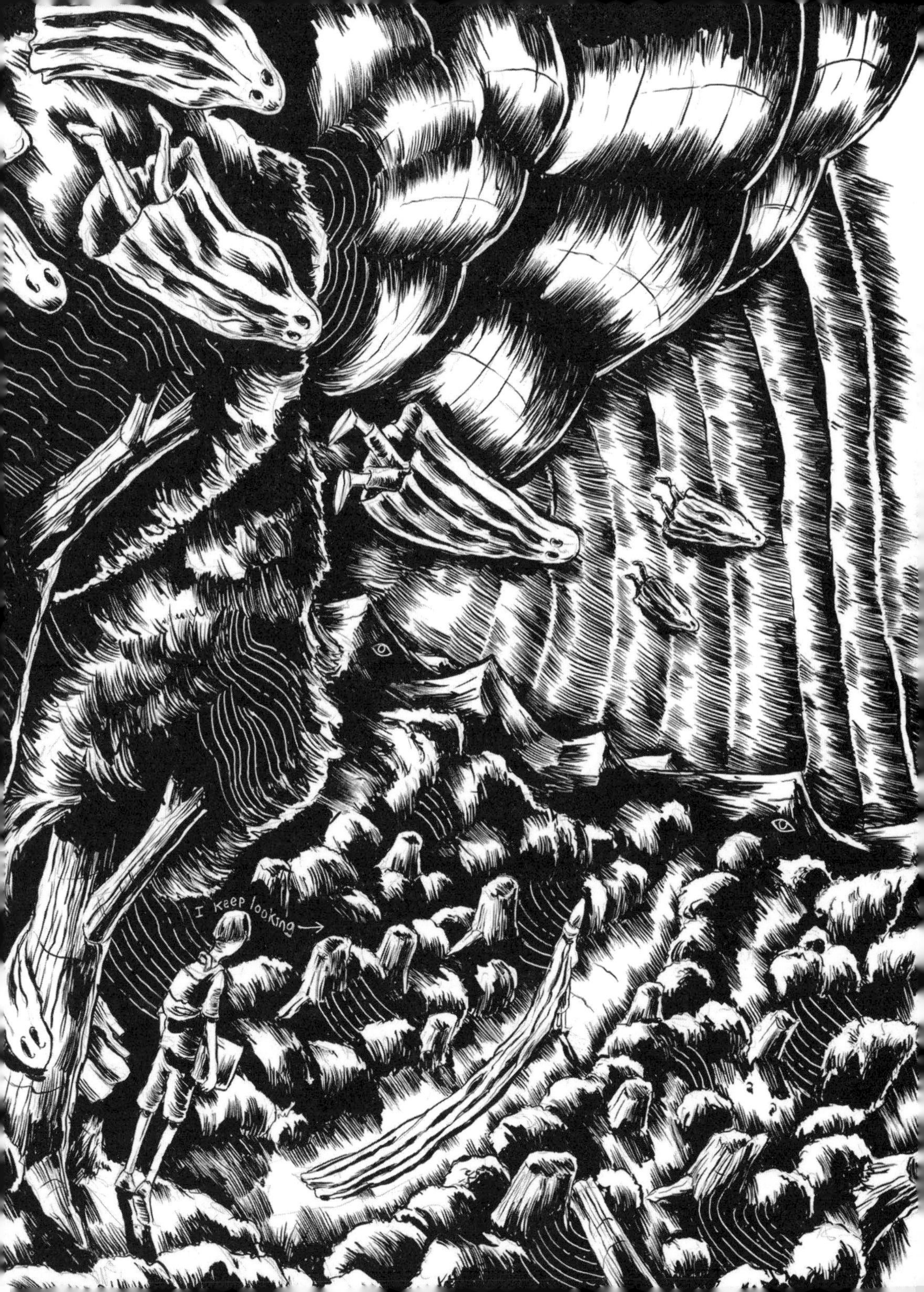
I keep looking →

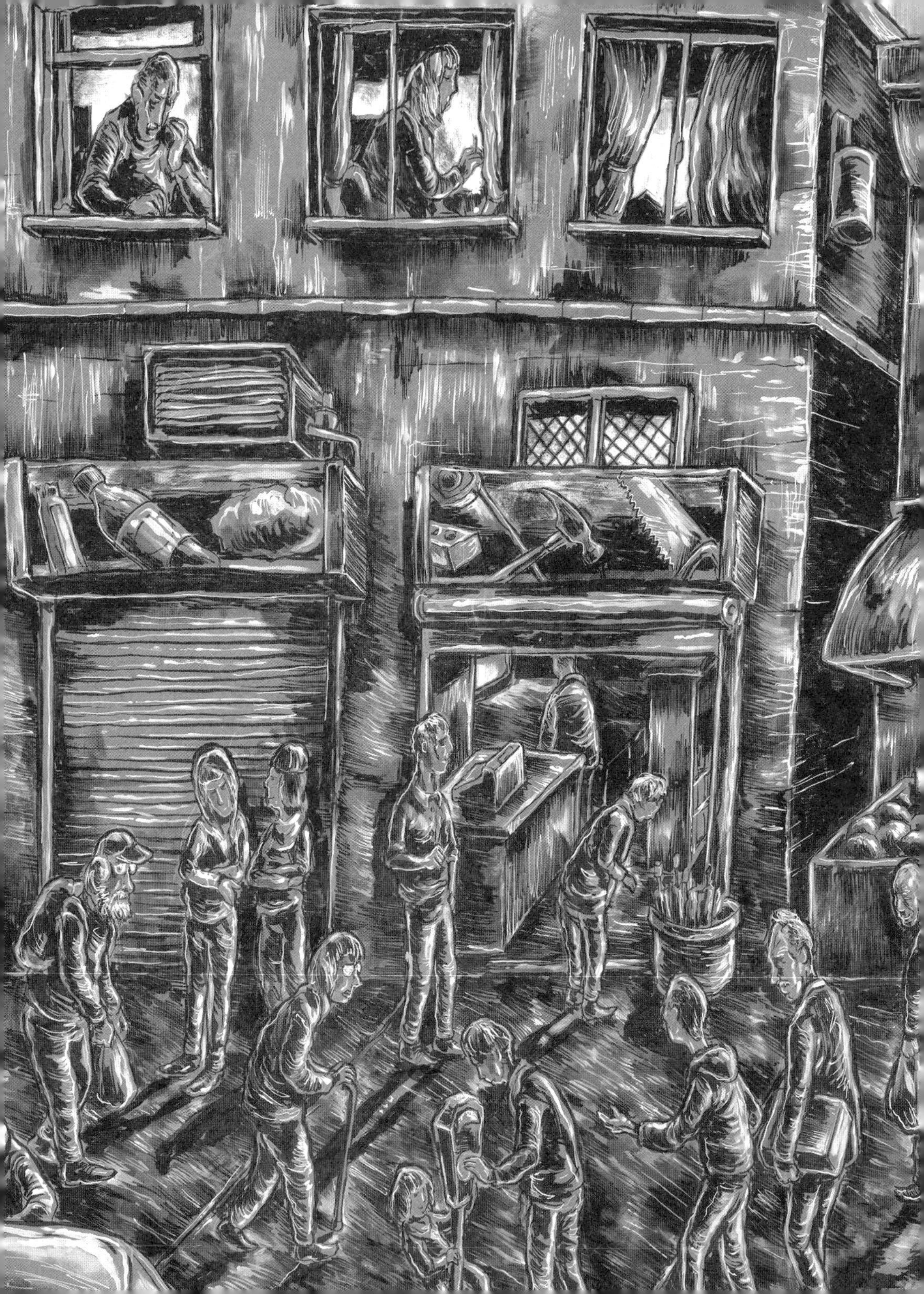

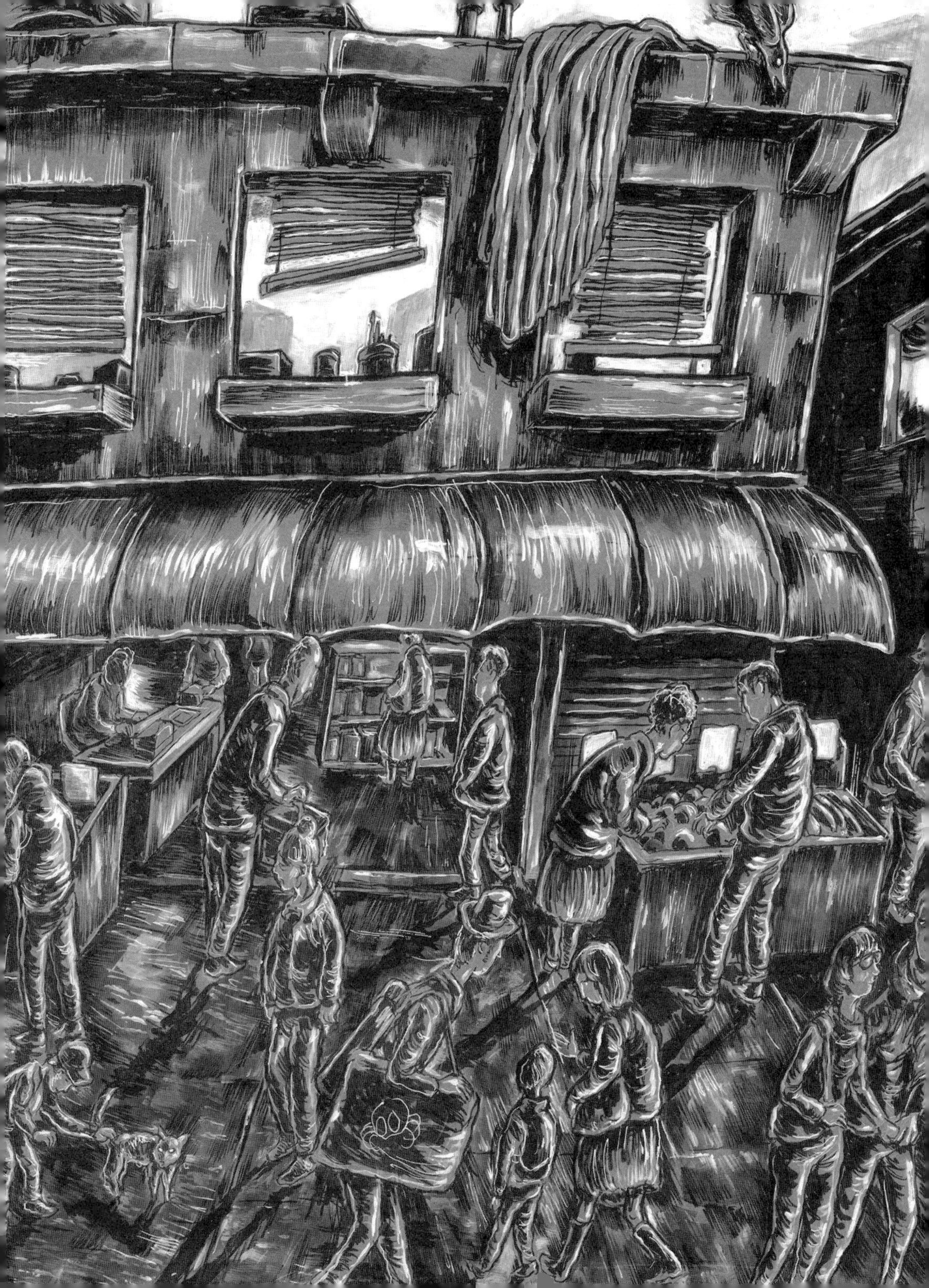

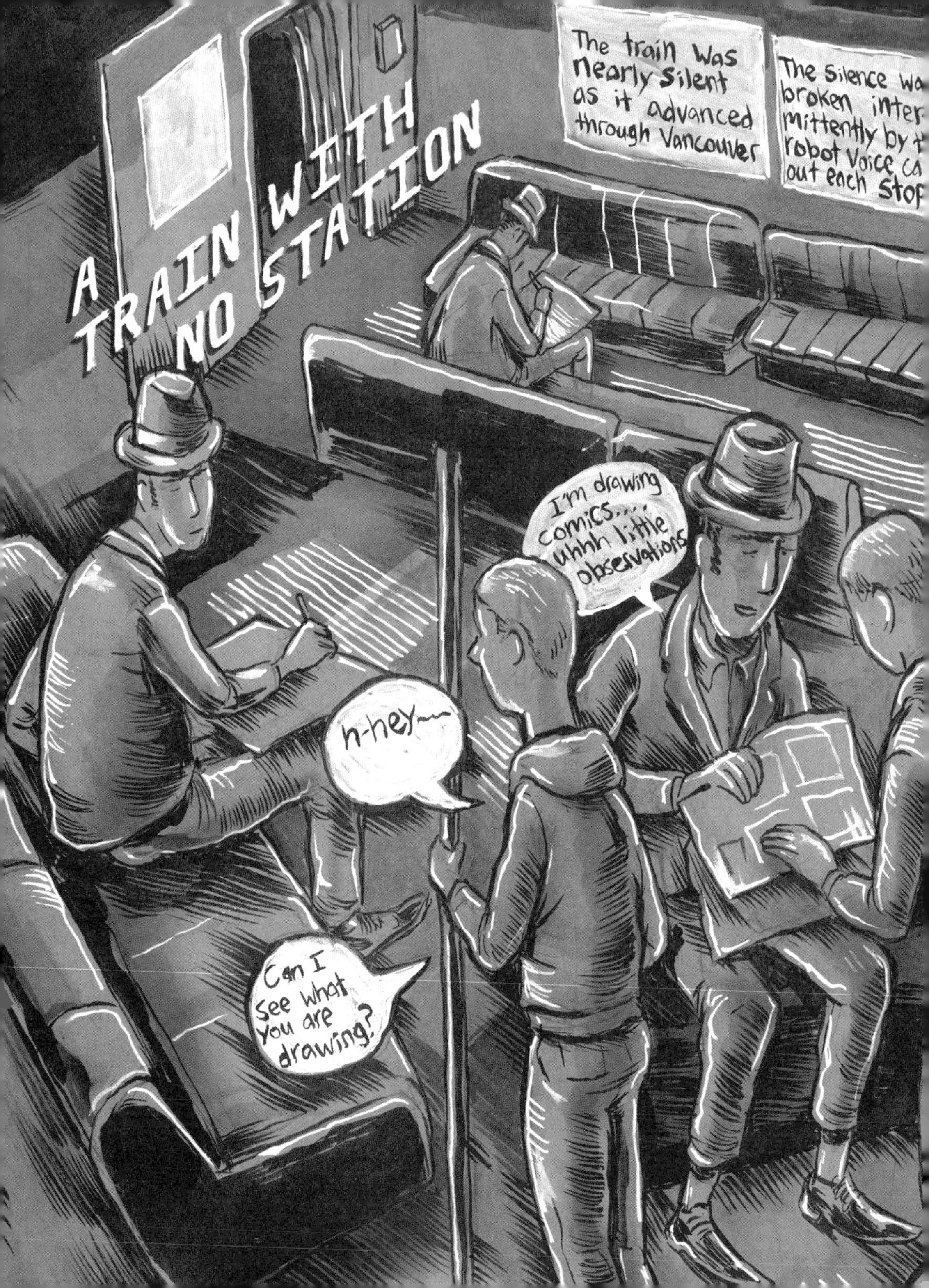
A TRAIN WITH NO STATION
The train was nearly silent as it advanced through Vancouver
The silence wa broken inter-mittently by t robot voice ca out each stop
h-hey—
Can I see what you are drawing?
I'm drawing comics.... uhhh little observations

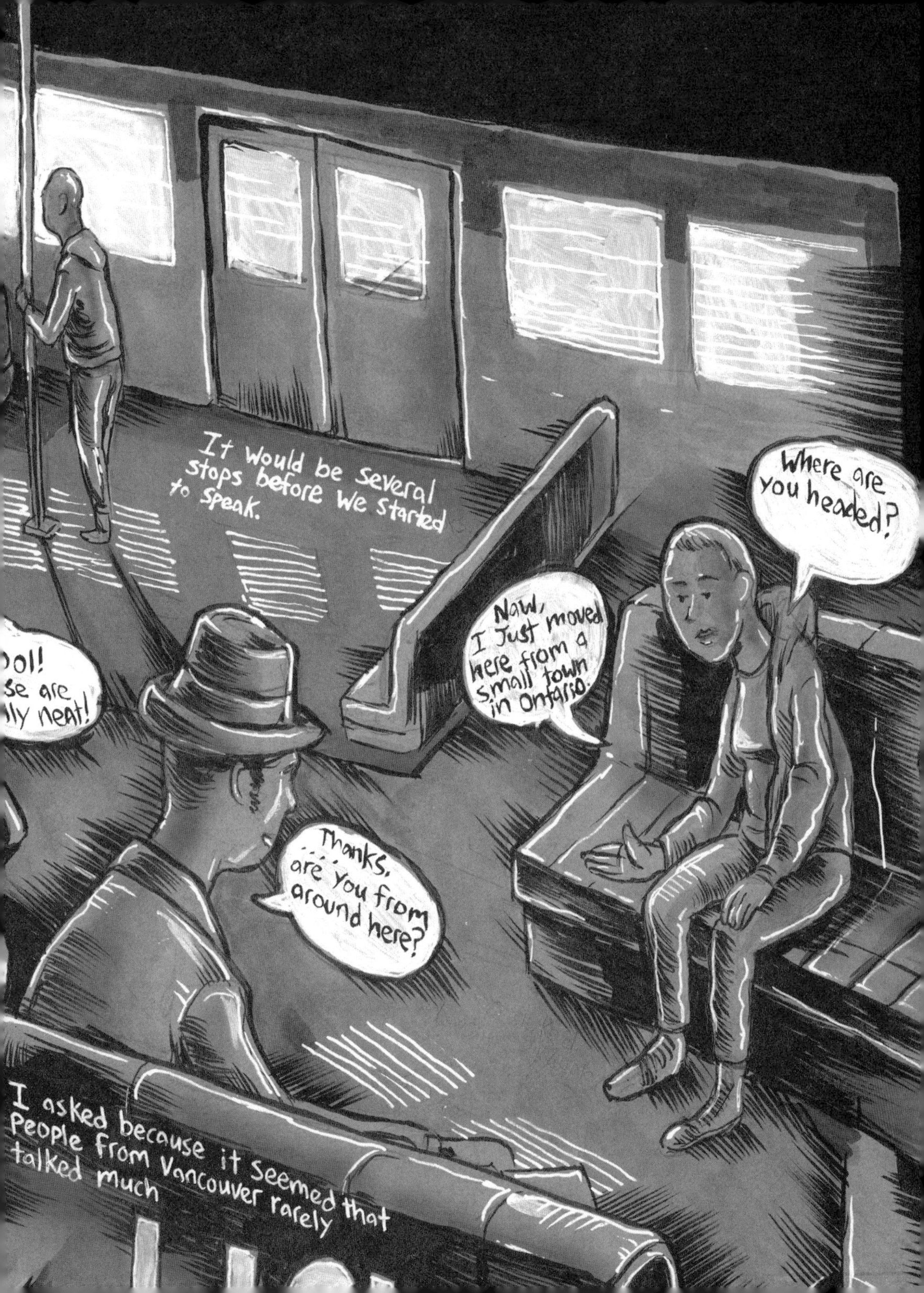

It would be several stops before we started to speak.
ool! se are lly neat!
Thanks, ... are you from around here?
Naw, I Just moved here from a small town in Ontario.
Where are you headed?
I asked because it seemed that people from Vancouver rarely talked much

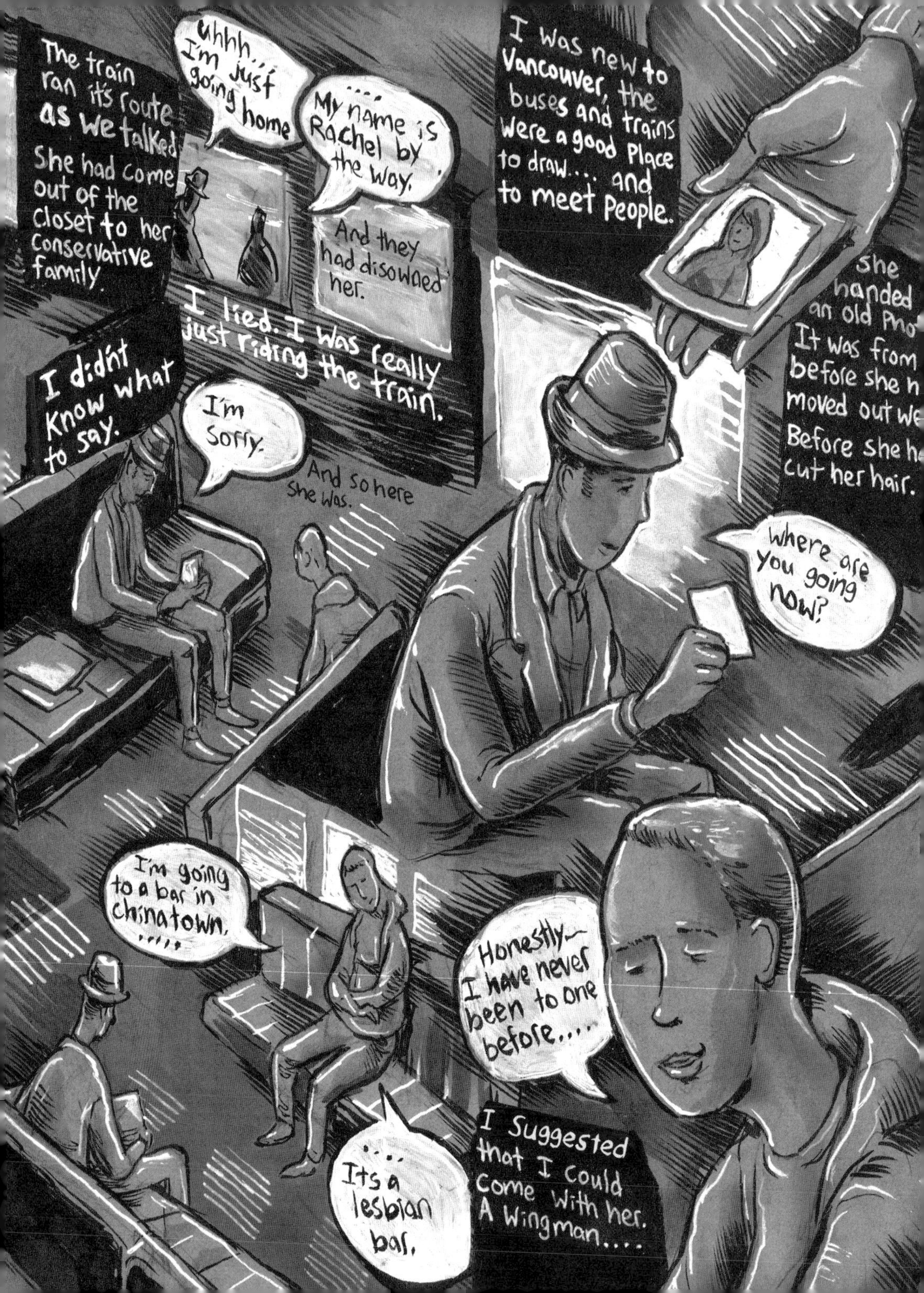
The train ran it's route as we talked.
Uhhh... I'm just going home
...
My name is Rachel by the way.
She had come out of the closet to her conservative family.
And they had disowned her.
I lied. I was really just riding the train.
I didn't know what to say.
I'm Sorry.
And so here she was.
I was new to Vancouver, the buses and trains were a good Place to draw.... and to meet People.
She handed an old Pho
It was from before she h
moved out we
Before she h
cut her hair.
Where are you going now?
I'm going to a bar in chinatown.
.....
Honestly— I have never been to one before....
.....
It's a lesbian bar.
I Suggested that I could come with her. A Wingman....

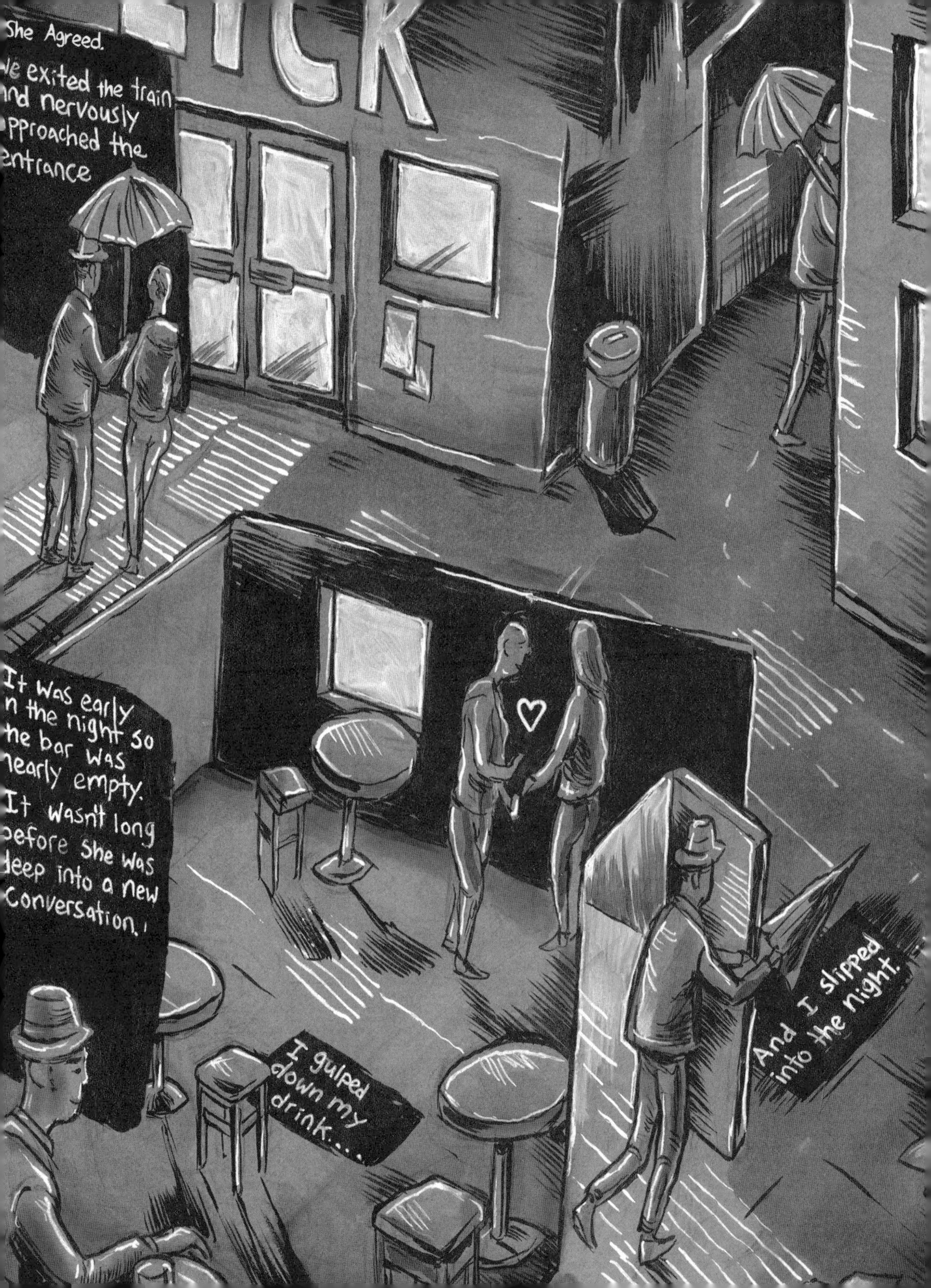

ICK
She Agreed.
e exited the train
nd nervously
pproached the
ntrance
It was early
n the night so
he bar was
nearly empty.
It wasn't long
efore she was
eep into a new
conversation.
I gulped down my drink....
And I slipped into the night.

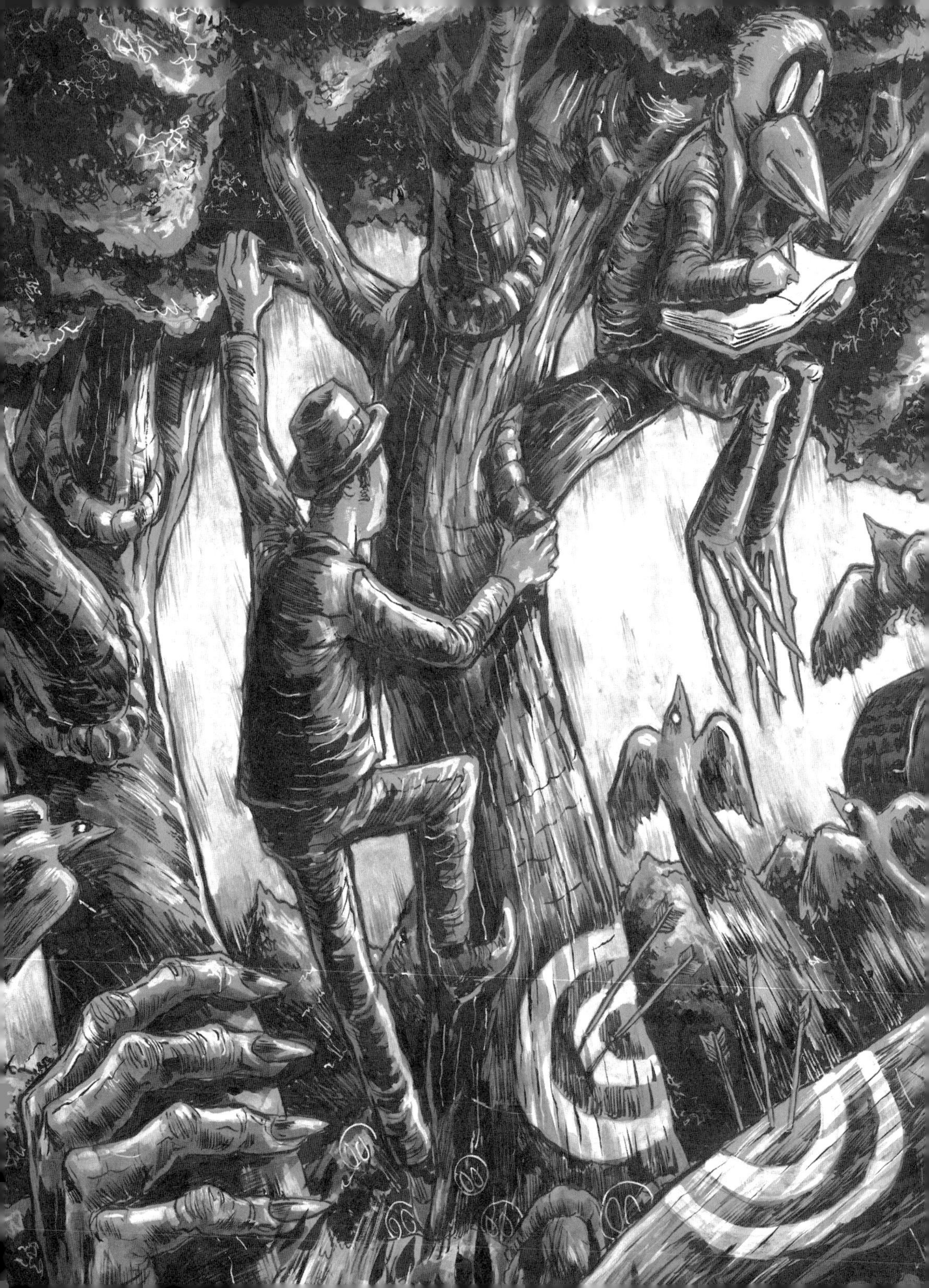

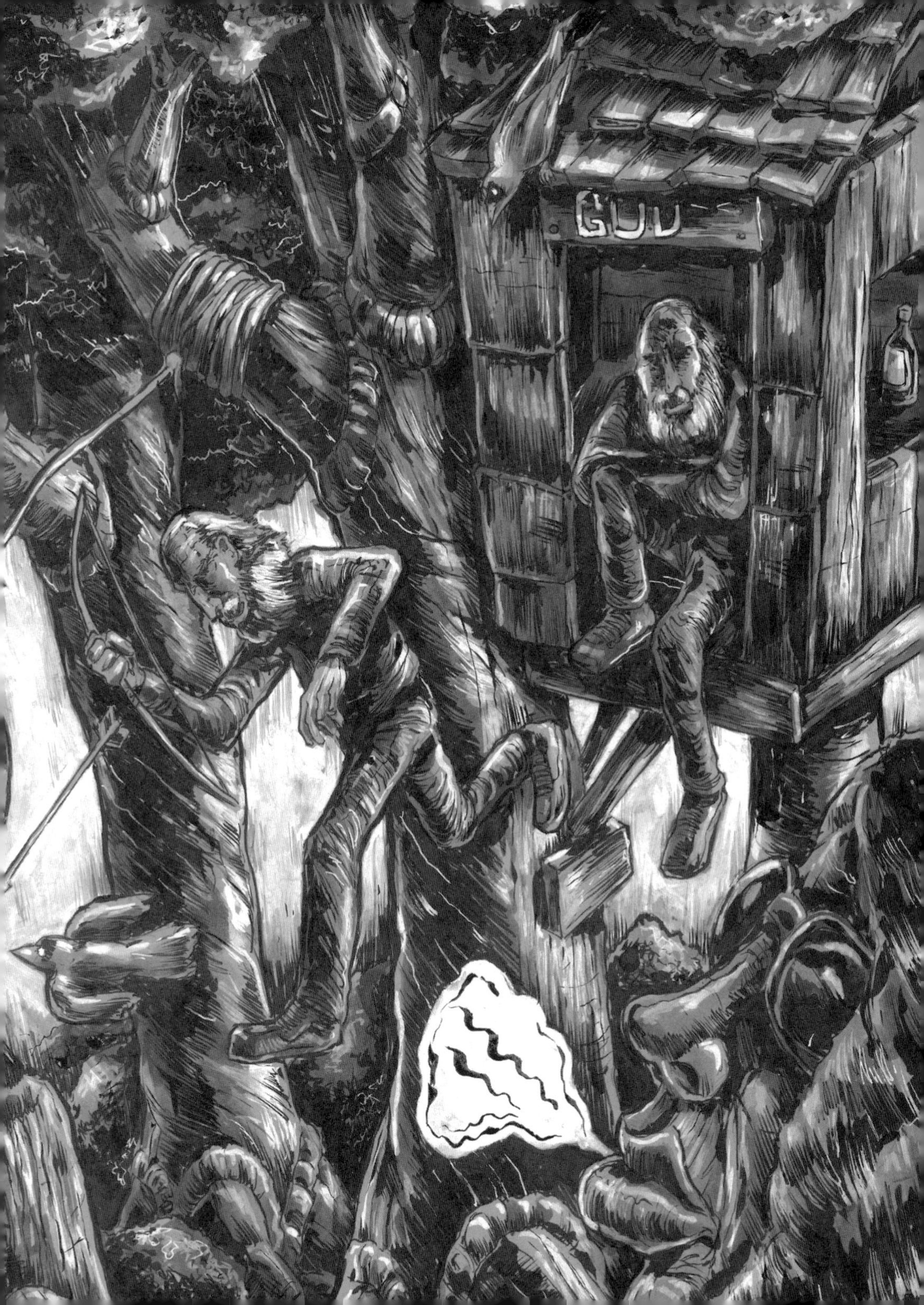
GUD

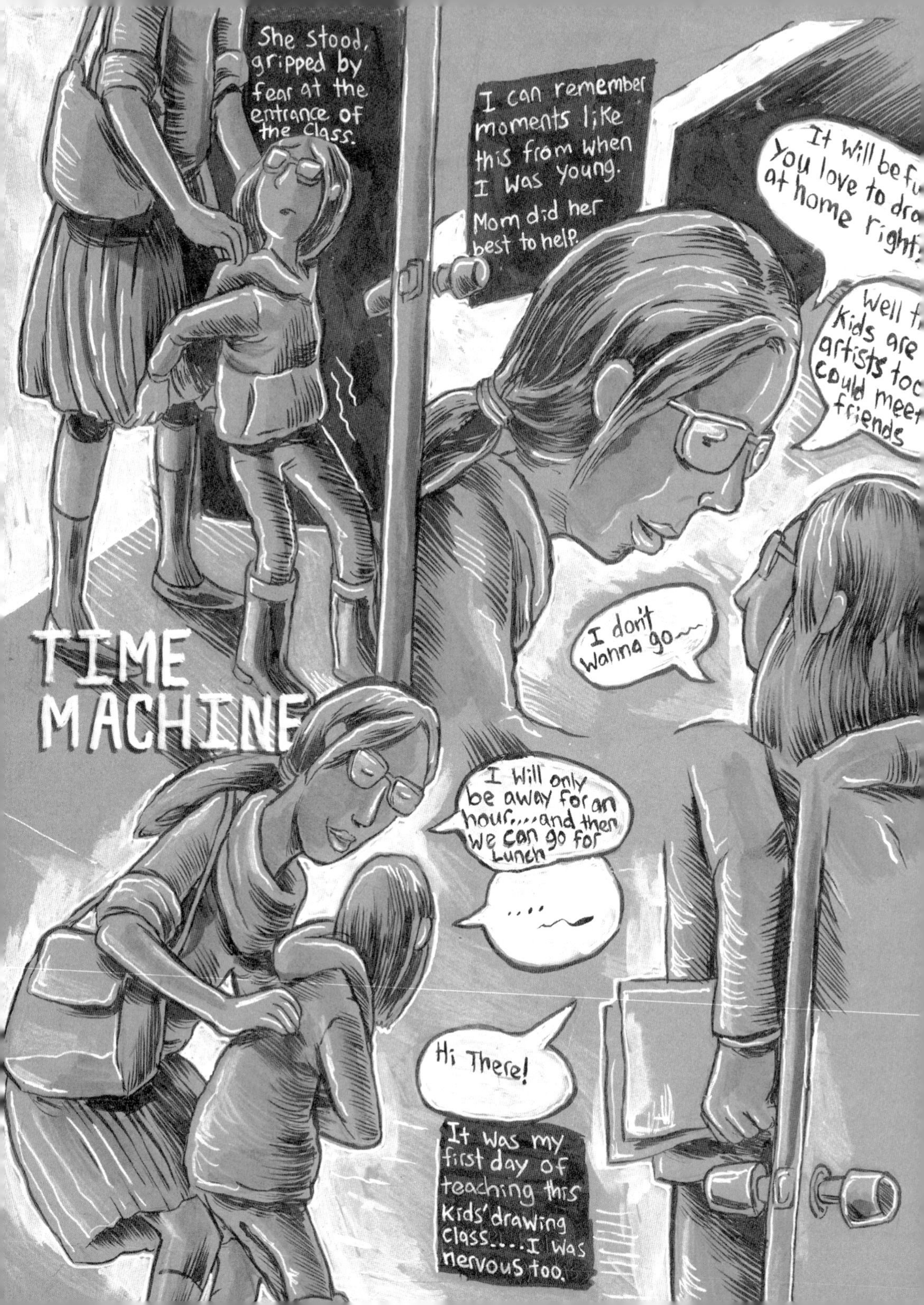 She stood, gripped by fear at the entrance of the class.
I can remember moments like this from when I was young. Mom did her best to help.
It will be fu You love to dra at home right
Well t Kids are artists toc could meet friends
I don't wanna go~~
TIME MACHINE
I will only be away for an hour....and then we can go for Lunch
....~
Hi There!
It was my first day of teaching this kids' drawing class....I was nervous too.

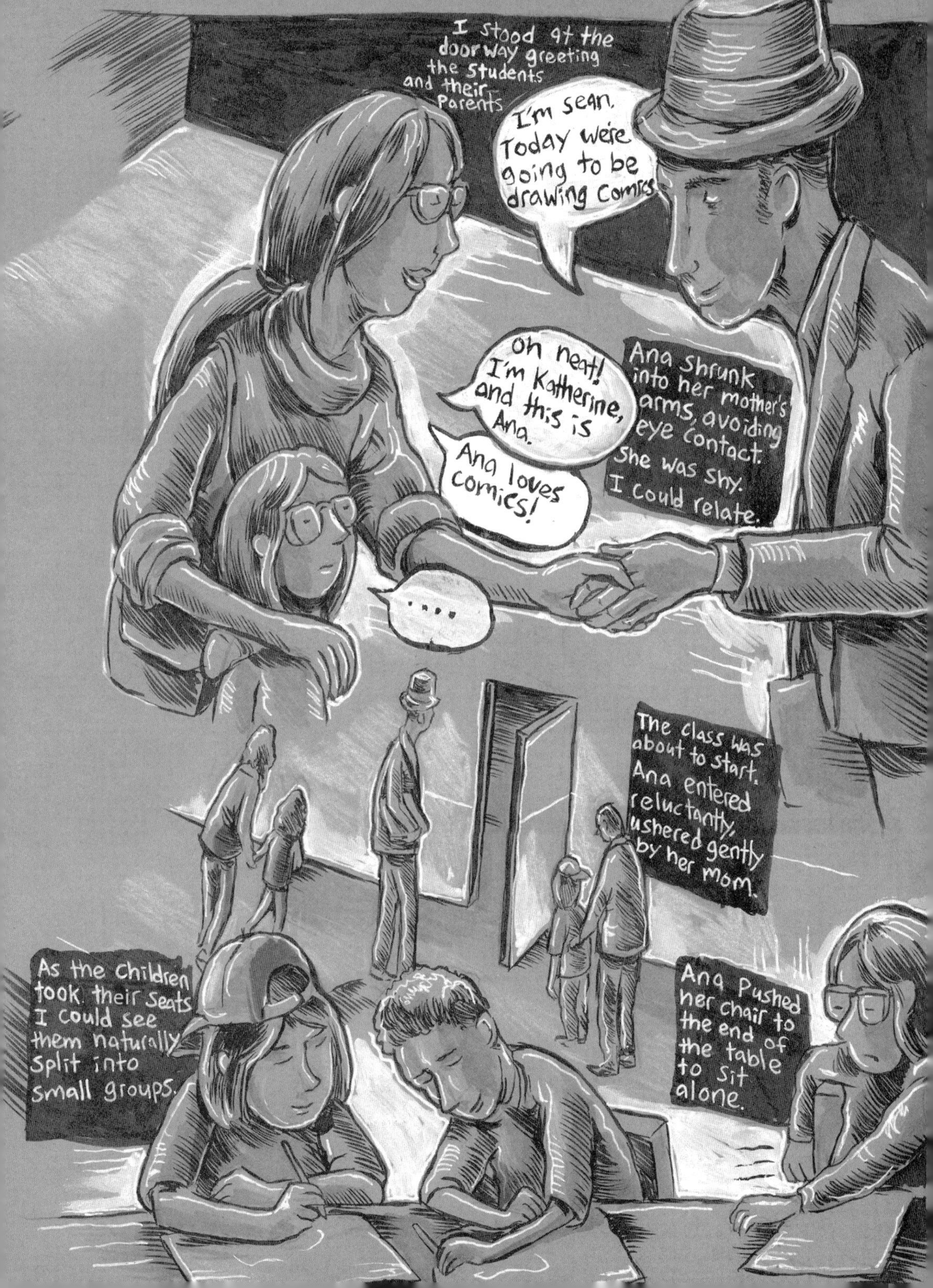
I stood at the doorway greeting the students and their parents
I'm Sean. Today we're going to be drawing comics.
Oh neat! I'm Katherine, and this is Ana.
Ana loves comics!
Ana shrunk into her mother's arms, avoiding eye contact. She was shy. I could relate.
....
The class was about to start. Ana entered reluctantly, ushered gently by her mom.
As the children took their seats I could see them naturally split into small groups.
Ana pushed her chair to the end of the table to sit alone.

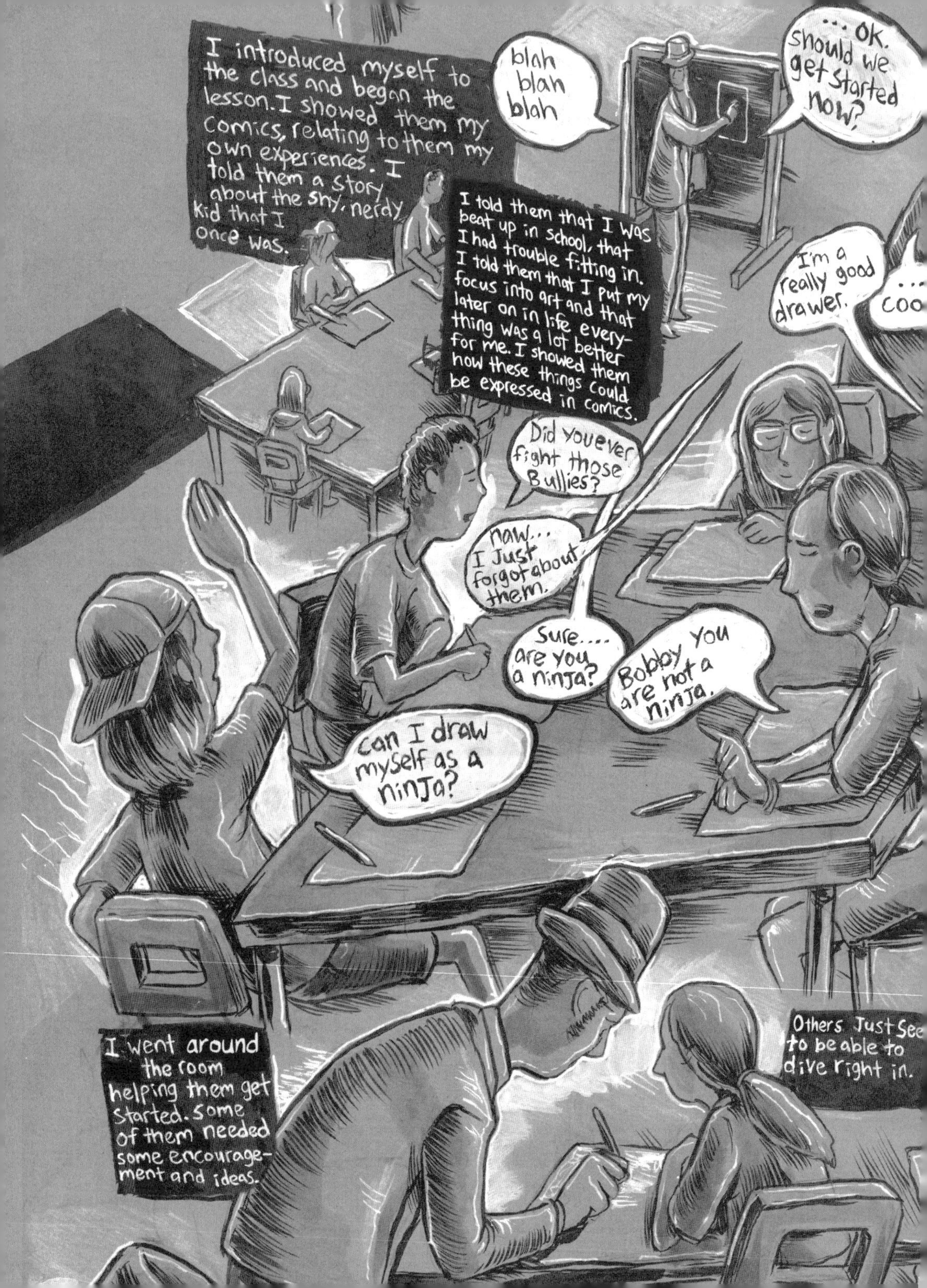
I introduced myself to the class and began the lesson. I showed them my comics, relating to them my own experiences. I told them a story about the shy, nerdy kid that I once was.
blah blah blah
... ok. should we get started now?
I told them that I was beat up in school, that I had trouble fitting in. I told them that I put my focus into art and that later on in life everything was a lot better for me. I showed them how these things could be expressed in comics.
I'm a really good drawer.
... coo
Did you ever fight those Bullies?
naw... I Just forgot about them.
Sure.... are you a ninja?
Bobby you are not a ninja.
Can I draw myself as a ninja?
I went around the room helping them get started. Some of them needed some encouragement and ideas.
Others Just See to be able to dive right in.

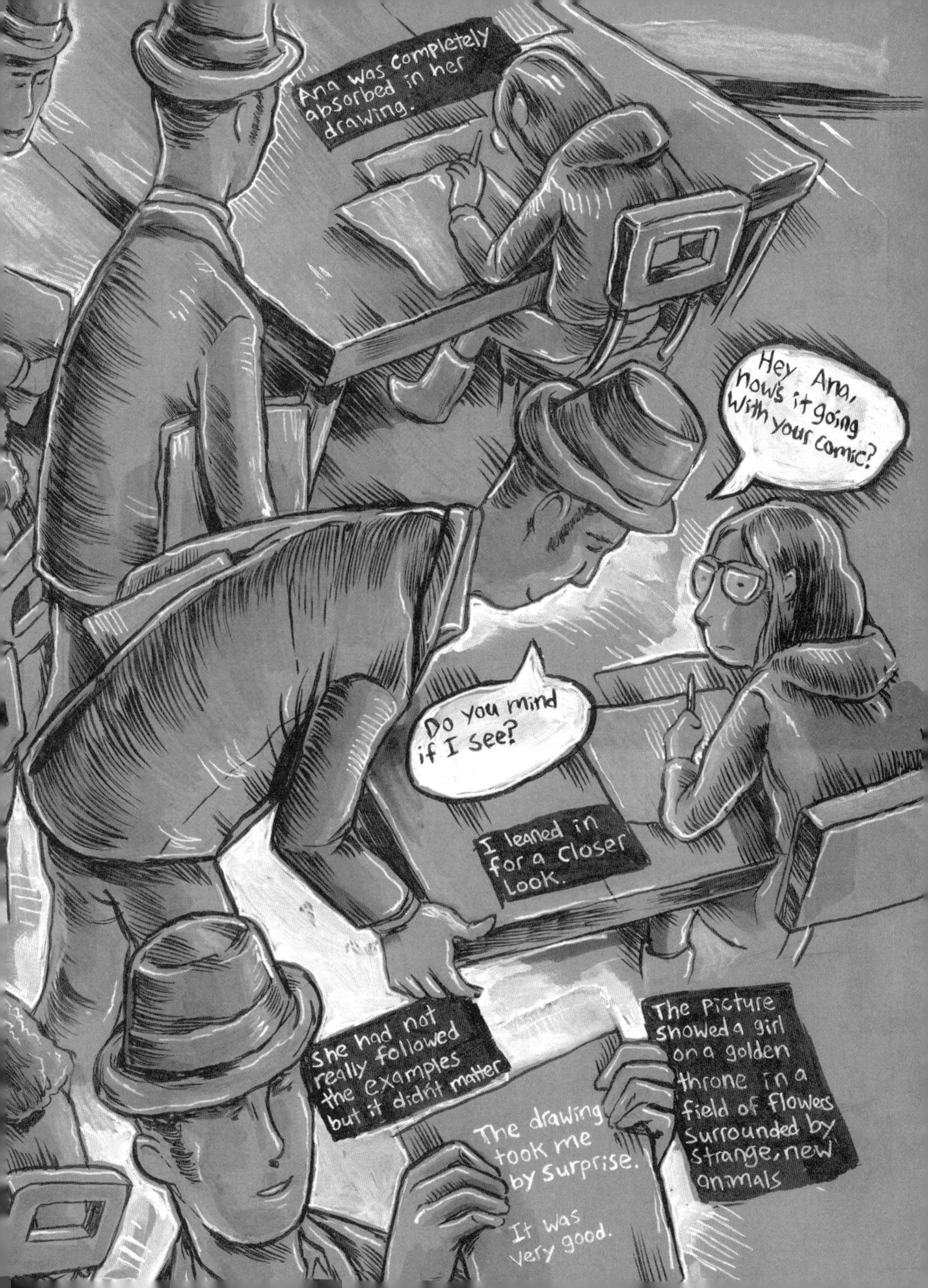
Ana was completely absorbed in her drawing.
Hey Ana, how's it going with your comic?
Do you mind if I see?
I leaned in for a closer look.
She had not really followed the examples but it didn't matter
The picture showed a girl on a golden throne in a field of flowers surrounded by strange, new animals
The drawing took me by surprise.
It was very good.

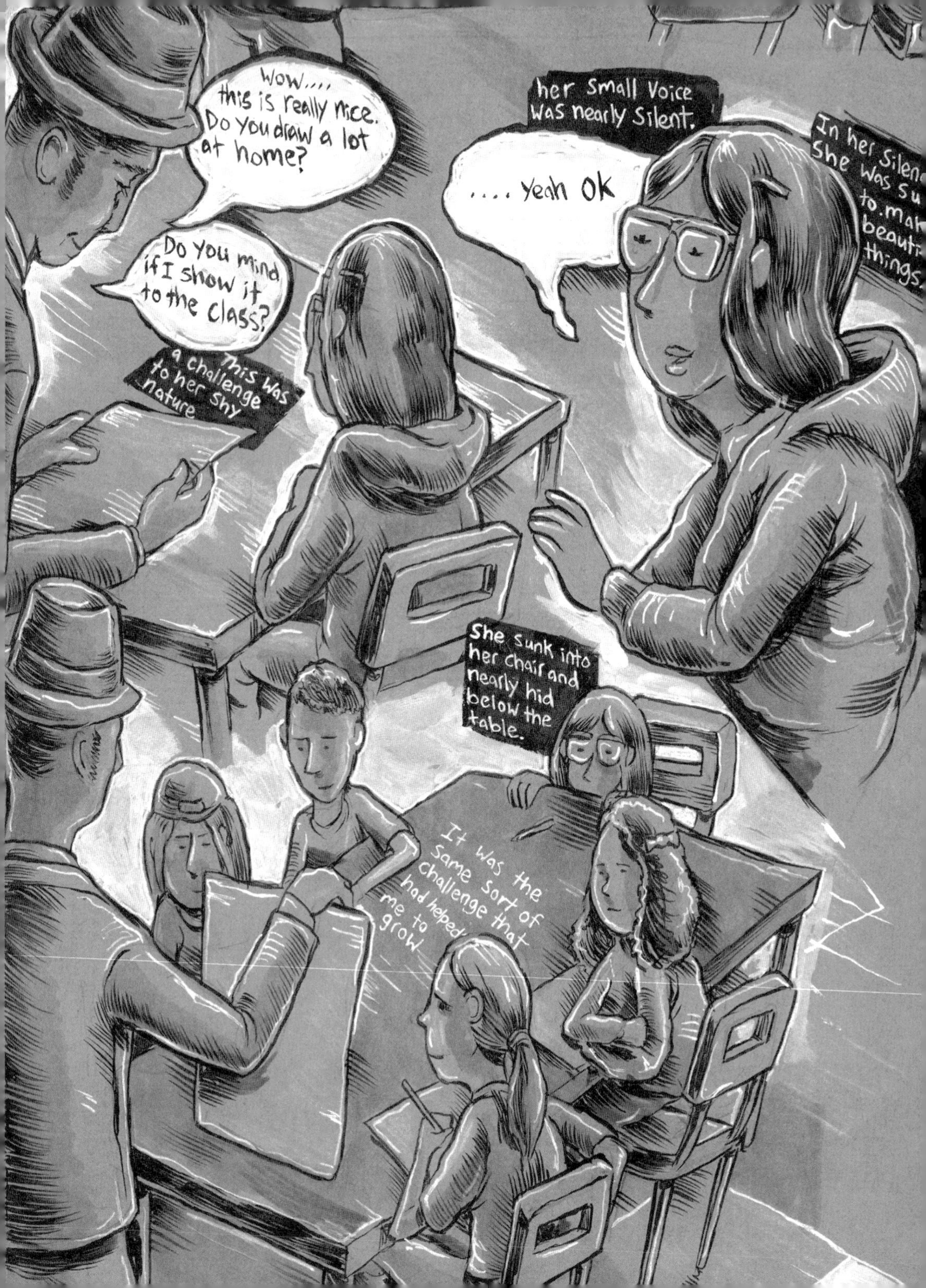
Wow.... this is really nice. Do you draw a lot at home?
Do you mind if I show it to the class?
This was a challenge to her shy nature
her small voice was nearly silent.
.... Yeah OK
In her Silen
She Was Su
to.ma
beauti
things.
She sunk into her chair and nearly hid below the table.
It was the same sort of challenge that had helped me to grow

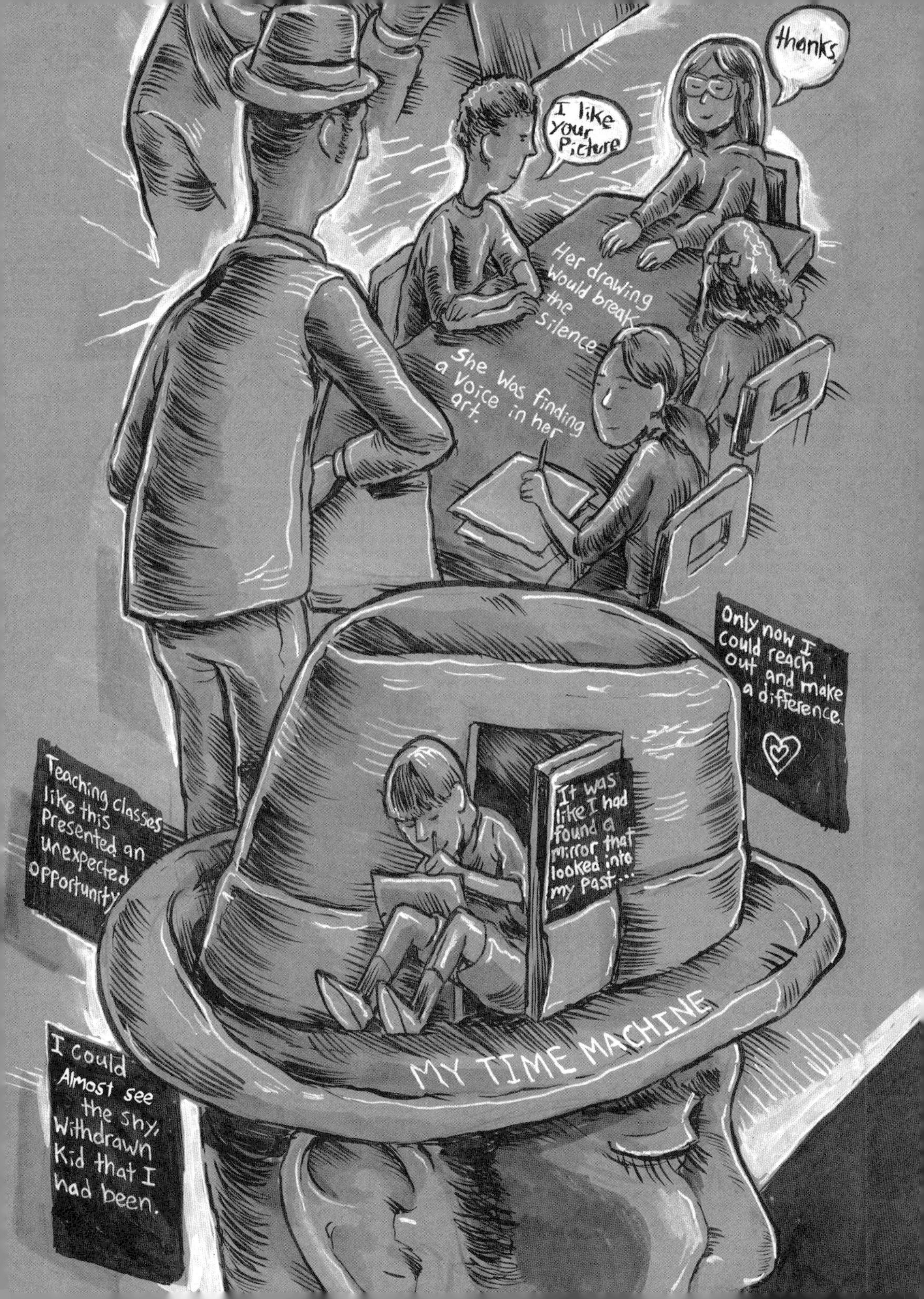
I like your Picture
thanks.
Her drawing would break the silence.
She was finding a voice in her art.
Only now I could reach out and make a difference.
Teaching classes like this Presented an unexpected opportunity
It was like I had found a mirror that looked into my past...
MY TIME MACHINE
I could Almost see the shy, Withdrawn Kid that I had been.

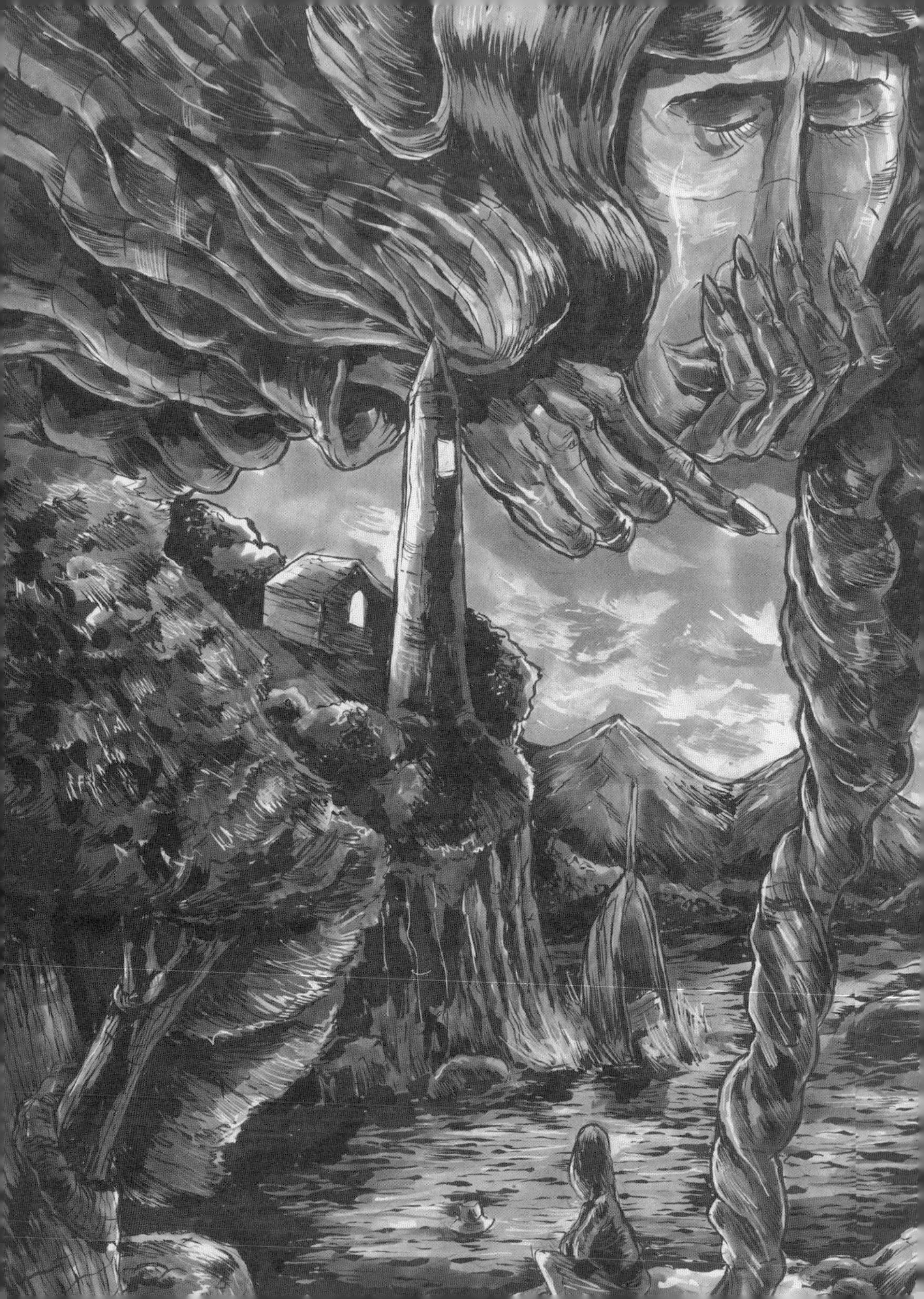

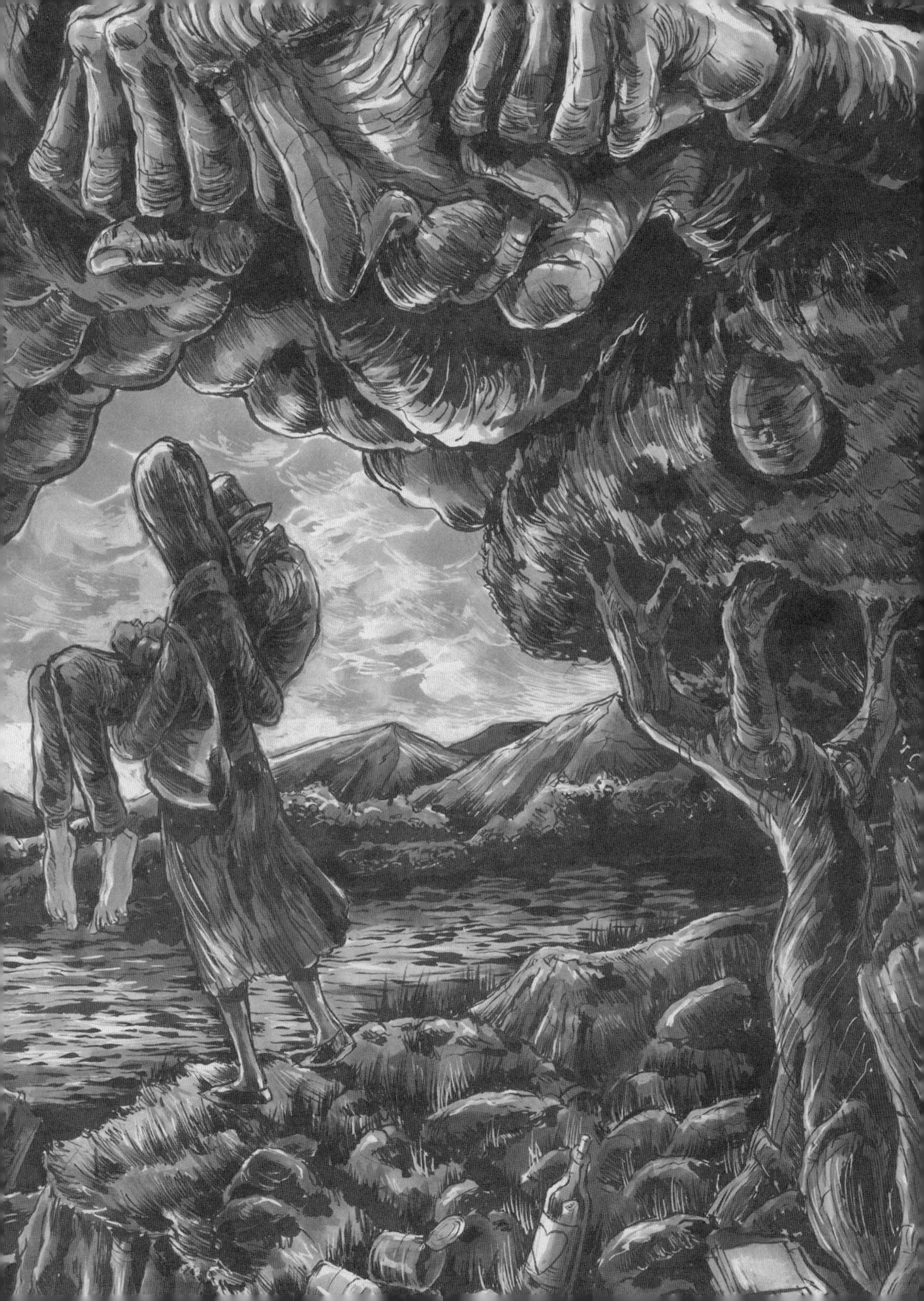

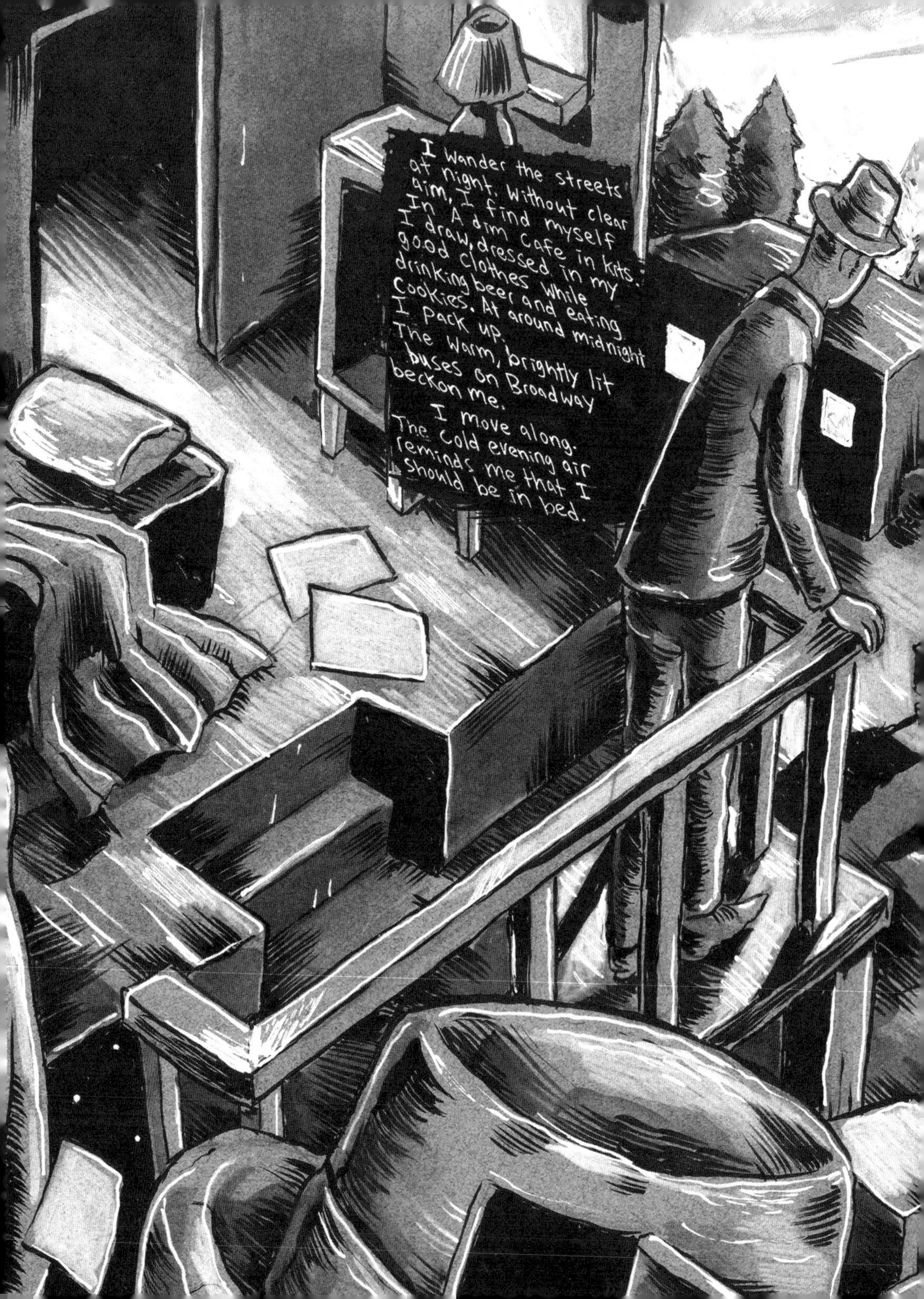
I wander the streets at night, without clear aim, I find myself In A dim cafe in kits. I draw, dressed in my good clothes while drinking beer and eating cookies. At around midnight I pack up. The warm, brightly lit buses on Broadway beckon me.
I move along. The cold evening air reminds me that I should be in bed.

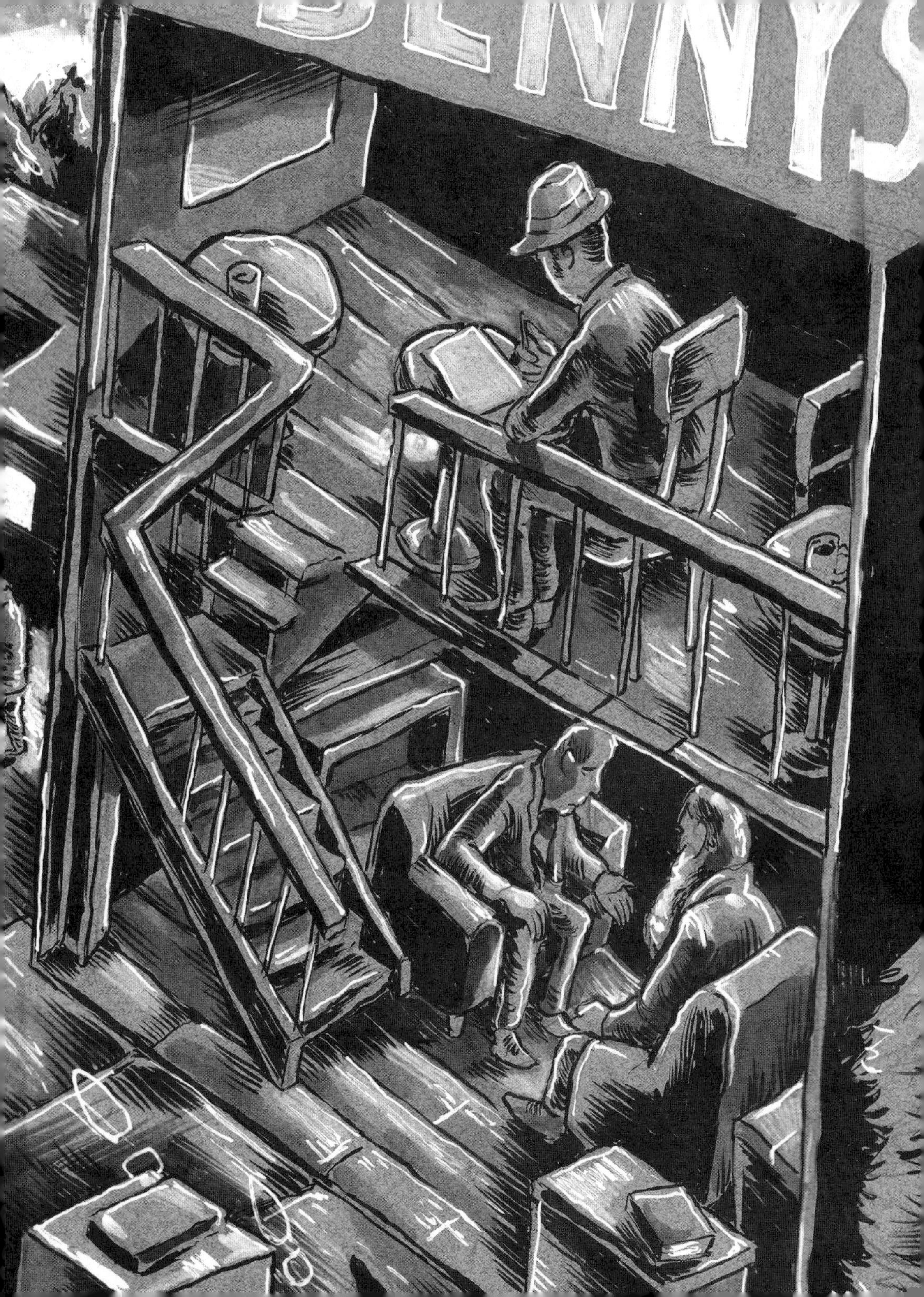

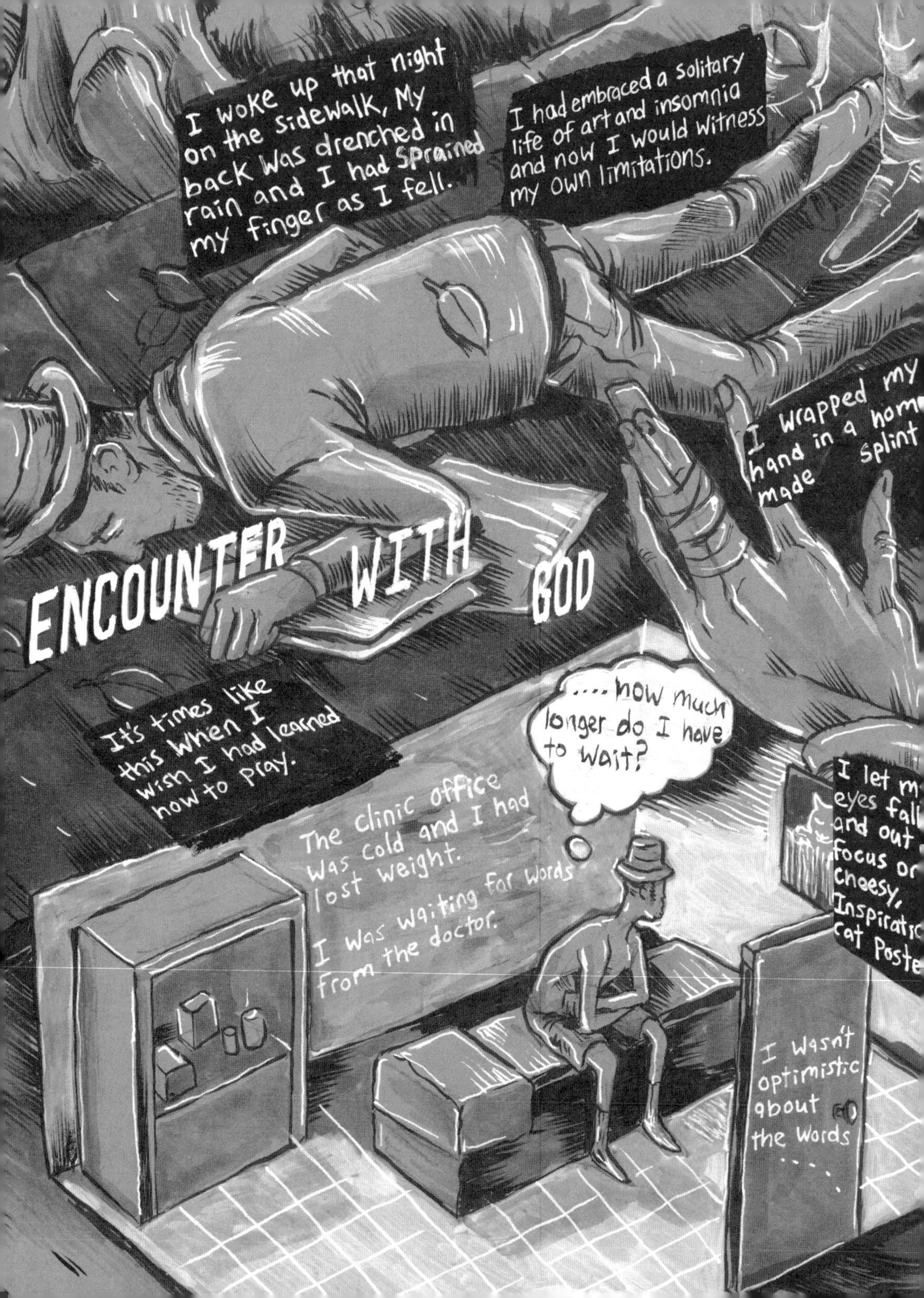

I woke up that night on the sidewalk, My back was drenched in rain and I had sprained my finger as I fell.
I had embraced a solitary life of art and insomnia and now I would witness my own limitations.
I wrapped my hand in a hom made splint
ENCOUNTER WITH GOD
It's times like this when I wish I had learned how to pray.
....how much longer do I have to wait?
The clinic office was cold and I had lost weight.
I was waiting for words from the doctor.
I let m eyes fall and out focus or cheesy, Inspiratio cat Poste
I wasn't optimistic about the words . . . .

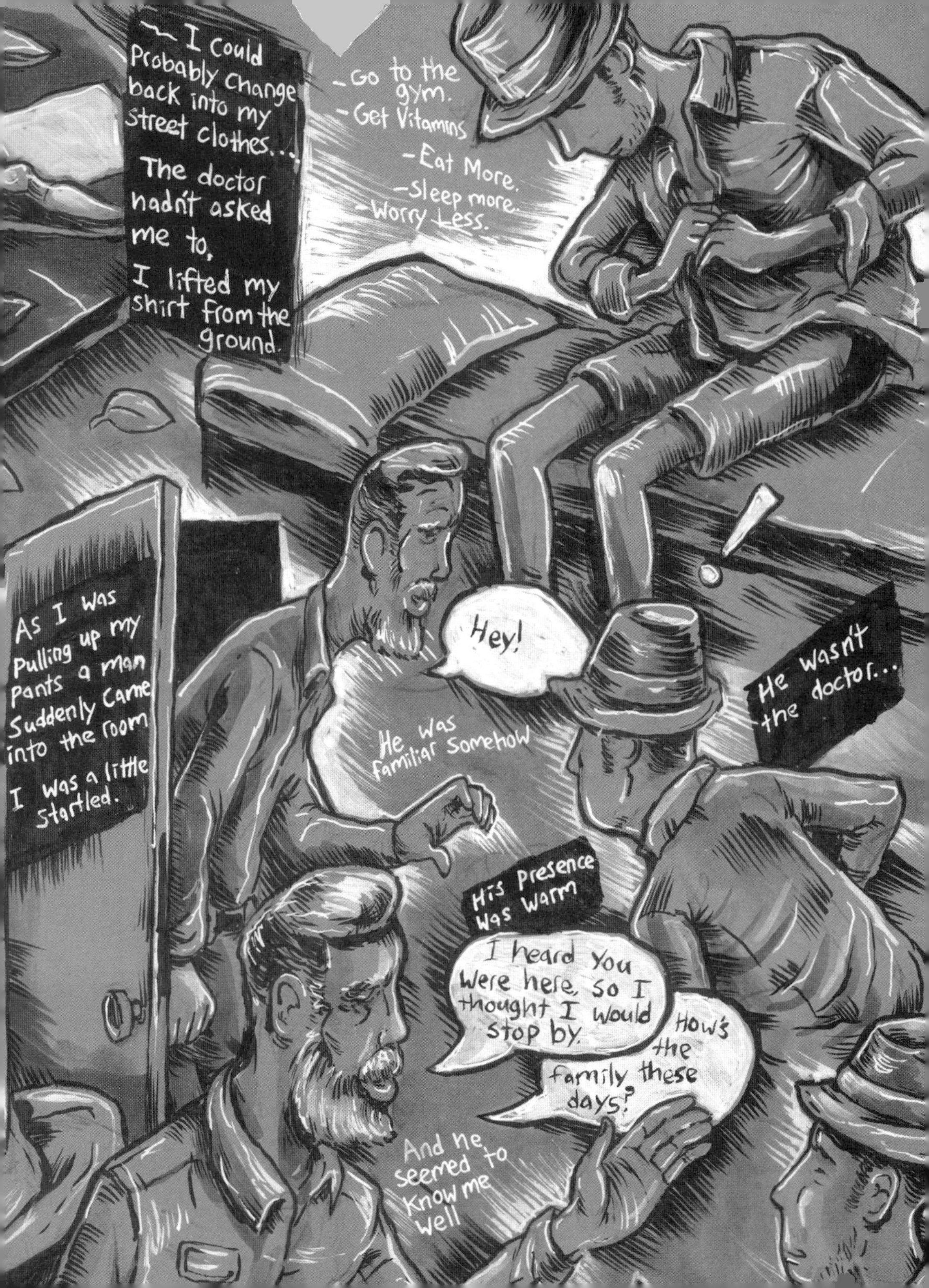
I could Probably change back into my street clothes...
The doctor hadn't asked me to,
I lifted my shirt from the ground.
-Go to the gym.
-Get Vitamins
-Eat More.
-Sleep more.
-Worry Less.
As I was pulling up my pants a man suddenly came into the room
I was a little startled.
Hey!
He wasn't the doctor...
He was familiar somehow
His Presence was warm
I heard you were here, so I thought I would stop by.
How's the family these days?
And he seemed to know me well

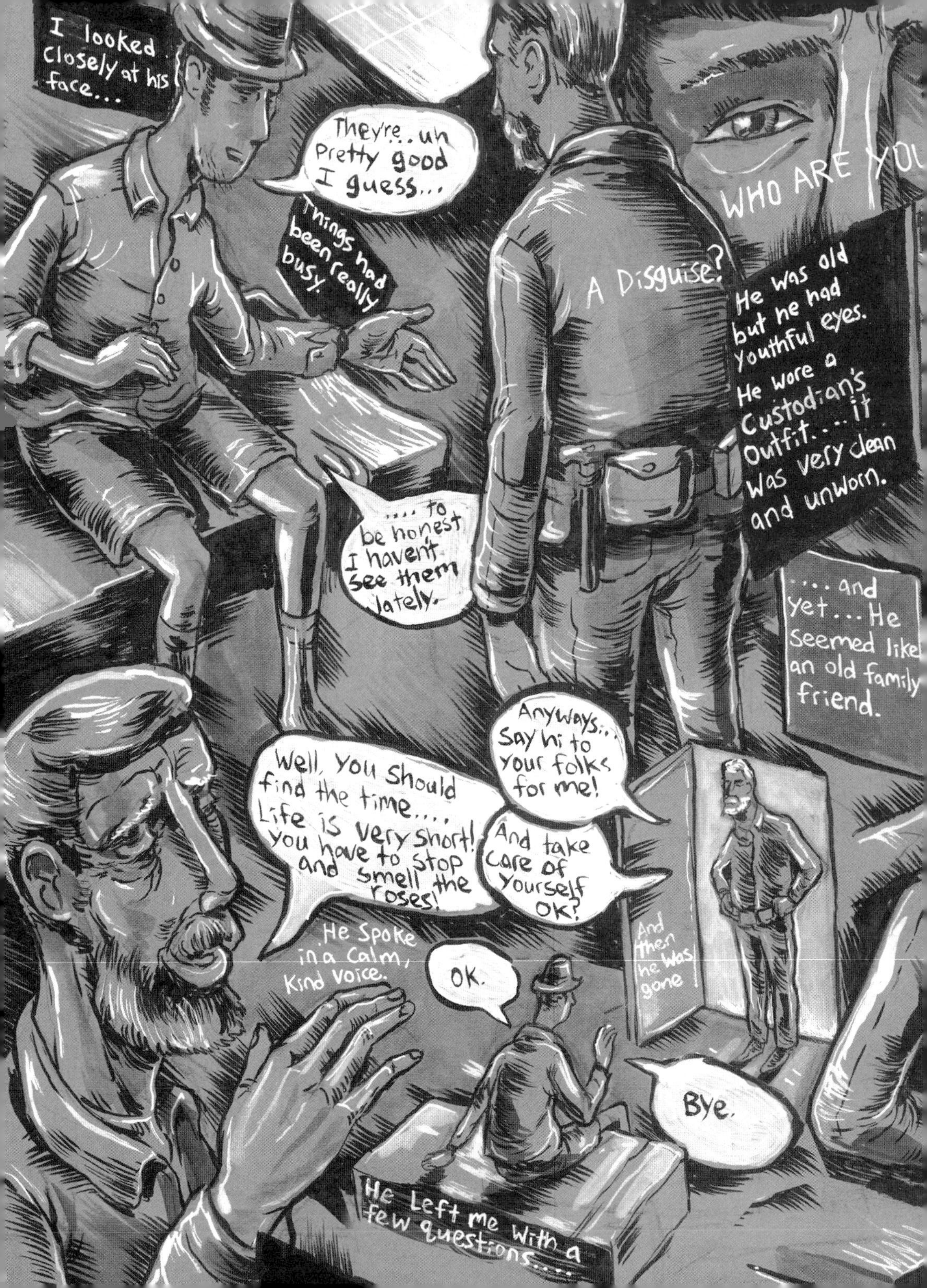
I looked closely at his face...
They're...uh pretty good I guess...
Things had been really busy.
WHO ARE YOU
A Disguise?
He was old but he had youthful eyes.
He wore a Custodian's Outfit...it was very clean and unworn.
...to be honest I haven't see them lately.
...and yet...He seemed like an old family friend.
Well, You should find the time.... Life is very short! you have to stop and smell the roses!
Anyways... Say hi to your folks for me!
And take care of yourself OK?
He Spoke in a calm, kind voice.
OK.
And then he was gone
Bye.
He Left me with a few questions....

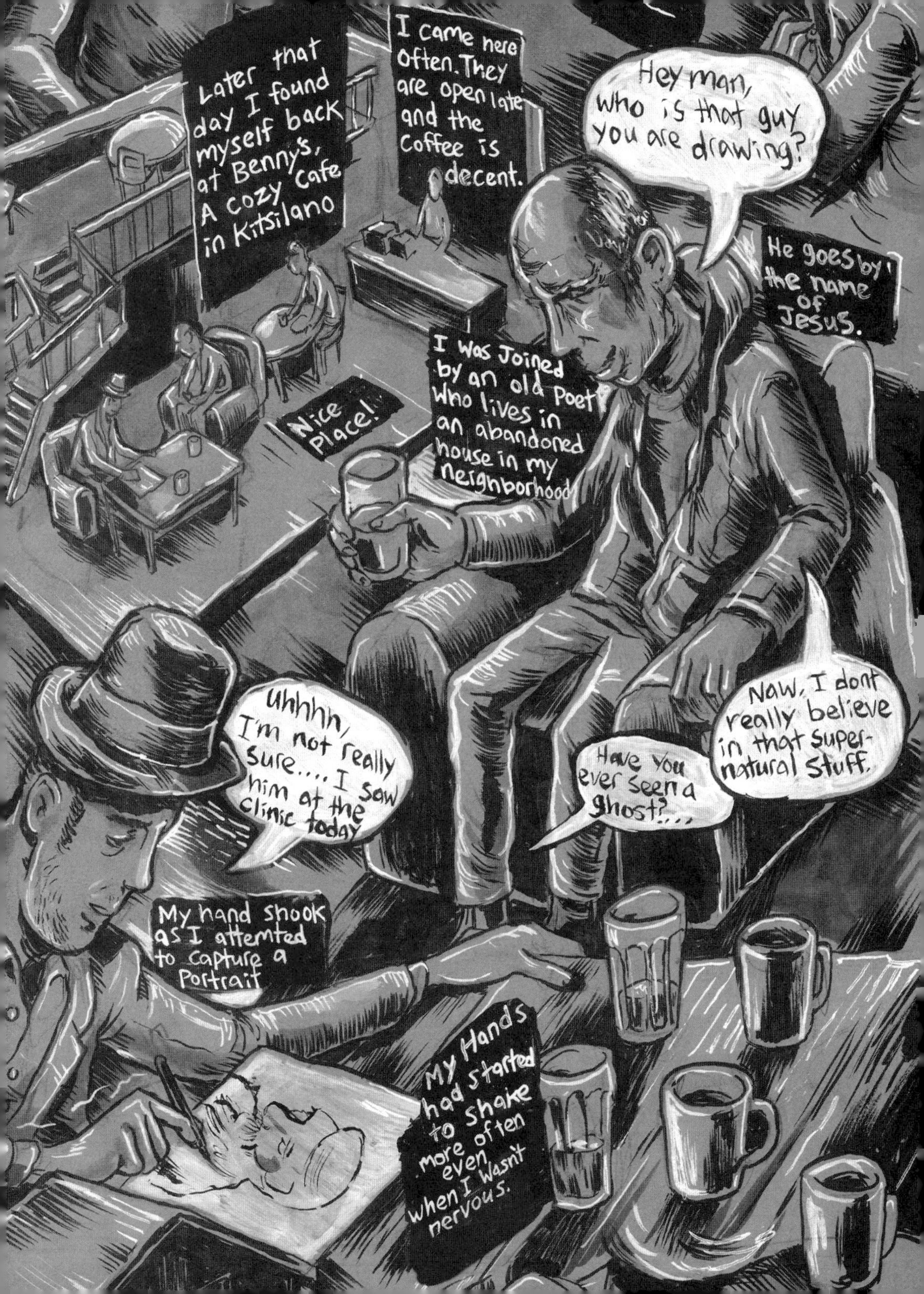
Later that day I found myself back at Benny's, A cozy cafe in Kitsilano
I came here often. They are open late and the Coffee is decent.
Hey man, who is that guy you are drawing?
He goes by the name of Jesus.
I was Joined by an old Poet who lives in an abandoned house in my neighborhood
Nice Place!
Uhhhh, I'm not really sure.... I saw him at the clinic today
Naw, I dont really believe in that super-natural stuff.
Have you ever seen a ghost?...
My hand shook as I attemted to capture a Portrait
My Hands had started to shake more often even when I wasn't nervous.

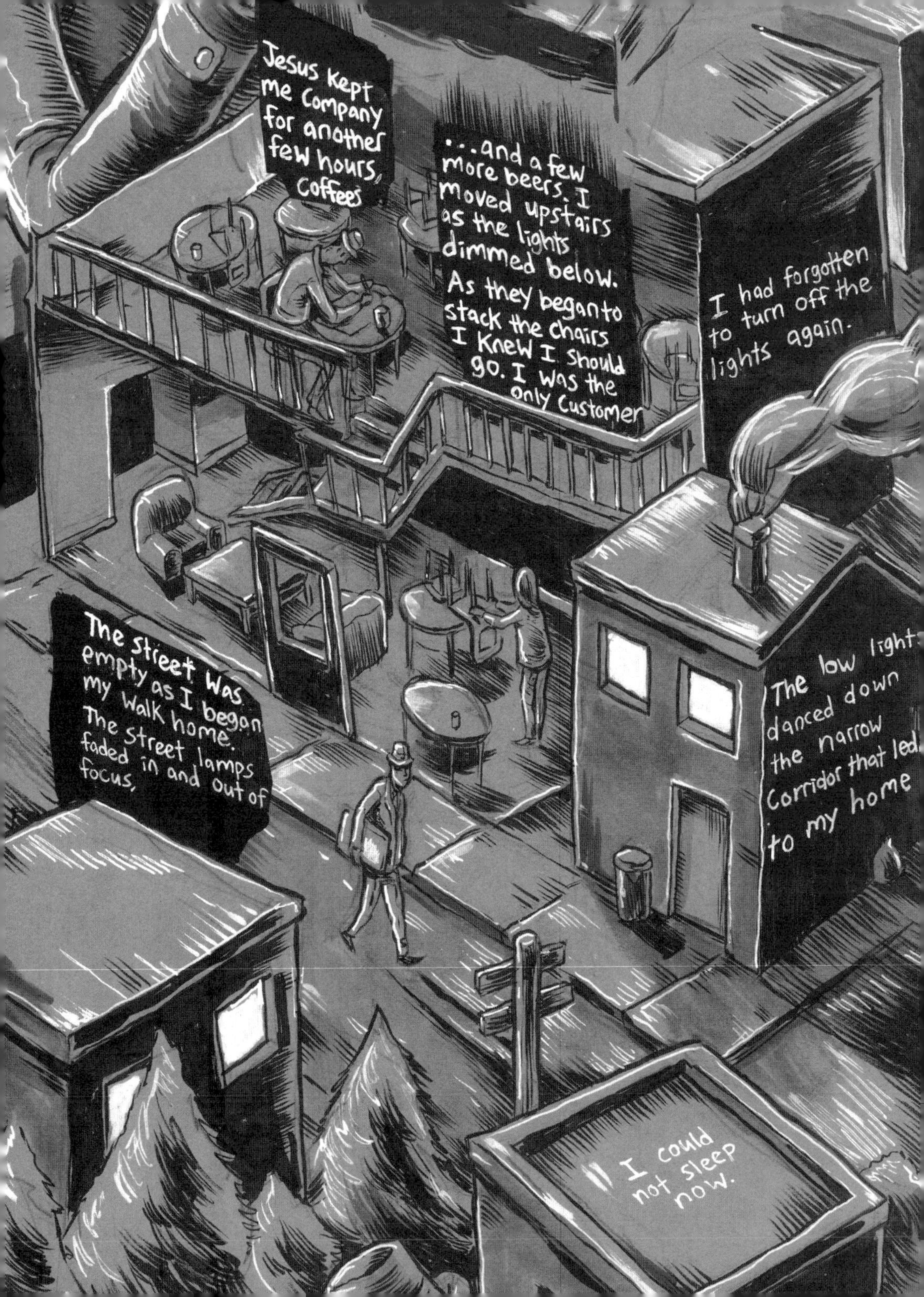
Jesus kept me company for another few hours, coffees
...and a few more beers. I moved upstairs as the lights dimmed below.
As they began to stack the chairs I knew I should go. I was the only customer
I had forgotten to turn off the lights again.
The street was empty as I began my walk home. The street lamps faded in and out of focus,
The low light danced down the narrow corridor that led to my home
I could not sleep now.

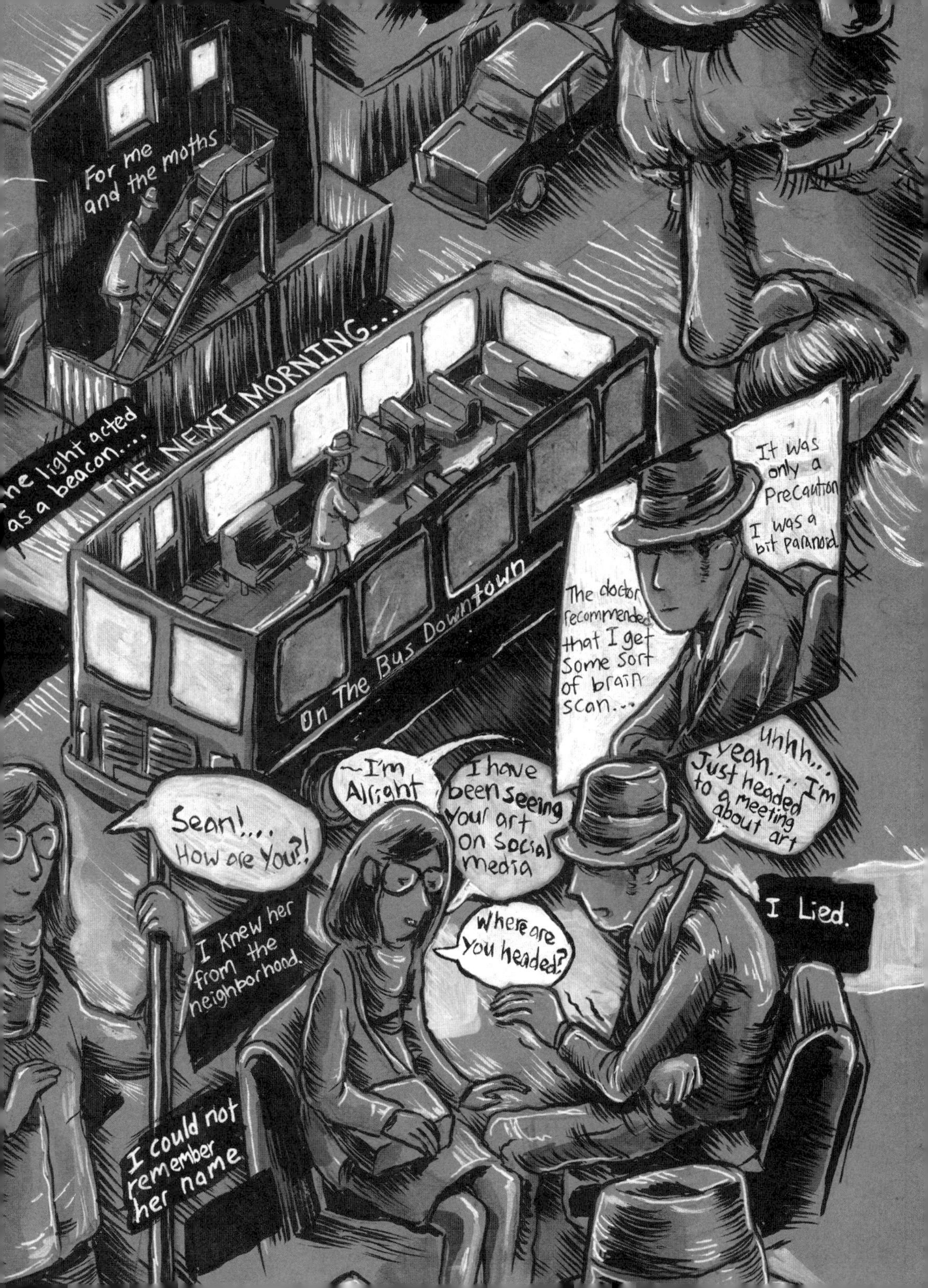
For me and the moths
...he light acted as a beacon....
THE NEXT MORNING...
On The Bus Downtown
It was only a Precaution I was a bit paranoid
The doctor recommended that I get some sort of brain scan...
Sean!... How are You?!
~I'm Alright
I have been seeing your art on Social media
Uhhh... yeah.... I'm Just headed to a meeting about art
I knew her from the neighborhood.
Where are you headed?
I Lied.
I could not remember her name

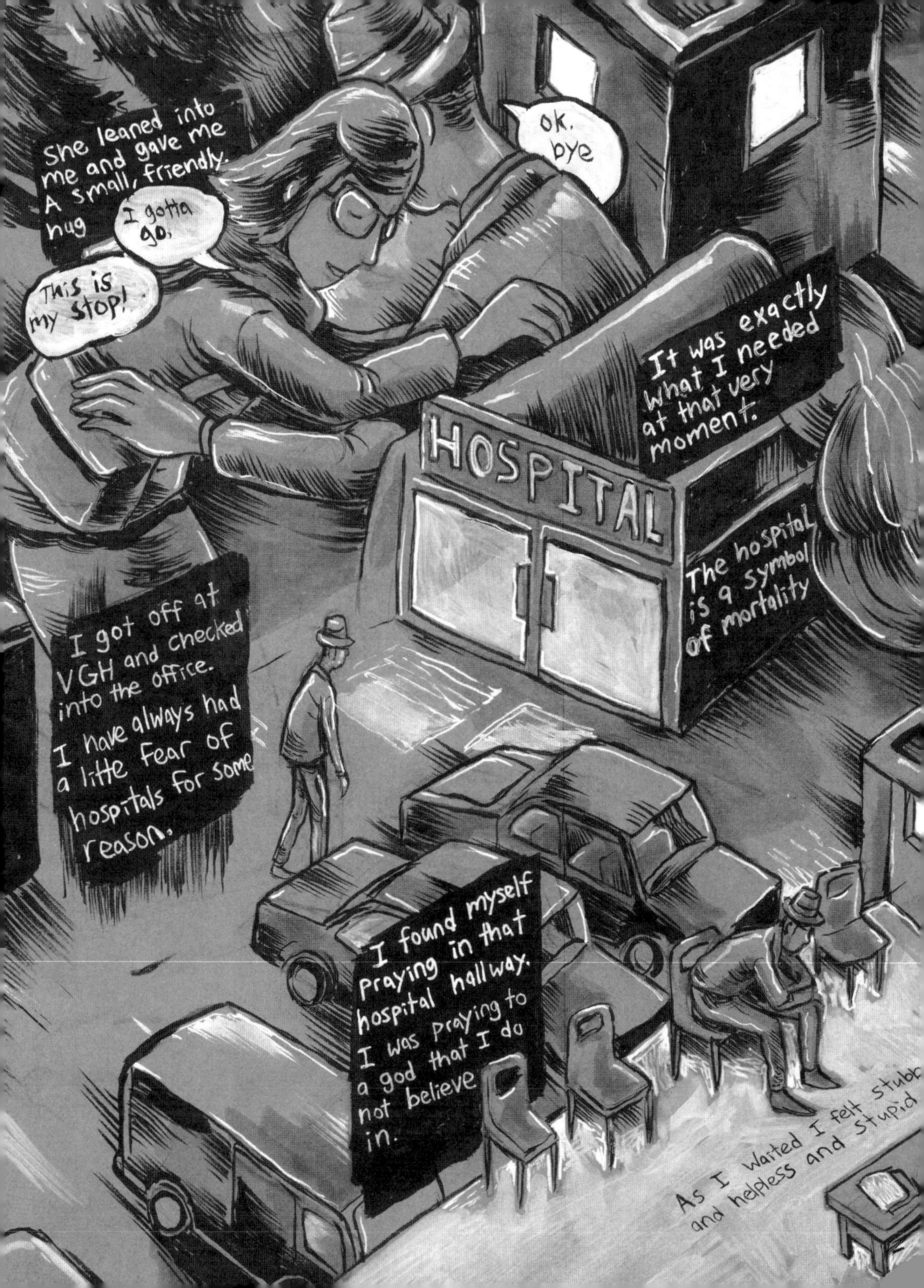
She leaned into me and gave me A small, friendly hug
I gotta go,
This is my stop!
ok, bye
It was exactly what I needed at that very moment.
HOSPITAL
The hospital is a symbol of mortality
I got off at VGH and checked into the office.
I have always had a little fear of hospitals for some reason.
I found myself praying in that hospital hallway. I was praying to a god that I do not believe in.
As I waited I felt stubb
and helpless and stupid

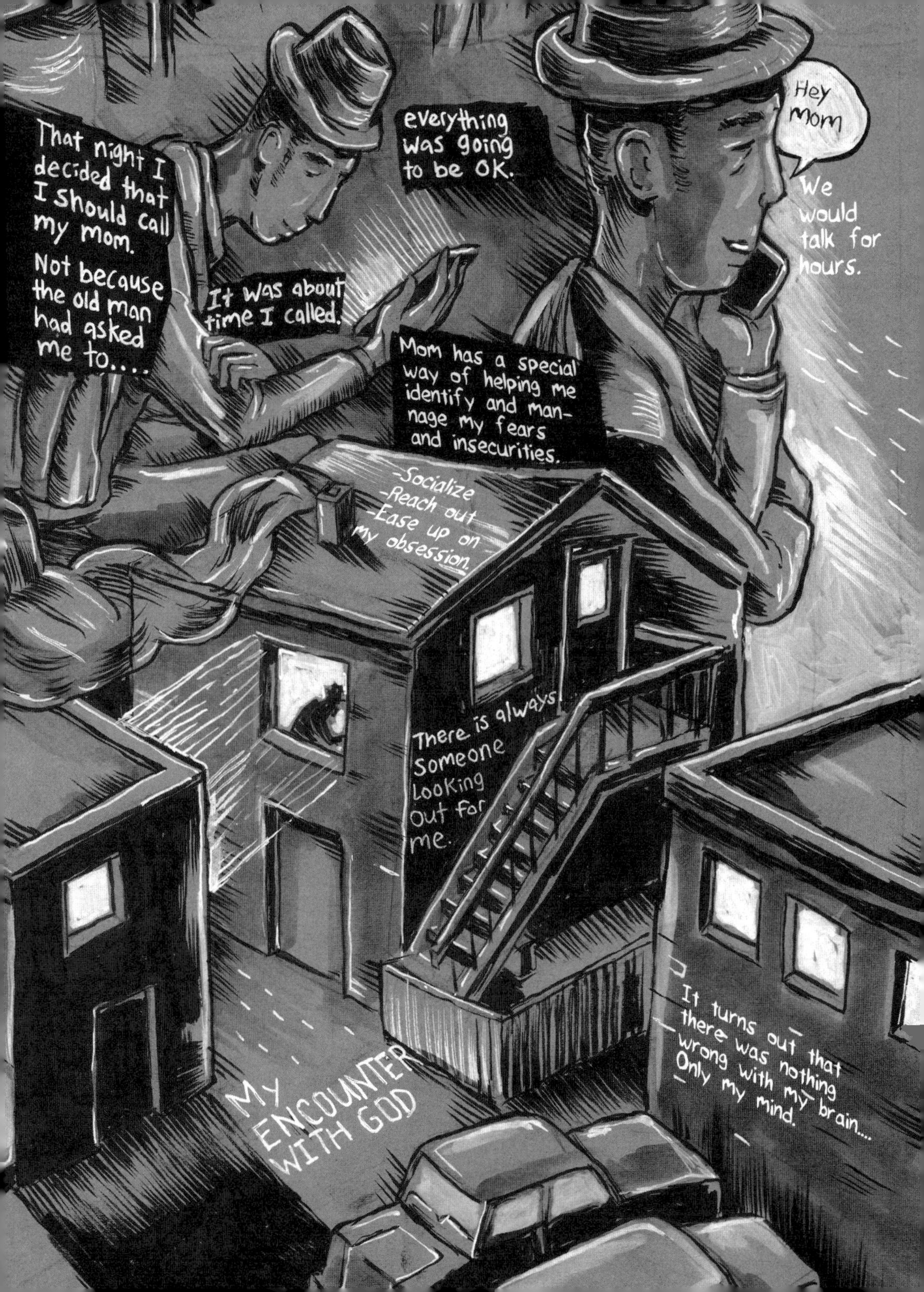

That night I decided that I should call my mom.
Not because the old man had asked me to....
It was about time I called.
everything was going to be OK.
Hey Mom
We would talk for hours.
Mom has a special way of helping me identify and manage my fears and insecurities.
-Socialize
-Reach out
-Ease up on my obsession.
There is always someone looking out for me.
It turns out that there was nothing wrong with my brain... Only my mind.
MY ENCOUNTER WITH GOD

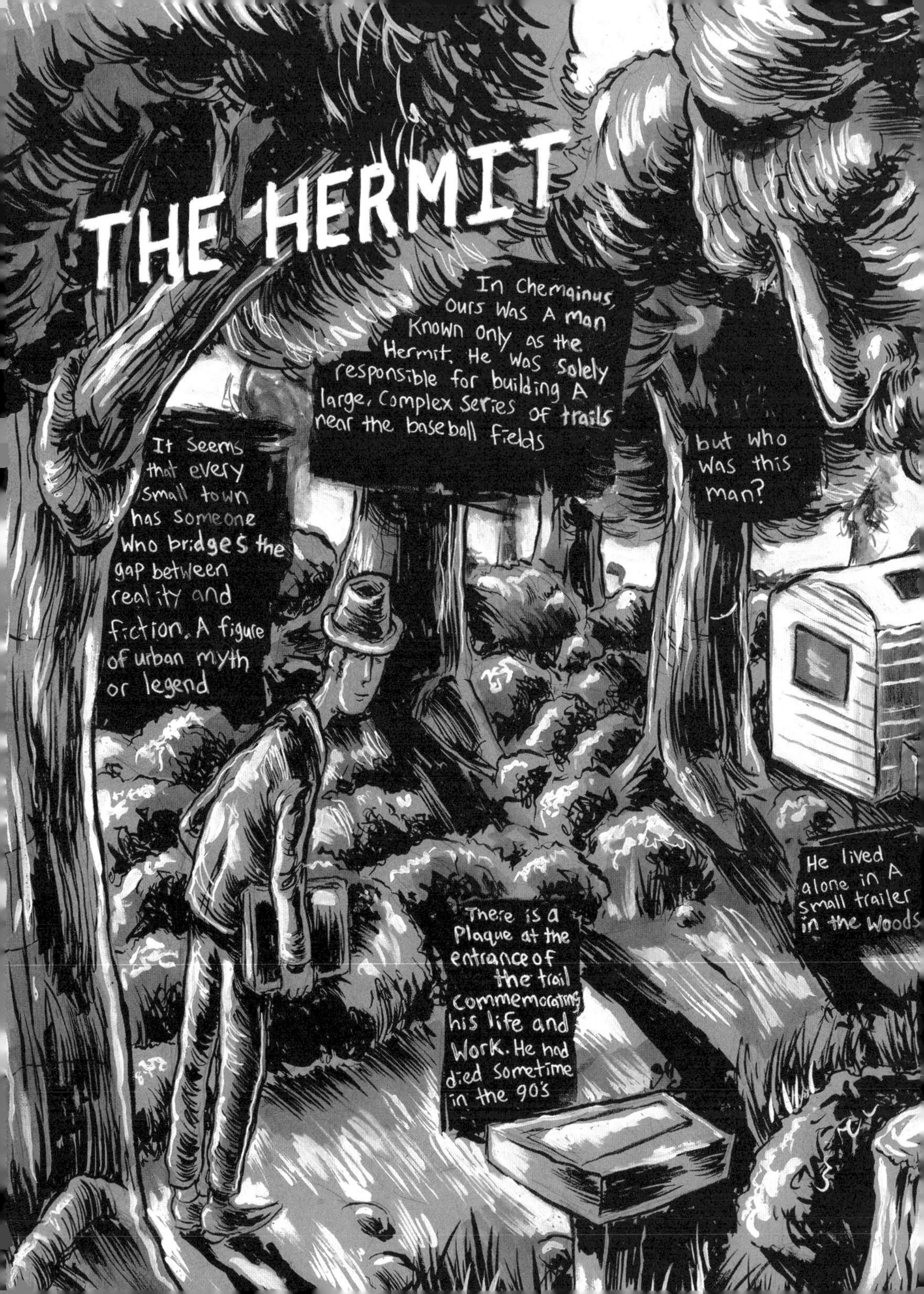
THE HERMIT
It seems that every small town has someone who bridges the gap between reality and fiction. A figure of urban myth or legend
In Chemainus, ours was a man known only as the Hermit. He was solely responsible for building a large, complex series of trails near the baseball fields
but who was this man?
He lived alone in a small trailer in the woods
There is a plaque at the entrance of the trail commemorating his life and work. He had died sometime in the 90's

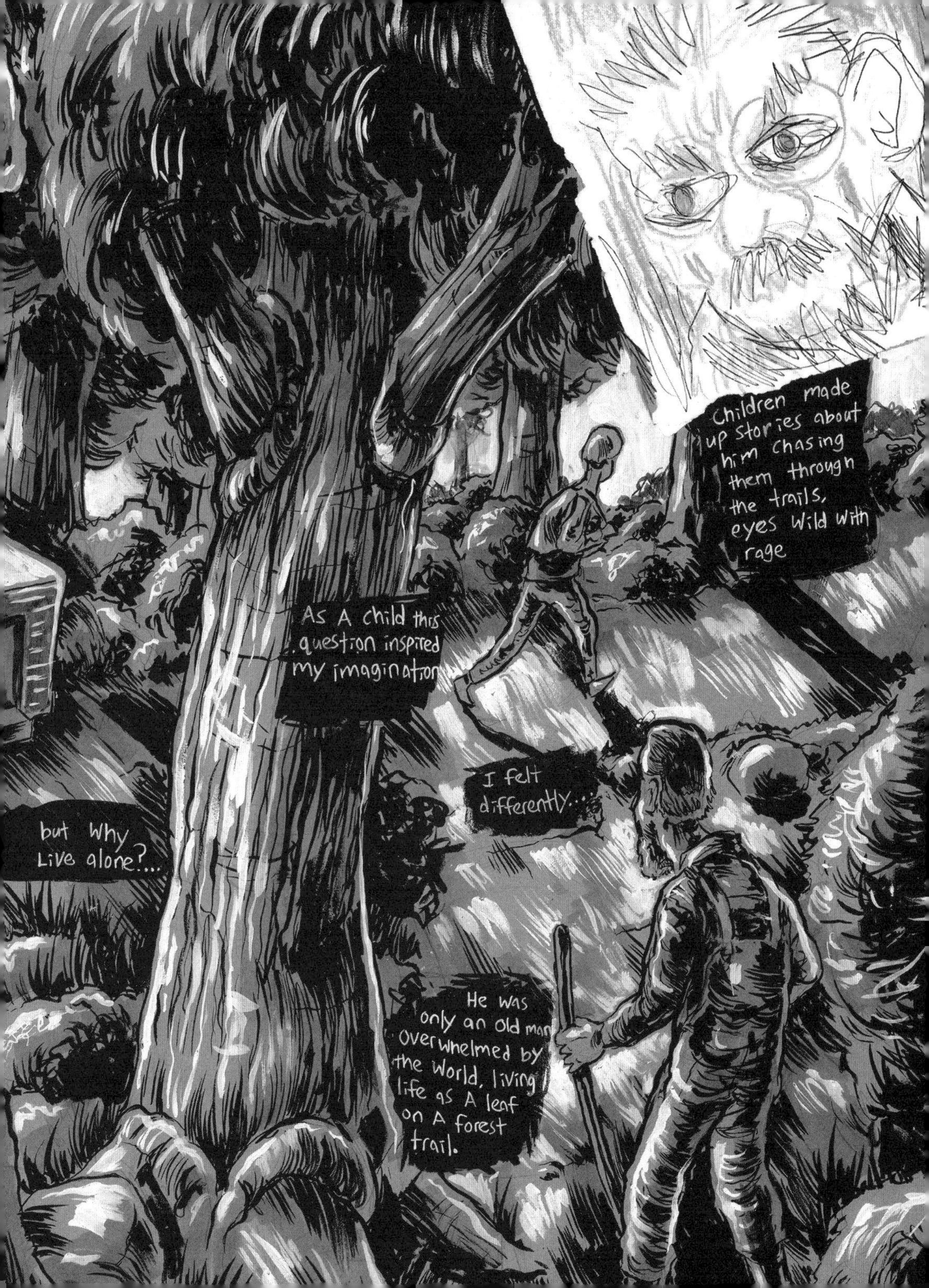

Children made up stories about him chasing them through the trails, eyes wild with rage
As A child this question inspired my imagination
I felt differently...
but why Live alone?...
He was only an old man overwhelmed by the world, living life as A leaf on A forest trail.

GORGE

the Ghost

-seank

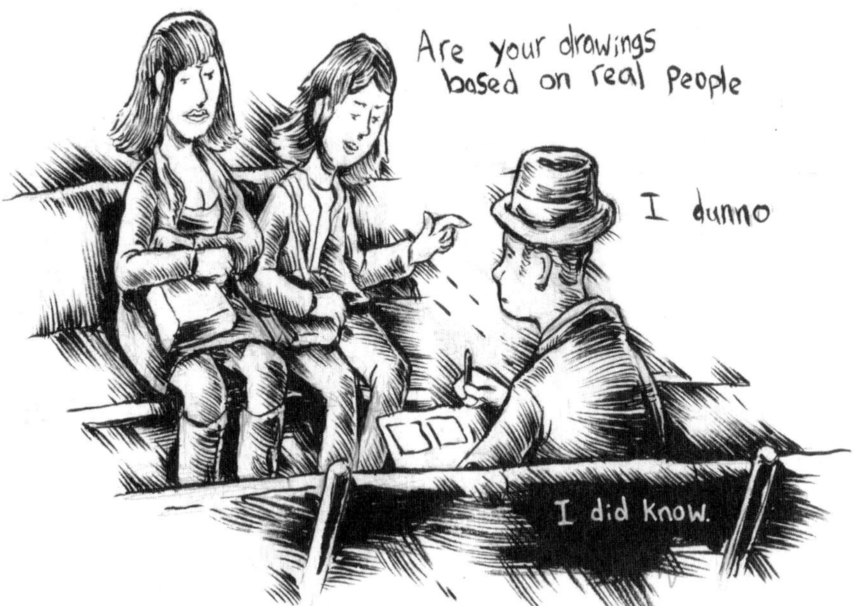

Are your drawings based on real people
I dunno
I did know.

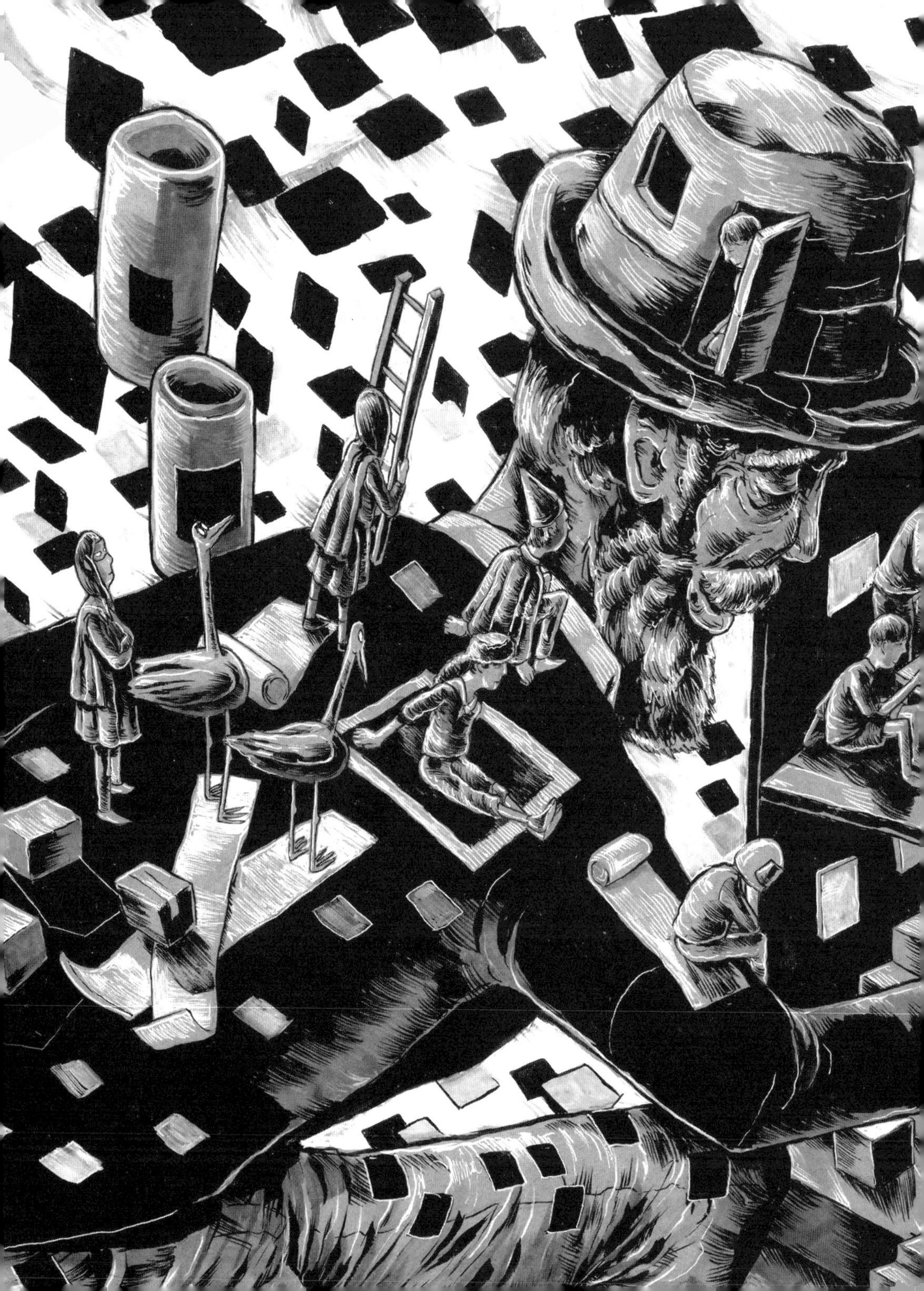

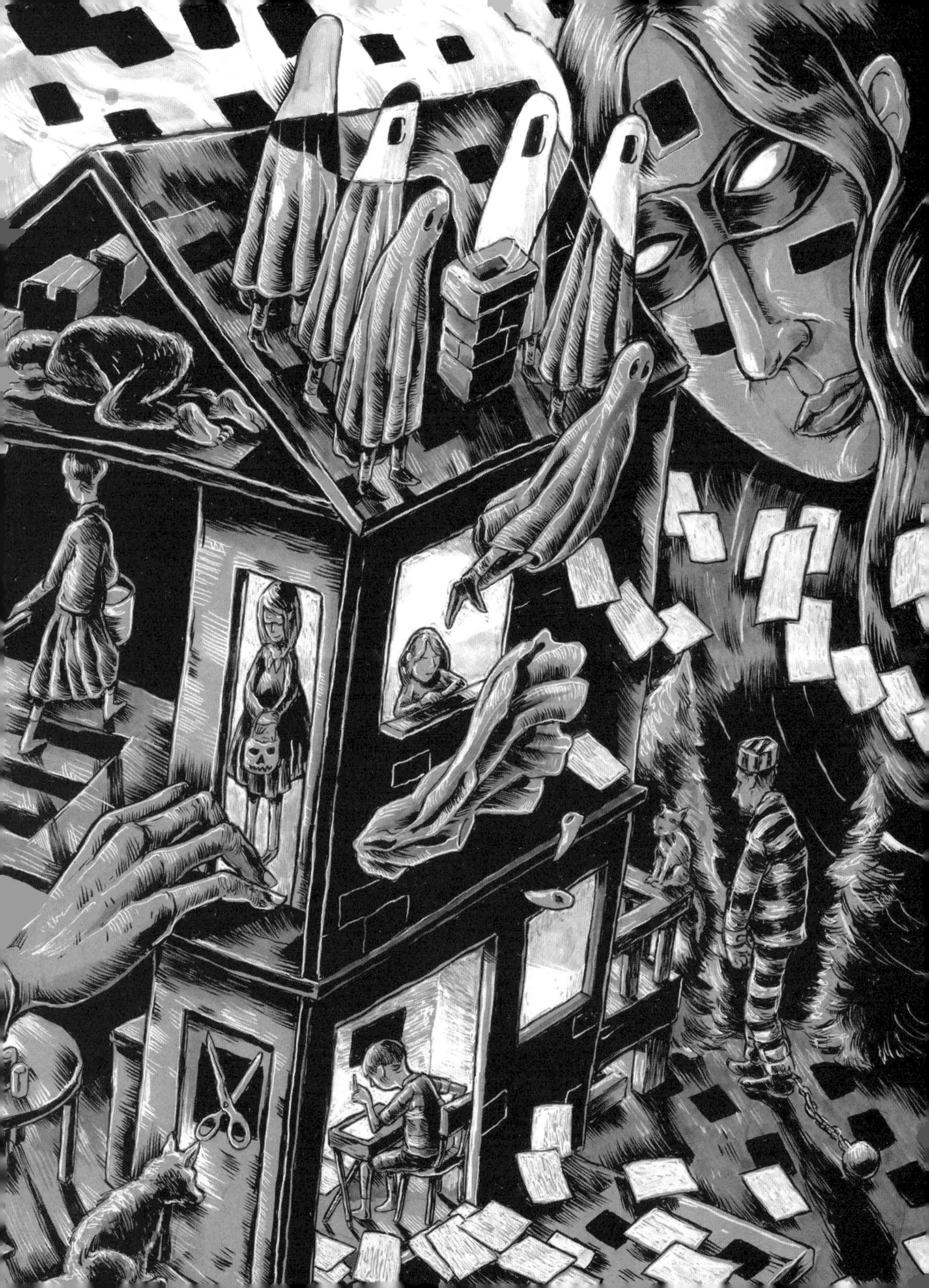

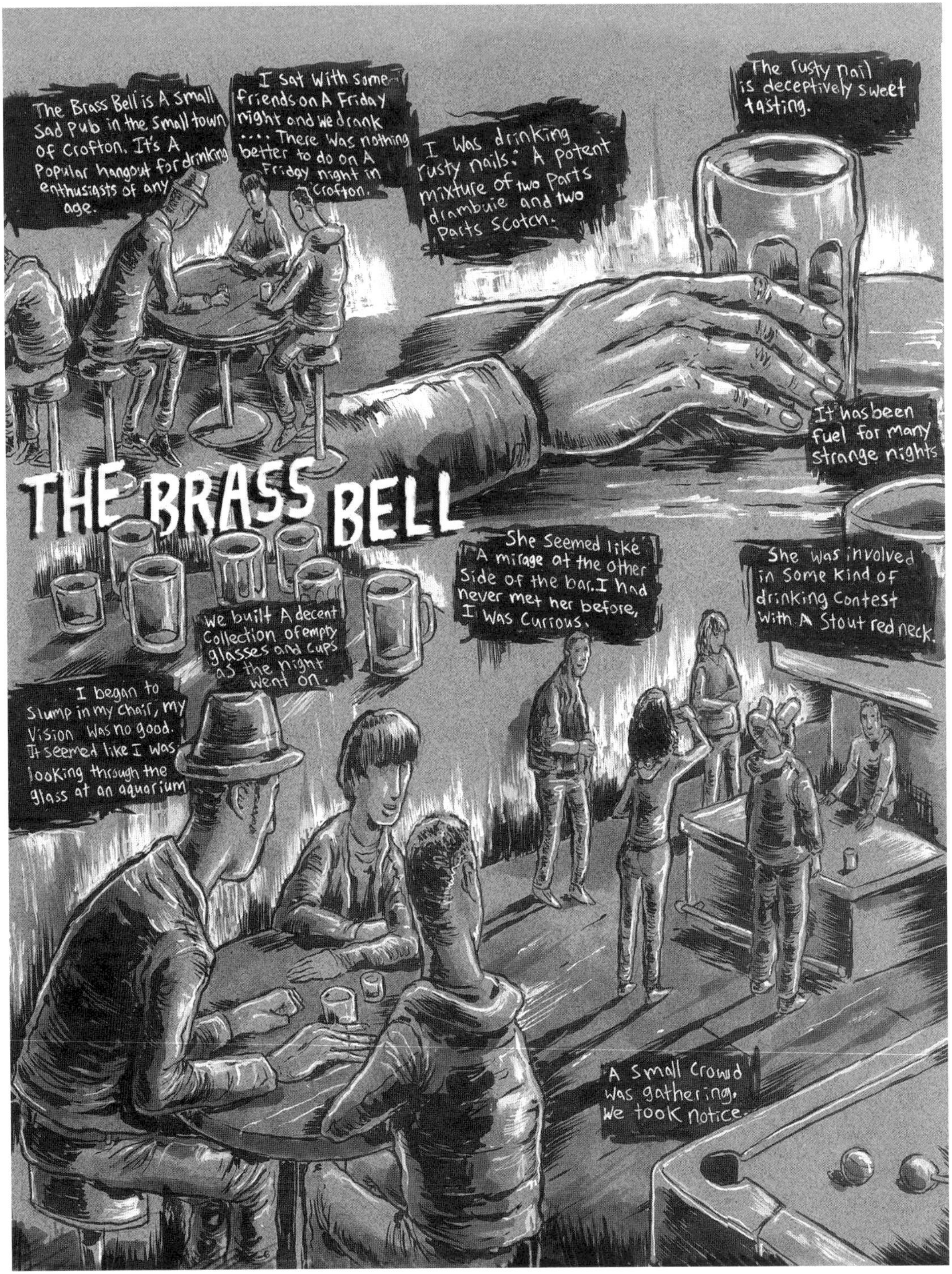

The Brass Bell is A small sad Pub in the small town of Crofton. It's A Popular hangout for drinking enthusiasts of any age.
I sat with some friends on A Friday night and we drank .... There was nothing better to do on A Friday night in Crofton.
I was drinking rusty nails: A potent mixture of two Parts drambuie and two Parts Scotch.
The rusty nail is deceptively sweet tasting.
It has been fuel for many strange nights
THE BRASS BELL
We built A decent Collection of empty glasses and cups as the night went on.
She seemed like A mirage at the other side of the bar. I had never met her before, I was Curious.
She was involved in some kind of drinking Contest with A stout red neck.
I began to slump in my chair, my vision was no good. It seemed like I was looking through the glass at an aquarium
A small crowd was gathering, we took notice.

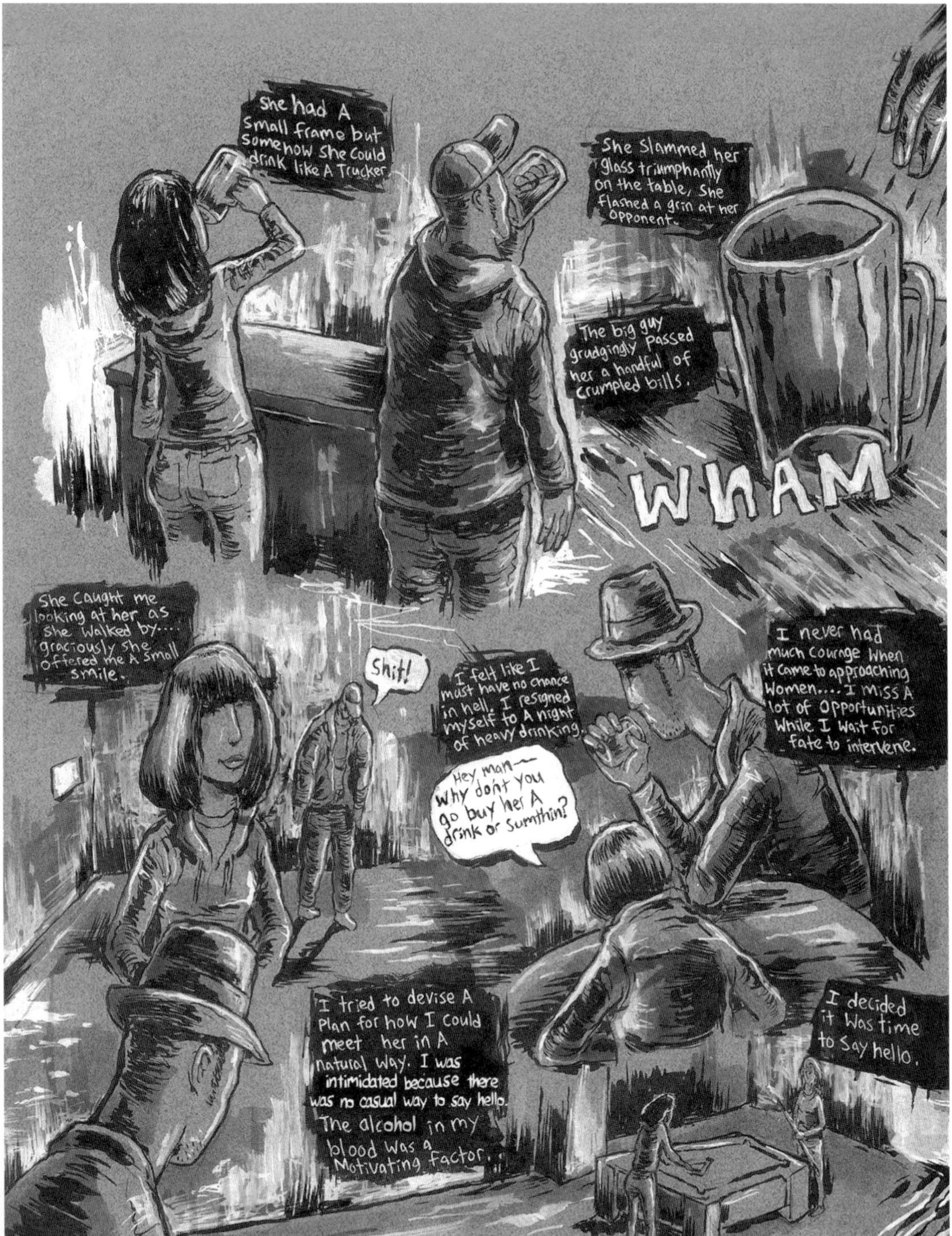
She had A Small frame but Somehow She could drink like A Trucker.
She Slammed her glass triumphantly on the table, She flashed a grin at her opponent.
The big guy grudgingly passed her a handful of crumpled bills.
WHAM
She Caught me looking at her as She Walked by... graciously she offered me A small smile.
Shit!
I felt like I must have no chance in hell. I resigned myself to A night of heavy drinking.
Hey man— Why don't you go buy her A drink or Sumthin?
I never had much courage When it came to approaching Women.... I Miss A lot of Opportunities While I Wait for fate to intervene.
I tried to devise A Plan for how I could meet her in A natural Way. I was intimidated because there was no casual way to say hello. The alcohol in my blood Was a Motivating factor.
I decided it Was time to Say hello.

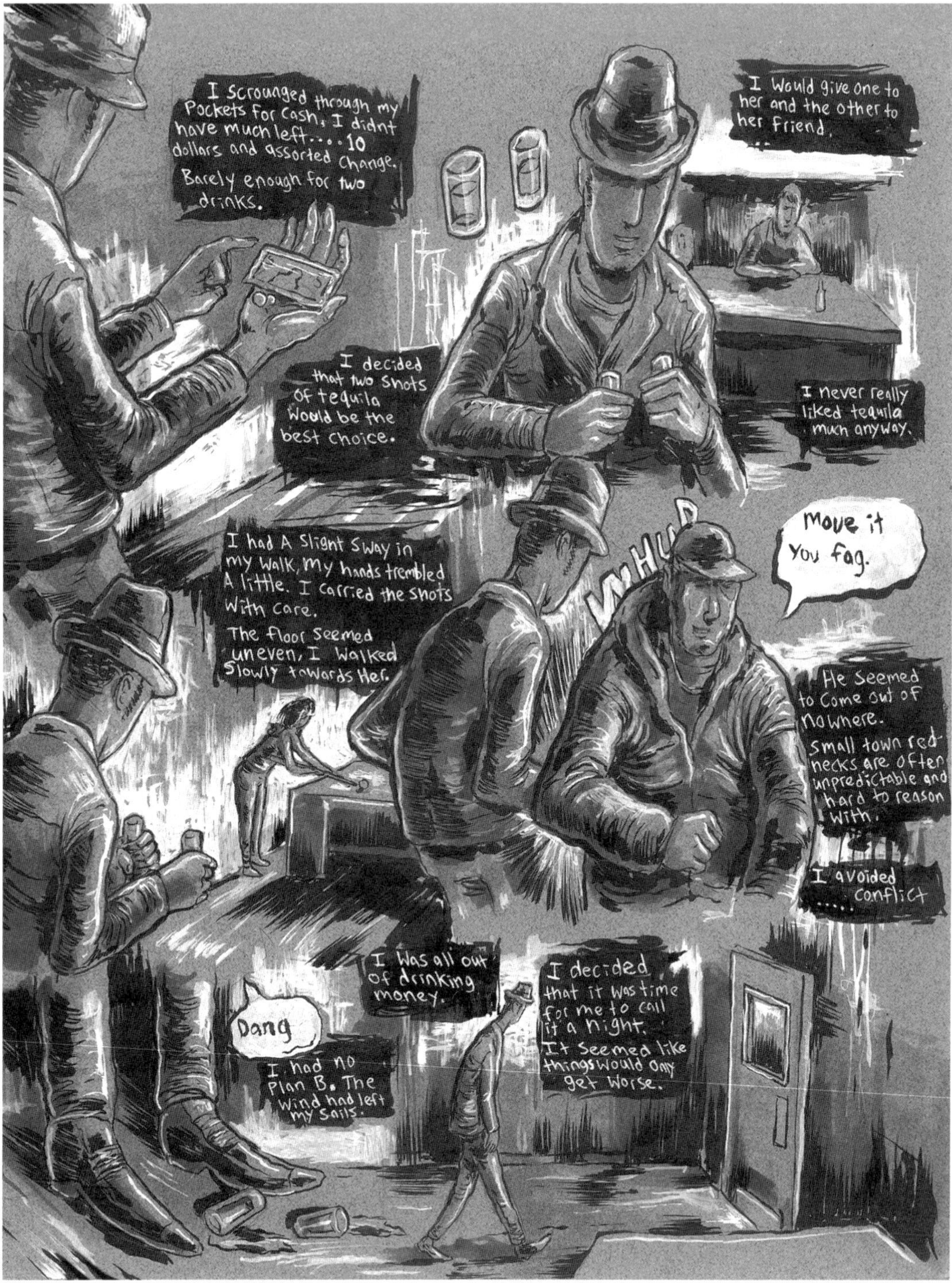
I Scrounged through my Pockets for Cash, I didnt have much left.....10 dollars and assorted Change.
Barely enough for two drinks.
I decided that two Shots of tequila Would be the best choice.
I Would give one to her and the other to her Friend.
I never really liked tequila much anyway.
I had A Slight Sway in my Walk, my hands trembled A little. I carried the Shots With care.
The floor Seemed uneven, I Walked Slowly towards Her.
WHUD
Move it You fag.
He Seemed to Come out of nowhere.
Small town red-necks are often unpredictable and hard to reason With.
I avoided conflict .....
I Was all out of drinking money.
Dang
I had no Plan B. The Wind had left my Sails.
I decided that it Was time for me to call it a night.
It Seemed like things Would Only get Worse.

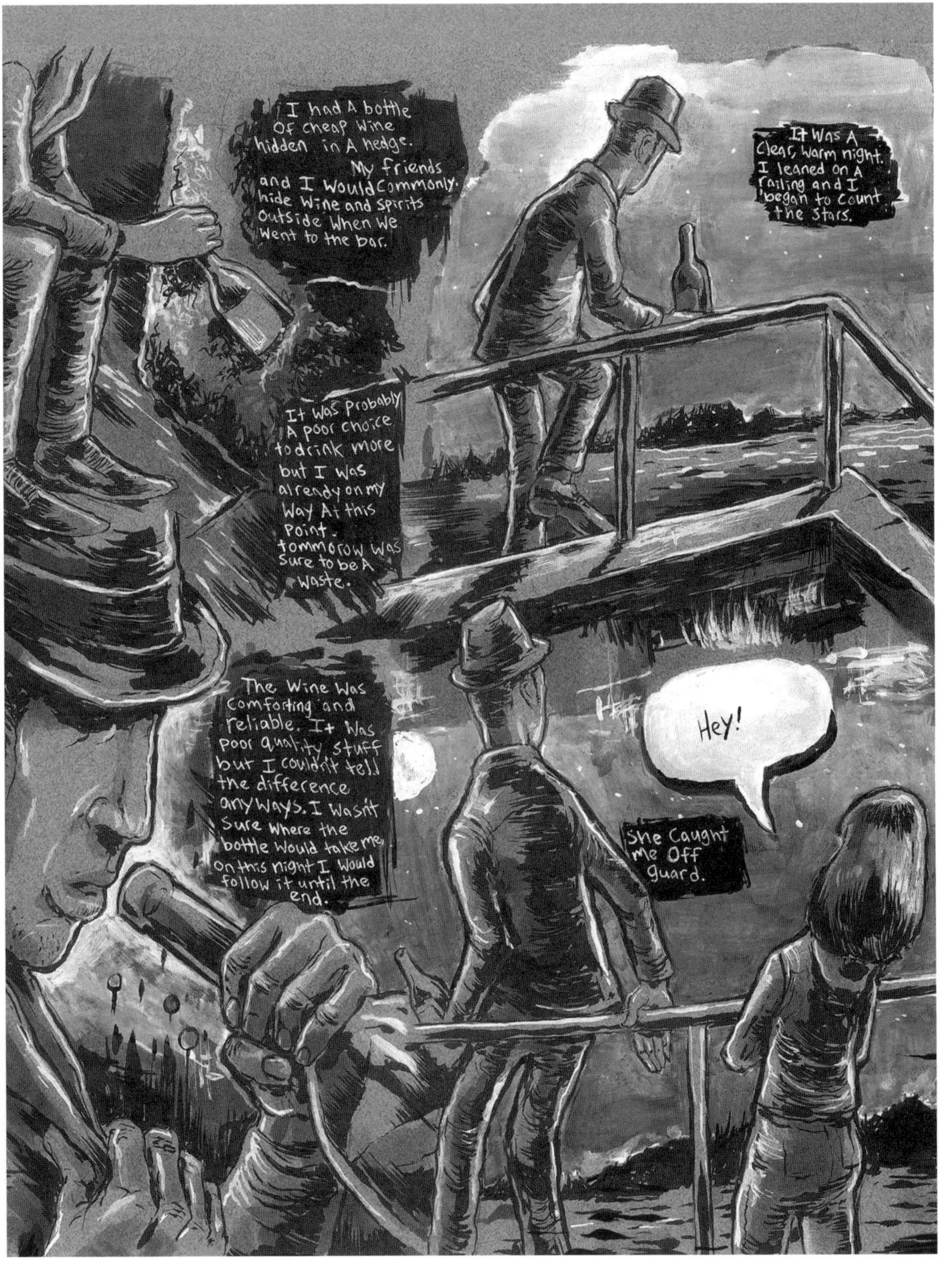
I had A bottle Of cheap Wine hidden in A hedge. My friends and I Would Commonly hide Wine and Spirits outside When We Went to the bar.
It Was A Clear, Warm night. I leaned on A railing and I began to Count the Stars.
It Was Probably A poor choice to drink more but I Was already on my Way At this Point. tommorow Was Sure to be A Waste.
The Wine Was Comforting and reliable. It Was poor quality stuff but I couldn't tell the difference anyways. I Wasn't Sure Where the bottle Would take me, on this night I Would follow it until the end.
Hey!
She Caught me Off guard.

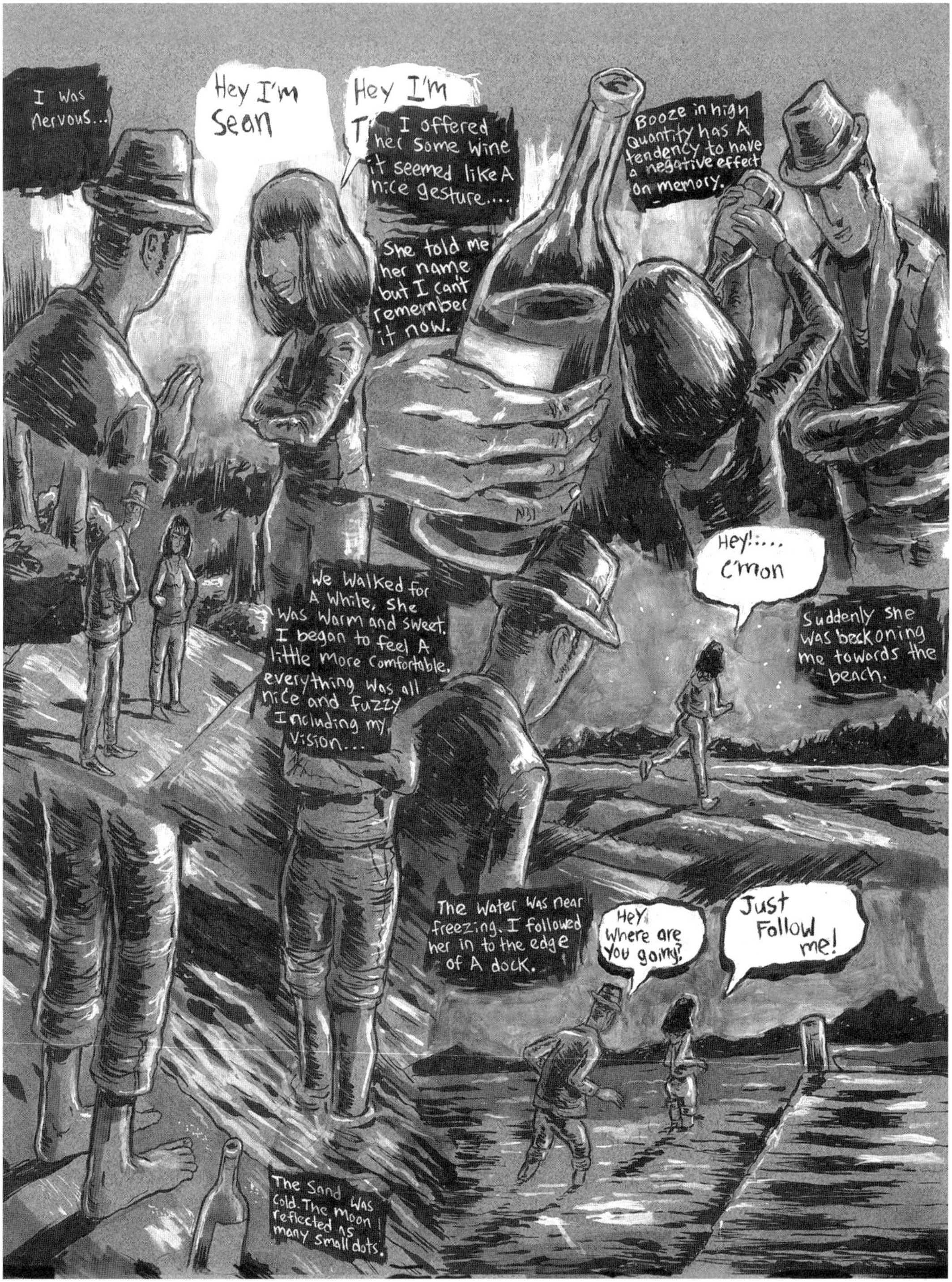
I was nervous...
Hey I'm Sean
Hey I'm T
I offered her some wine it seemed like A nice gesture....
She told me her name but I can't remember it now.
Booze in high Quantity has A tendency to have a negative effect on memory.
We walked for A while, she was warm and sweet. I began to feel A little more comfortable, everything was all nice and fuzzy Including my vision...
Hey!.... C'mon
Suddenly she was beckoning me towards the beach.
The water was near freezing. I followed her in to the edge of A dock.
Hey! Where are you going?
Just Follow me!
The Sand was cold. The moon reflected as many small dots.

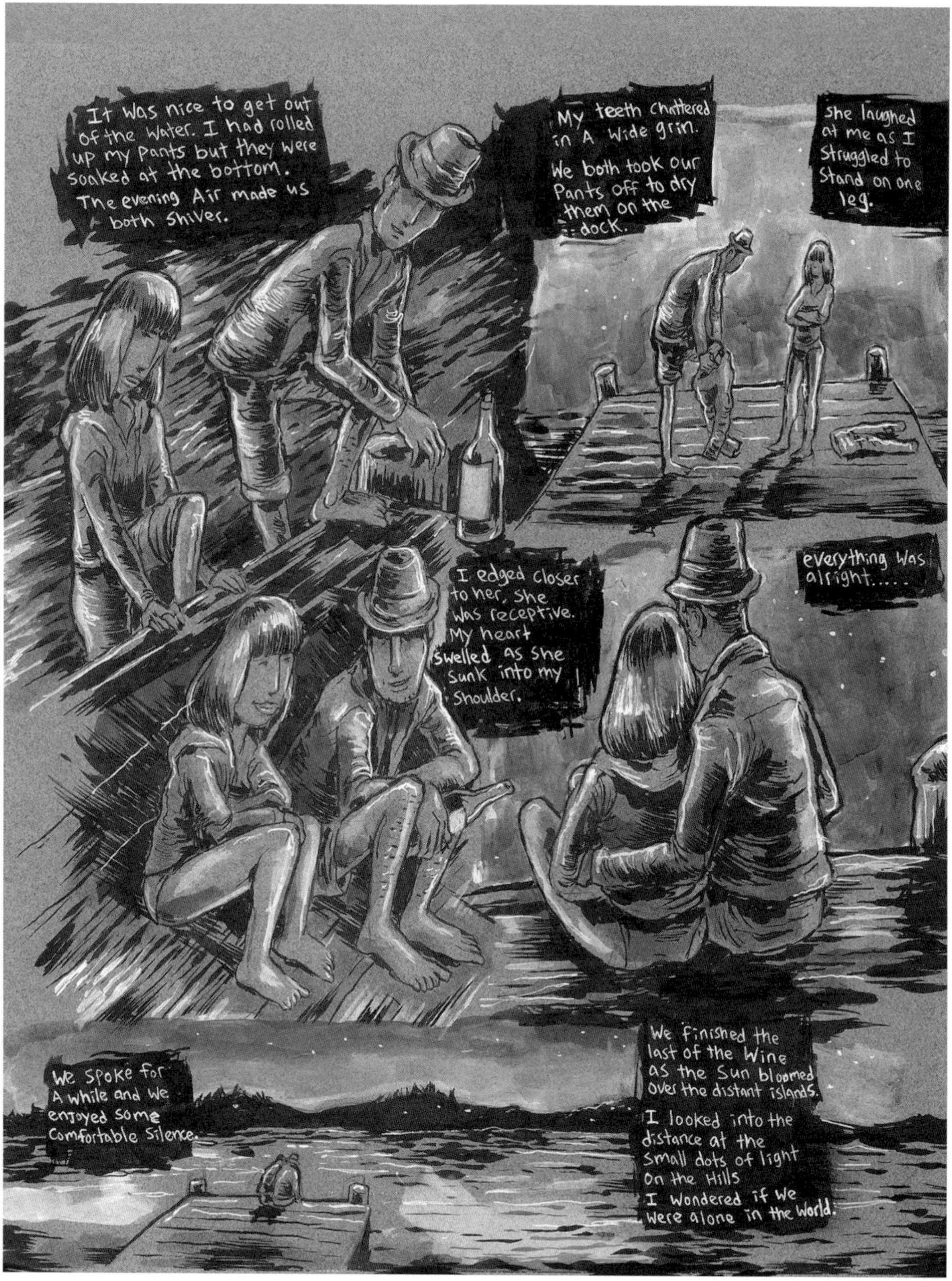
It was nice to get out of the water. I had rolled up my pants but they were soaked at the bottom. The evening Air made us both Shiver.
My teeth chattered in A wide grin.
We both took our Pants off to dry them on the dock.
She laughed at me as I Struggled to Stand on one leg.
I edged closer to her, she was receptive. My heart swelled as she sunk into my Shoulder.
everything was alright.....
We spoke for A while and we enjoyed some Comfortable Silence.
We finished the last of the Wine as the Sun bloomed over the distant islands.
I looked into the distance at the Small dots of light on the Hills
I wondered if we were alone in the World.

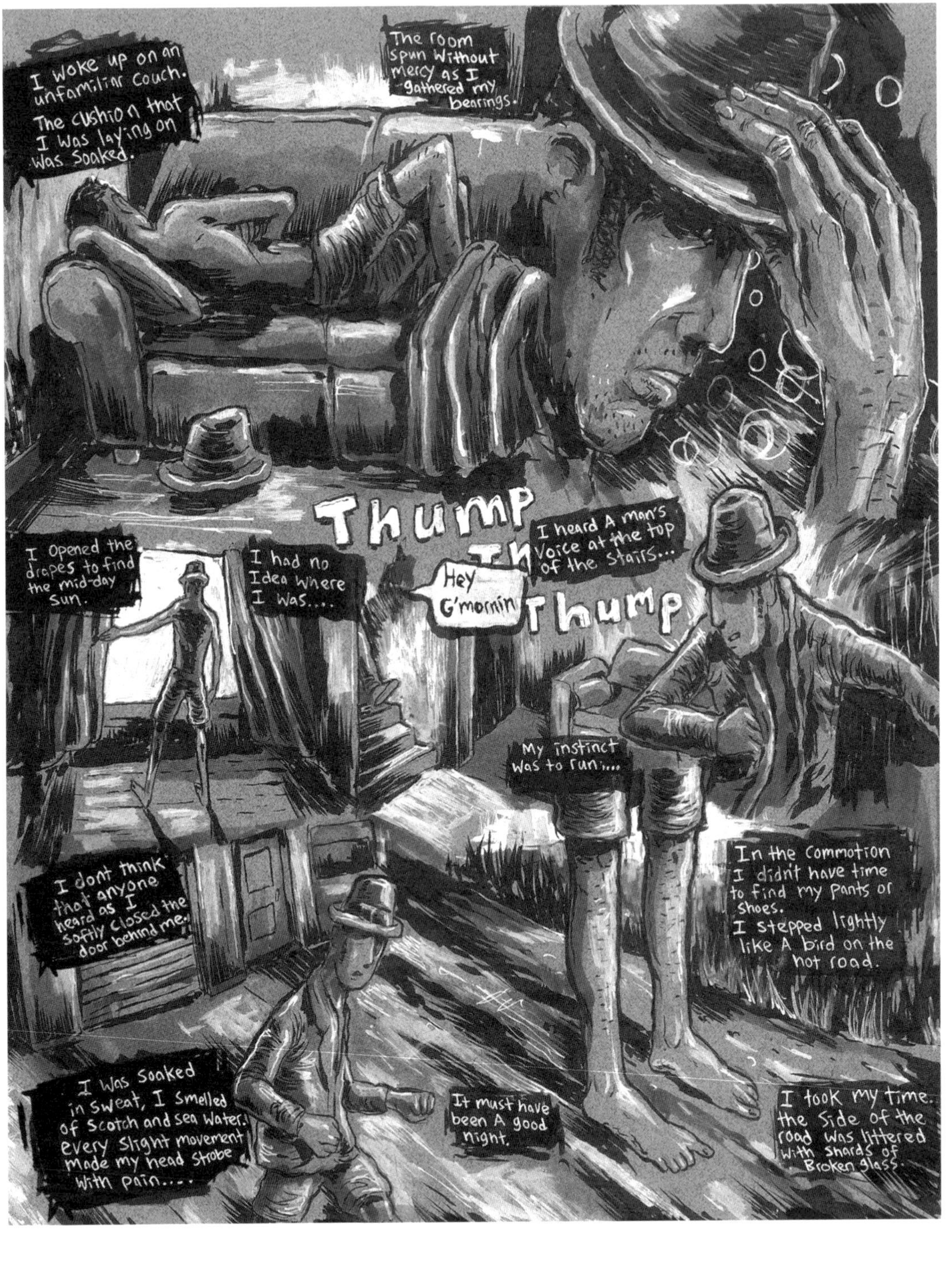
I woke up on an unfamiliar couch.
The cushion that I was laying on was soaked.
The room spun without mercy as I gathered my bearings.
Thump
Th
Thump
I heard A man's voice at the top of the stairs...
Hey G'mornin
I opened the drapes to find the mid-day sun.
I had no Idea where I was....
My instinct was to run....
I dont think that anyone heard as I softly closed the door behind me.
In the commotion I didn't have time to find my pants or shoes.
I stepped lightly like A bird on the hot road.
I was soaked in sweat, I smelled of Scotch and sea water. every slight movement made my head strobe with pain....
It must have been A good night.
I took my time. the side of the road was littered with shards of Broken glass.

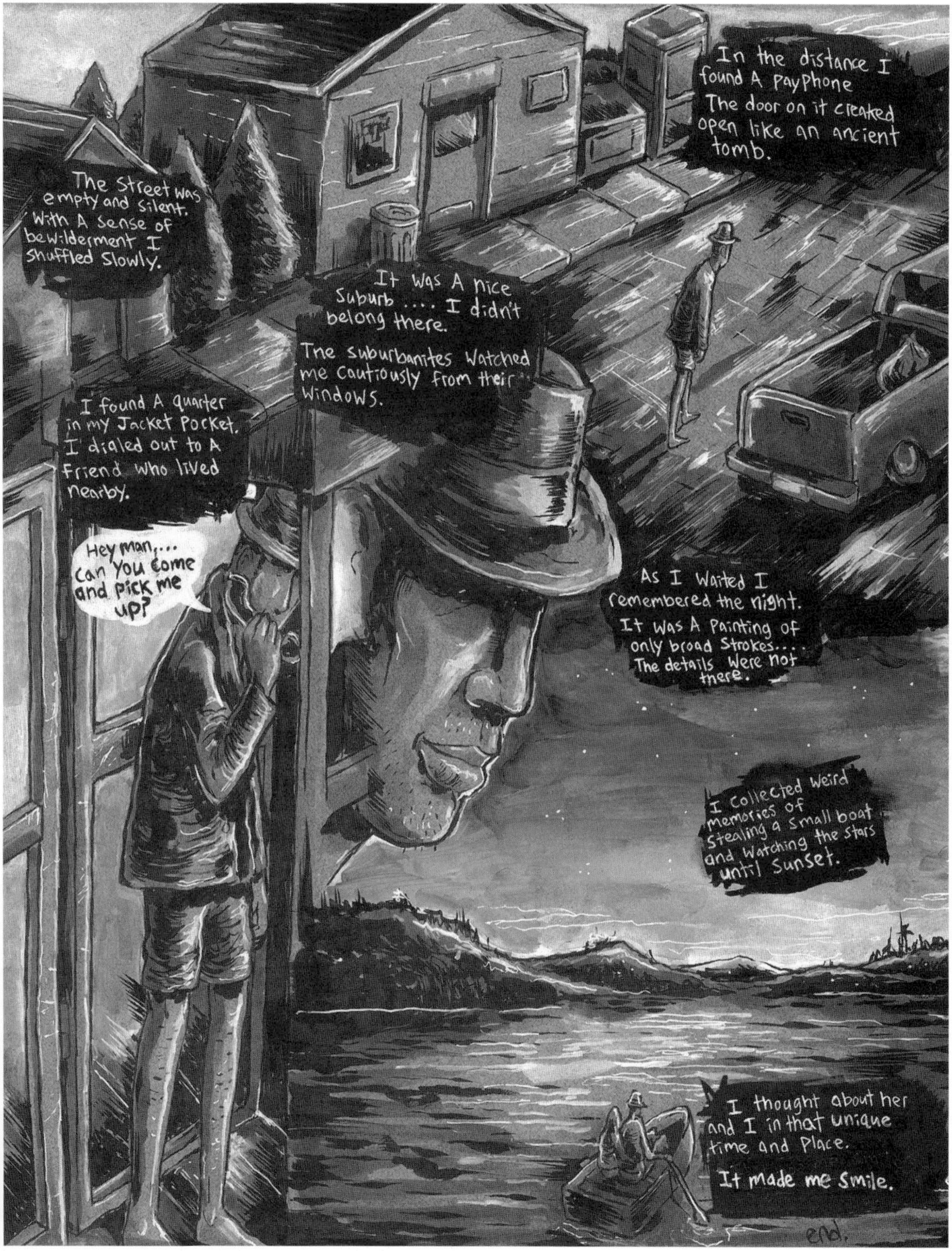
The Street was empty and Silent. With A sense of bewilderment I shuffled Slowly.
It was A nice Suburb .... I didn't belong there.
The suburbanites Watched me cautiously from their windows.
In the distance I found A payphone
The door on it creaked open like an ancient tomb.
I found A quarter in my Jacket Pocket. I dialed out to A Friend who lived nearby.
Hey man,... can you come and pick me up?
As I Waited I remembered the night.
It was A Painting of only broad Strokes.... The details were not there.
I collected weird memories of stealing a small boat and watching the stars until Sunset.
I thought about her and I in that unique time and Place.
It made me Smile.
end.

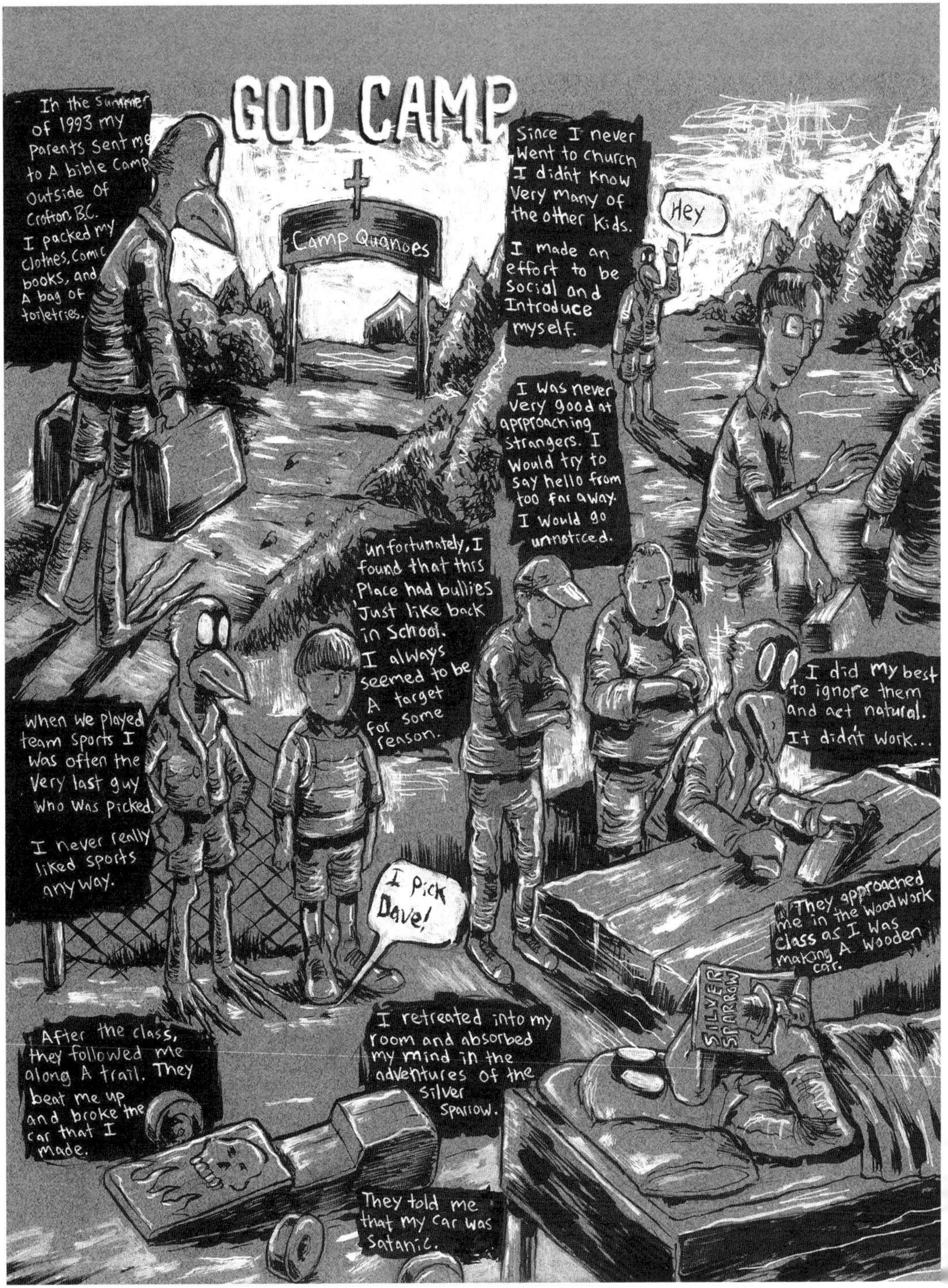
GOD CAMP
In the summer of 1993 my parents sent me to A bible camp outside of Crofton, B.C. I packed my clothes, comic books, and A bag of toiletries.
Camp Quanoes
Since I never went to church I didn't know very many of the other kids.
I made an effort to be social and introduce myself.
Hey
I was never very good at approaching strangers. I would try to say hello from too far away. I would go unnoticed.
unfortunately, I found that this place had bullies just like back in School.
I always seemed to be A target for some reason.
When we played team sports I was often the very last guy who was picked.
I never really liked sports anyway.
I pick Dave!
I did my best to ignore them and act natural.
It didn't work...
They approached me in the woodwork class as I was making A wooden car.
After the class, they followed me along A trail. They beat me up and broke the car that I made.
I retreated into my room and absorbed my mind in the adventures of the silver sparrow.
SILVER SPARROW
They told me that my car was satanic.

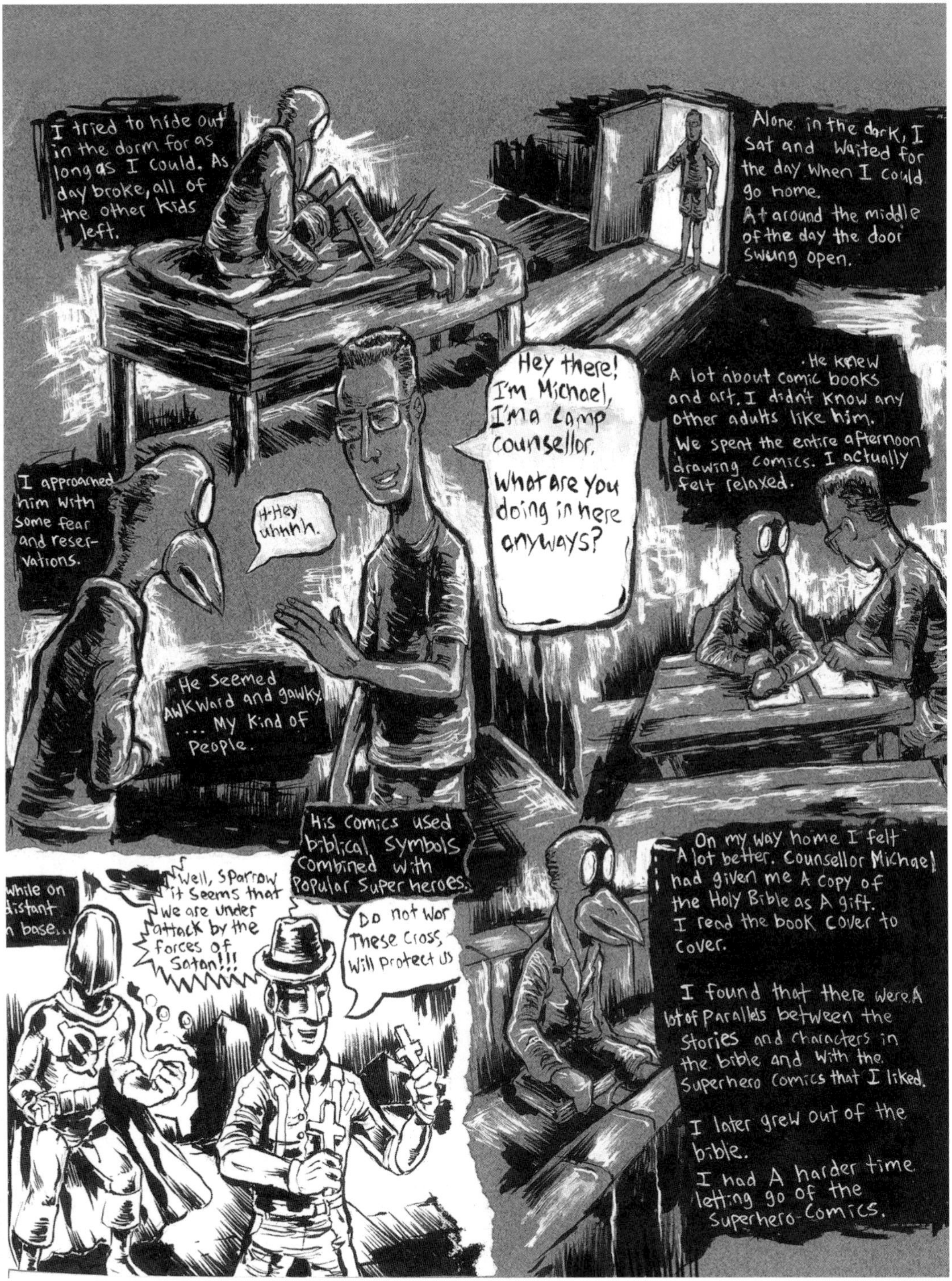
I tried to hide out in the dorm for as long as I could. As day broke, all of the other kids left.
Alone in the dark, I sat and waited for the day when I could go home.
At around the middle of the day the door swung open.
Hey there! I'm Michael, I'm a camp counsellor.
What are you doing in here anyways?
I approached him with some fear and reservations.
H-Hey uhhhh.
He seemed awkward and gawky. .... My kind of people.
. He knew a lot about comic books and art. I didn't know any other adults like him.
We spent the entire afternoon drawing comics. I actually felt relaxed.
His comics used biblical symbols combined with popular super heroes.
while on distant n base...
Well, Sparrow it seems that we are under attack by the forces of Satan!!!
Do not wor These cross, will protect us
On my way home I felt a lot better. Counsellor Michael had given me a copy of the Holy Bible as a gift.
I read the book cover to cover.
I found that there were a lot of parallels between the stories and characters in the bible and with the superhero comics that I liked.
I later grew out of the bible.
I had a harder time letting go of the superhero comics.

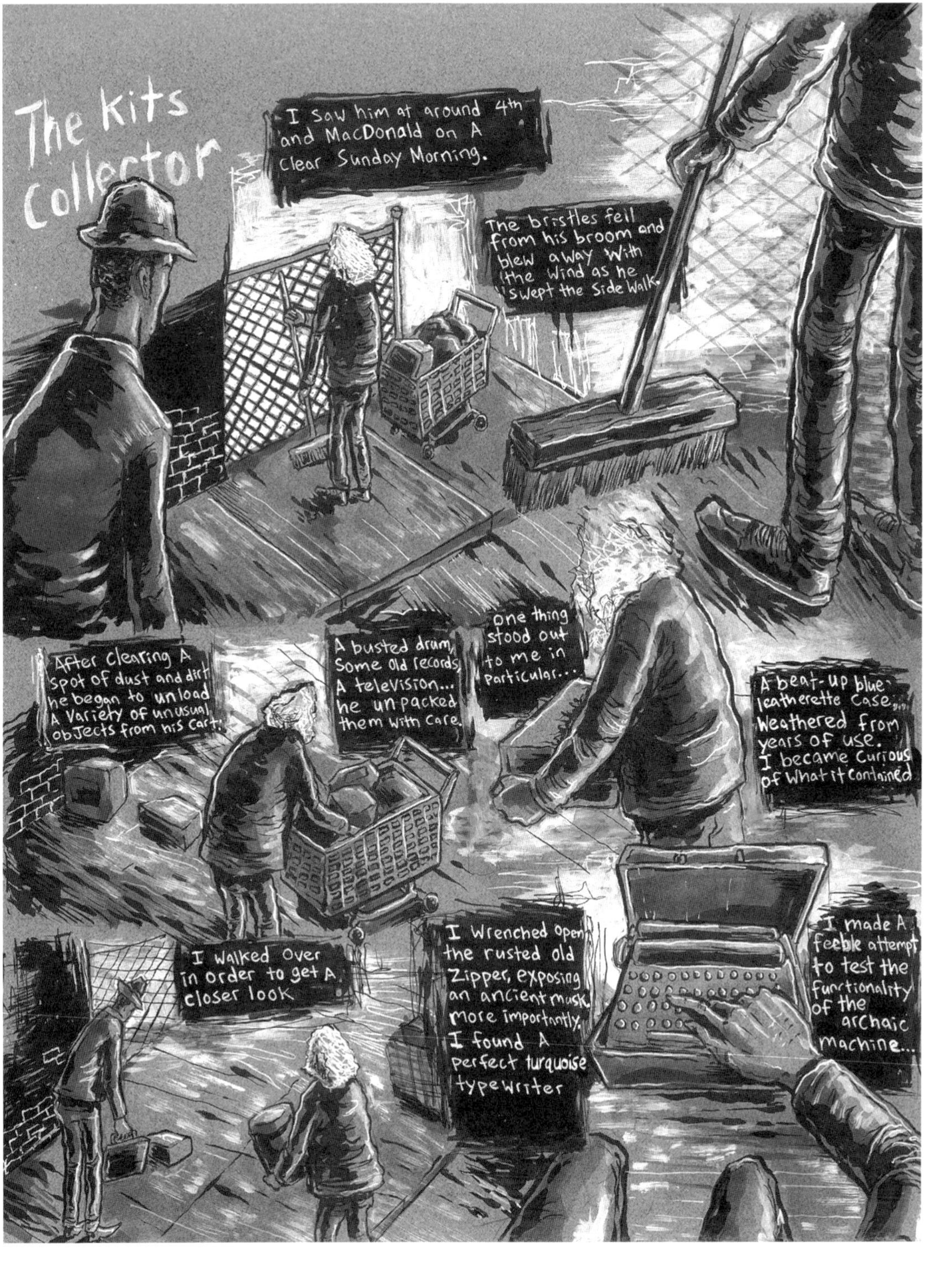
The Kits Collector
I saw him at around 4th and MacDonald on A clear Sunday Morning.
The bristles fell from his broom and blew away with the wind as he swept the side walk.
After clearing A spot of dust and dirt he began to unload A variety of unusual objects from his cart.
A busted drum, some old records, A television... he unpacked them with care.
One thing stood out to me in particular...
A beat-up blue leatherette case... weathered from years of use. I became curious of what it contained
I walked over in order to get A closer look
I wrenched open the rusted old zipper, exposing an ancient musk. more importantly, I found A perfect turquoise typewriter
I made A feeble attempt to test the functionality of the archaic machine...

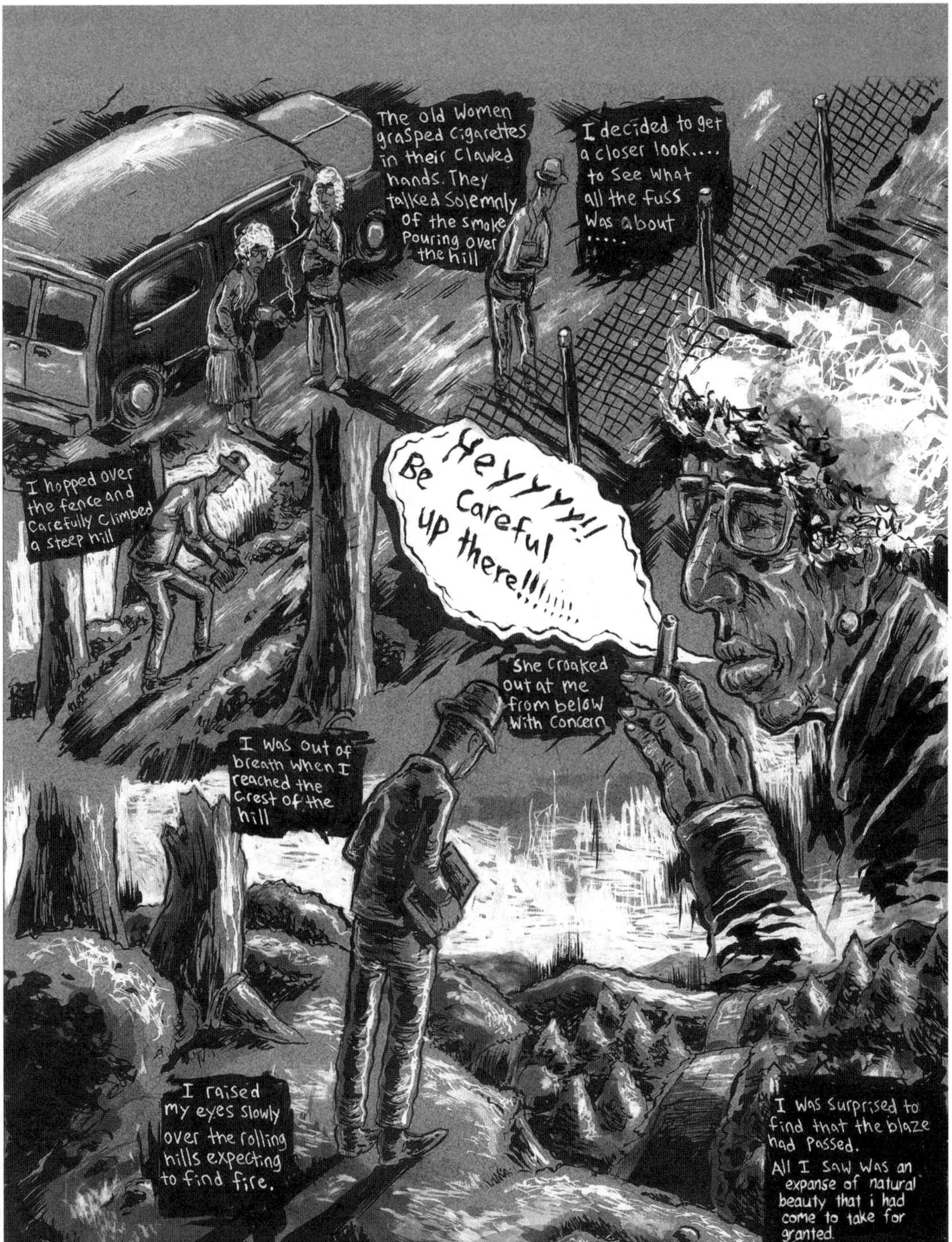

The old Women grasped Cigarettes in their Clawed hands. They talked Solemnly of the smoke pouring over the hill
I decided to get a closer look.... to see What all the fuss Was about .....
I hopped over the fence and Carefully Climbed a steep hill
Heyyyy!! Be careful up there!!!!!!!
She croaked out at me from below With Concern
I was out of breath when I reached the crest of the hill
I raised my eyes slowly over the rolling hills expecting to find fire.
I was surprised to find that the blaze had passed.
All I saw was an expanse of natural beauty that i had come to take for granted.

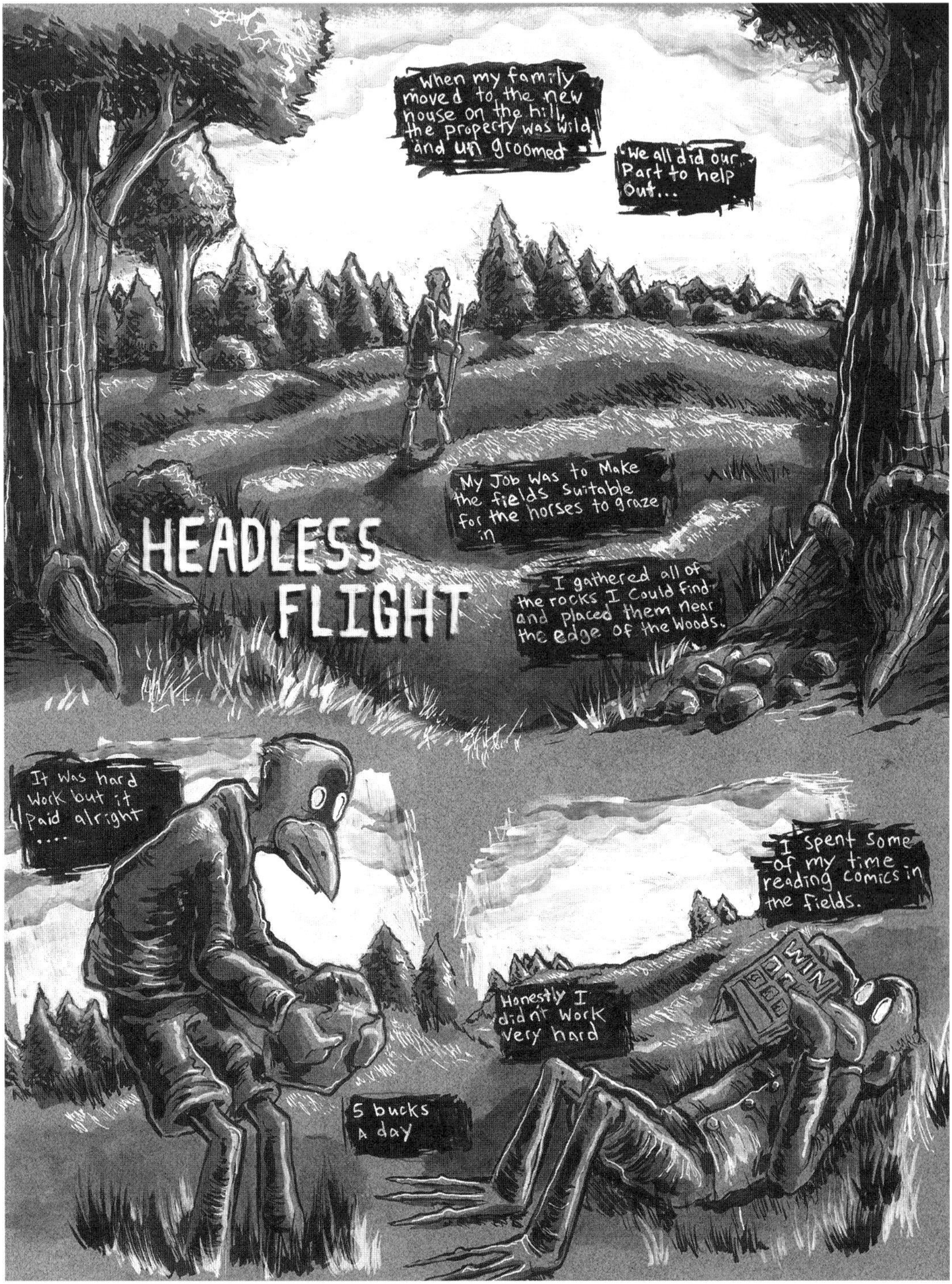
When my family moved to the new house on the hill, the property was wild and un groomed
We all did our Part to help out...
My Job was to Make the fields Suitable for the horses to graze in
HEADLESS FLIGHT
I gathered all of the rocks I Could find and placed them near the edge of the Woods.
It was hard Work but it Paid alright ....
5 bucks A day
I spent some of my time reading comics in the fields.
Honestly I did n't Work very hard

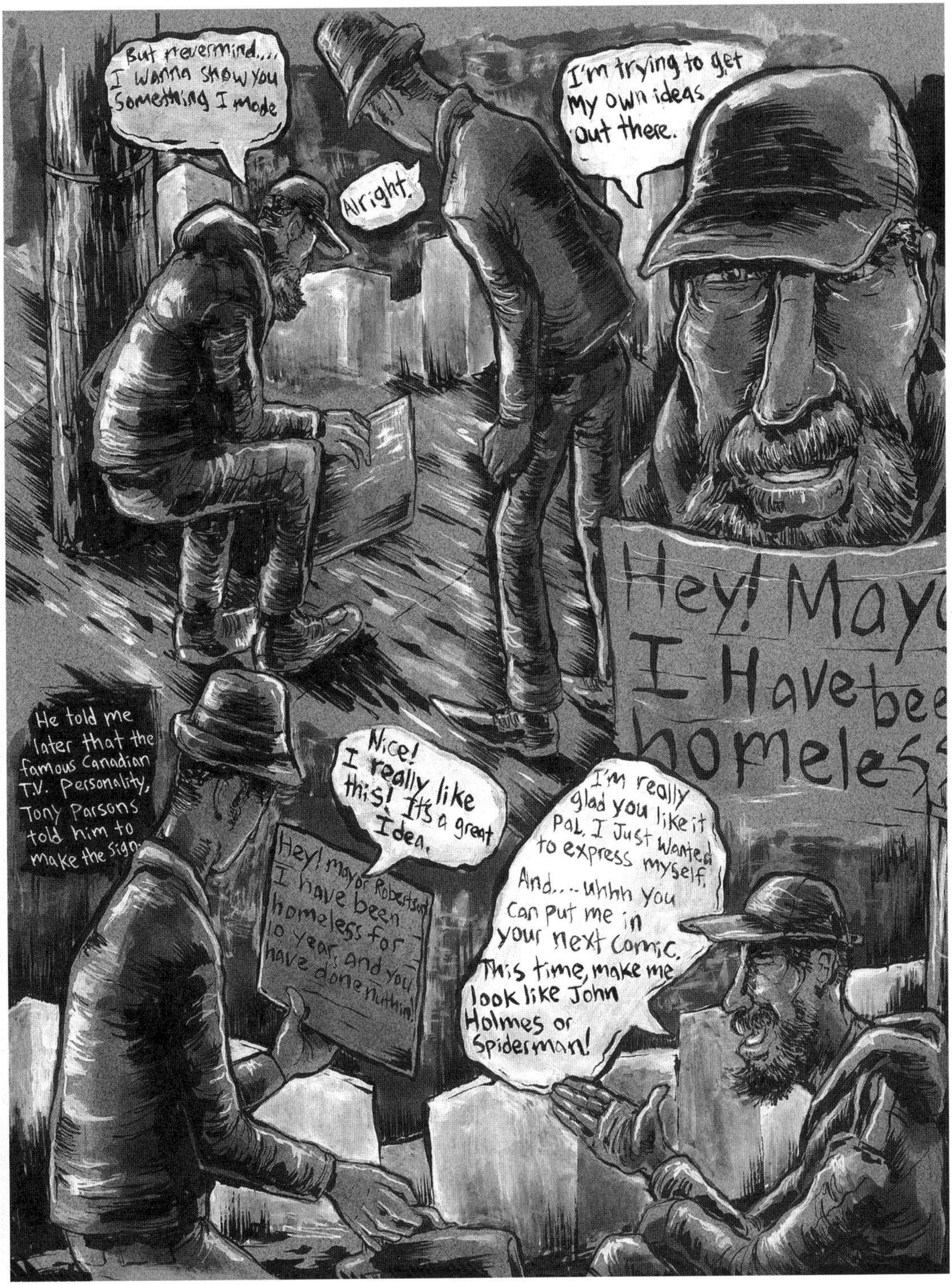
But nevermind....
I wanna show you
Something I made
Alright.
I'm trying to get
my own ideas
out there.
Hey! Mayo
I Have bee
homeless
He told me
later that the
famous Canadian
T.V. Personality,
Tony Parsons
told him to
make the Sign.
Nice!
I really like
this! It's a great
Idea.
Hey! mayor Robertson
I have been
homeless for
10 years and you
have done nuthin!
I'm really
glad you like it
Pal. I Just wanted
to express myself.
And.... uhhh you
can put me in
your next Comic.
This time, make me
look like John
Holmes or
Spiderman!

MY LIFE AS A LEAF

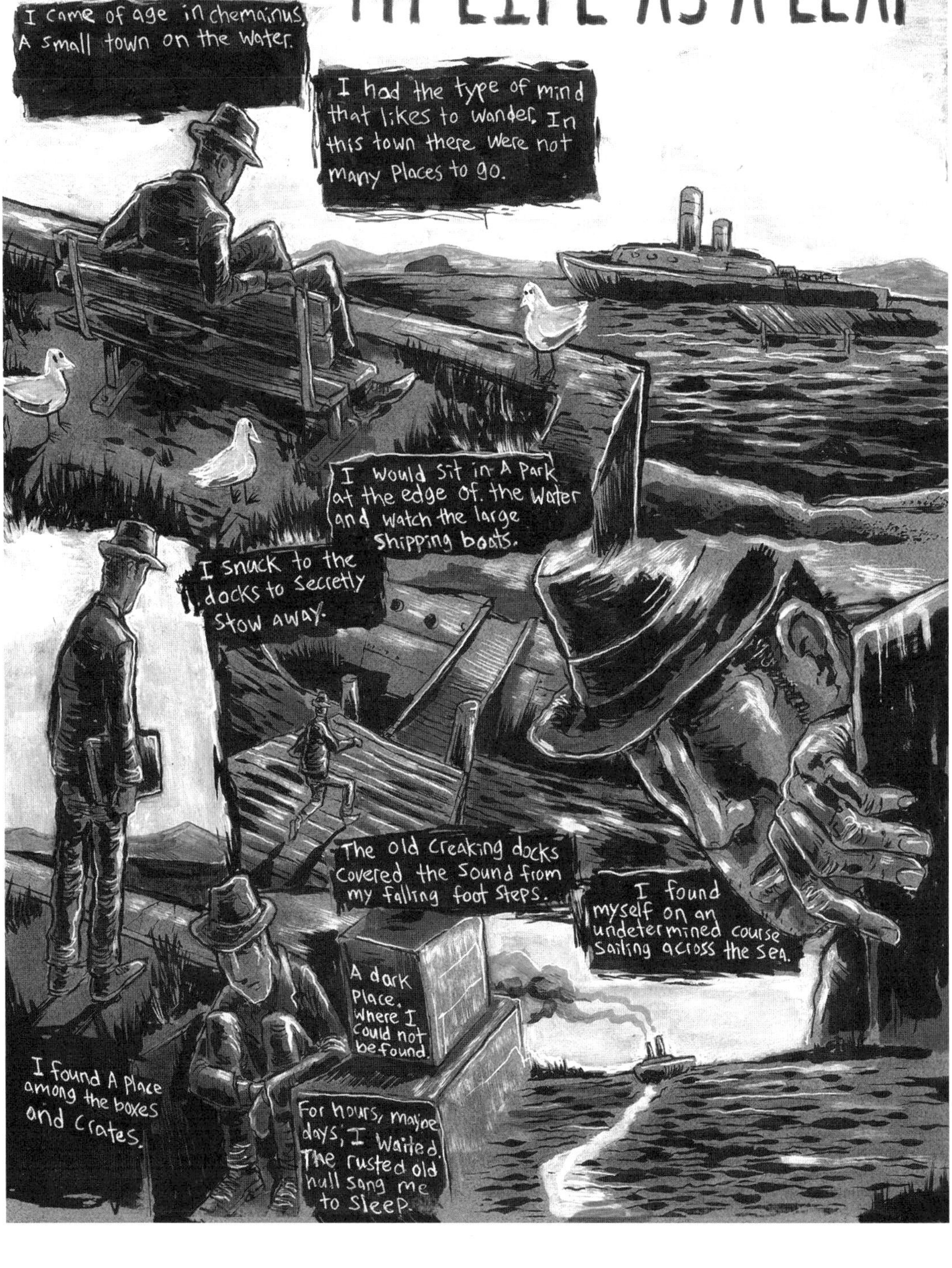
I came of age in chemainus, A small town on the water.
I had the type of mind that likes to wander. In this town there were not many places to go.
I would sit in A park at the edge of the water and watch the large shipping boats.
I snuck to the docks to secretly stow away.
The old creaking docks covered the sound from my falling foot steps.
I found myself on an undetermined course sailing across the sea.
A dark place, where I could not be found.
I found A place among the boxes and crates.
For hours, maybe days, I waited. The rusted old hull sang me to sleep.

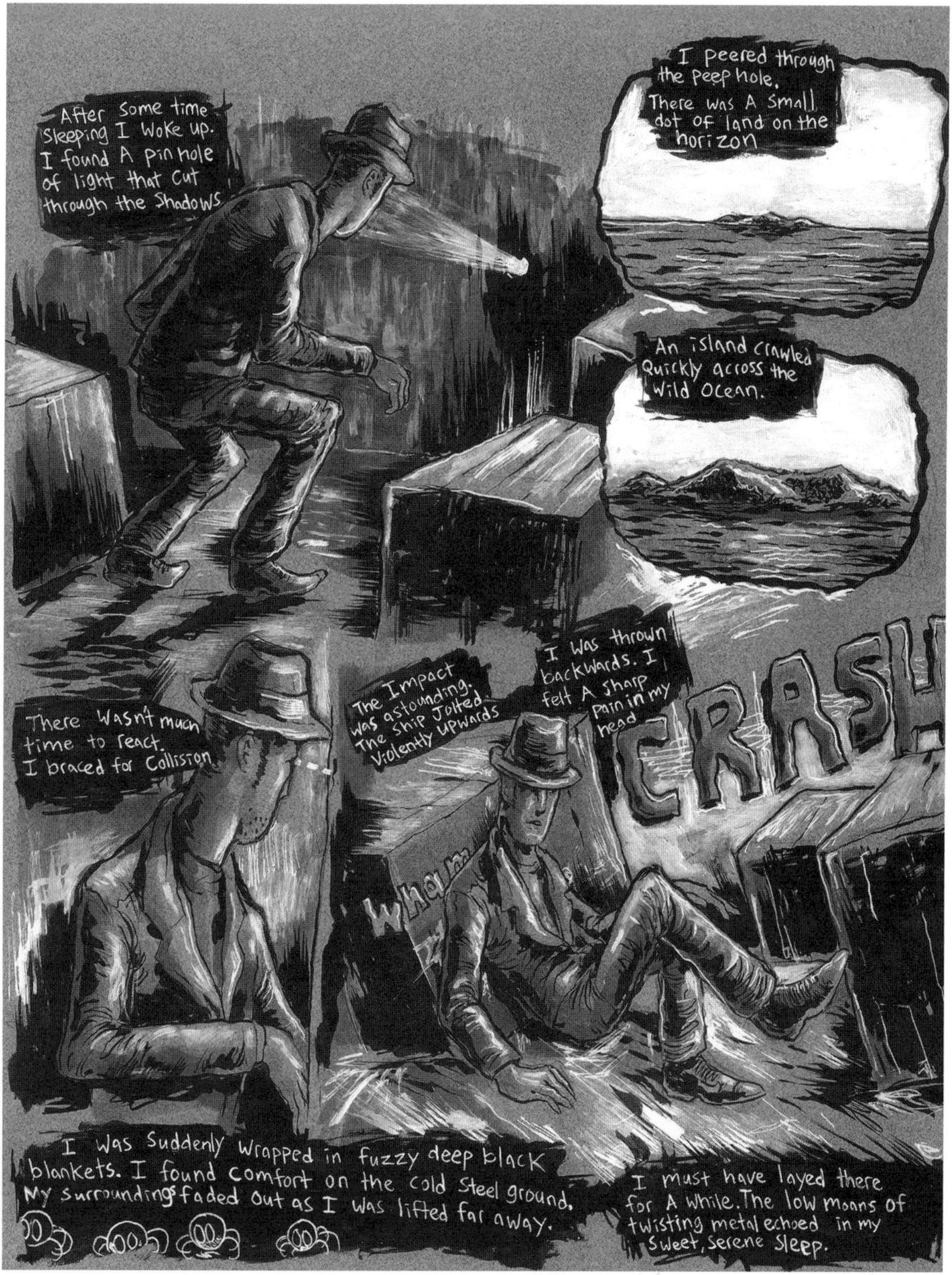
After some time sleeping I woke up. I found A pin hole of light that cut through the Shadows
I peered through the peep hole. There was A small dot of land on the horizon
An island crawled Quickly across the Wild Ocean.
There wasn't much time to react. I braced for Collision
The Impact was astounding. The ship Jolted Violently upwards
I was thrown backwards. I felt A sharp pain in my head
CRASH
I was Suddenly Wrapped in fuzzy deep black blankets. I found comfort on the cold Steel ground. My surroundings faded out as I was lifted far away.
I must have layed there for A while. The low moans of twisting metal echoed in my Sweet, Serene Sleep.

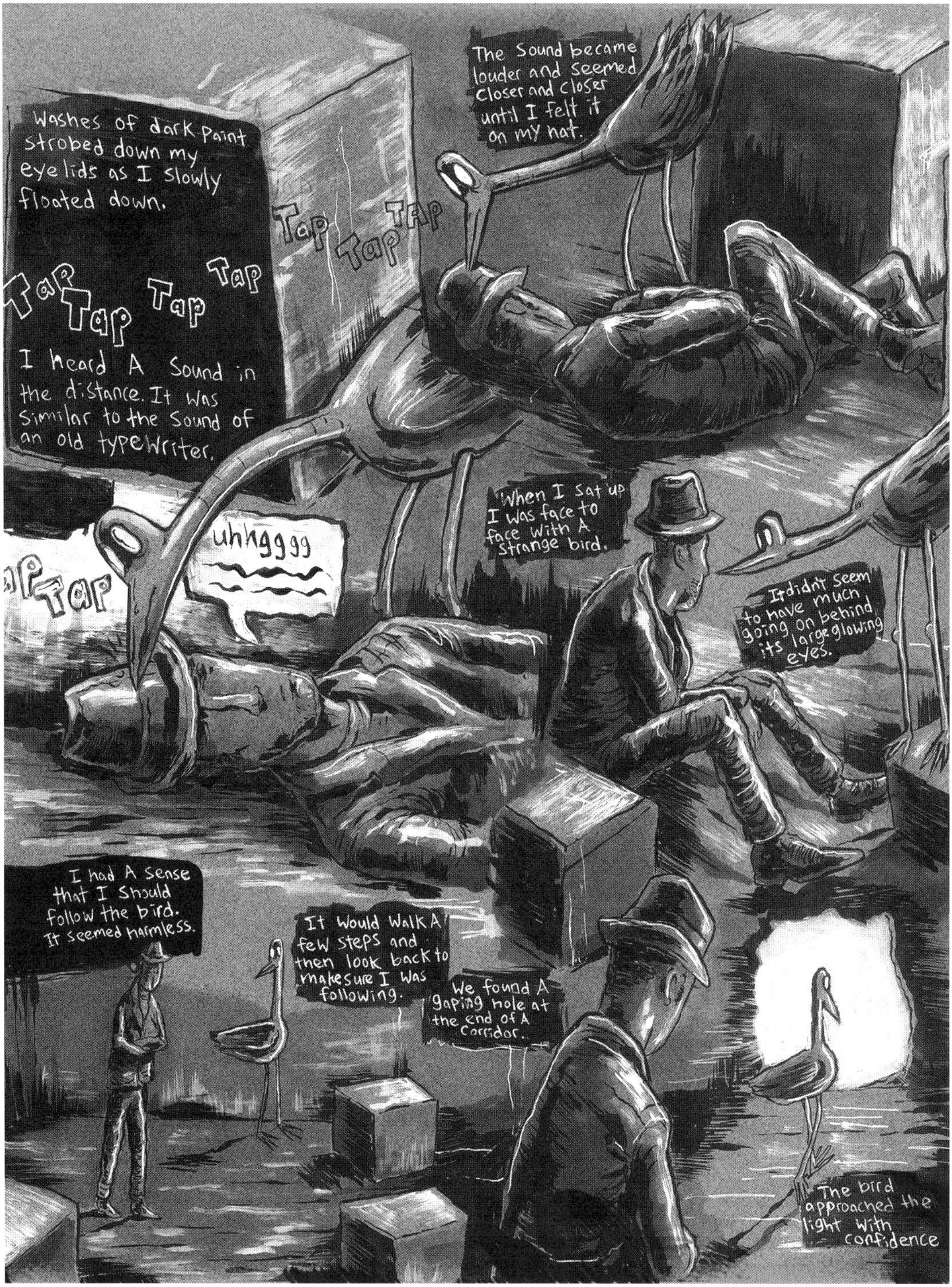

Washes of dark Paint strobed down my eyelids as I slowly floated down.
Tap Tap Tap Tap
I heard A Sound in the distance. It was similar to the Sound of an old typeWriter.
Tap Tap TAP
The Sound became louder and seemed closer and closer until I felt it on my hat.
Tap Tap
uhhgggg
When I sat up I was face to face with A strange bird.
It didn't seem to have much going on behind its large glowing eyes.
I had A sense that I should follow the bird. It seemed harmless.
It would WalkA few steps and then look back to makesure I was following.
We found A gaping hole at the end of A corridor.
The bird approached the light with confidence

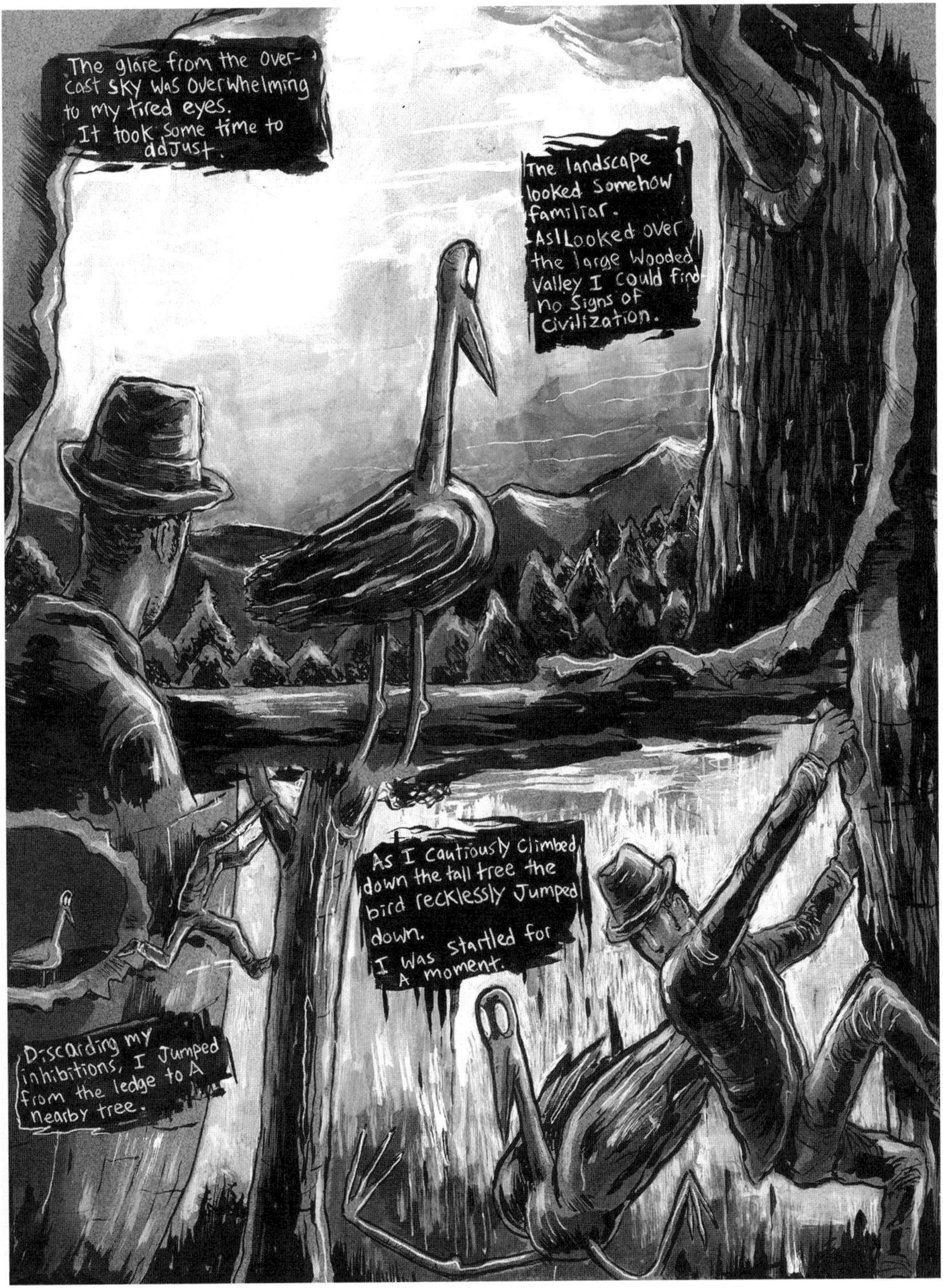
The glare from the over-cast SKY was OverWhelming to my tired eyes. It took Some time to adJust.
The landscape looked Somehow familiar. AsILooked over the large Wooded Valley I could find no Signs of civilization.
As I cautiously climbed down the tall tree the bird recklessly Jumped down. I was startled for A moment.
Discarding my inhibitions, I Jumped from the ledge to A nearby tree.

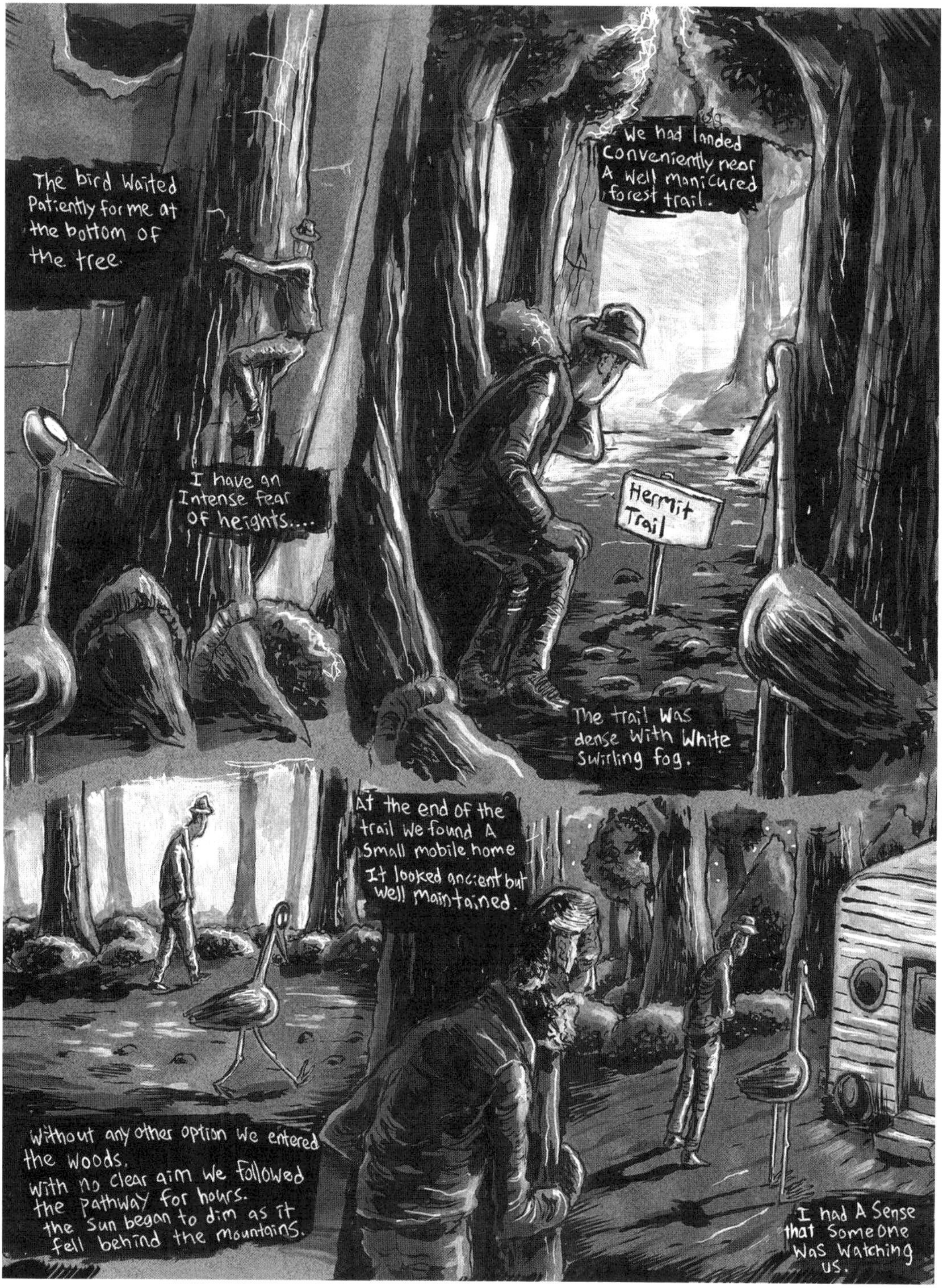
The bird Waited Patiently for me at the bottom of the tree.
I have an Intense fear of heights....
We had landed Conveniently near A well manicured forest trail.
Hermit Trail
The trail Was dense With White Swirling fog.
Without any other option We entered the woods.
With no clear aim we followed the Pathway for hours.
the Sun began to dim as it fell behind the mountains.
At the end of the trail We found A Small mobile home
It looked ancient but Well maintained.
I had A Sense that Some One Was Watching us.

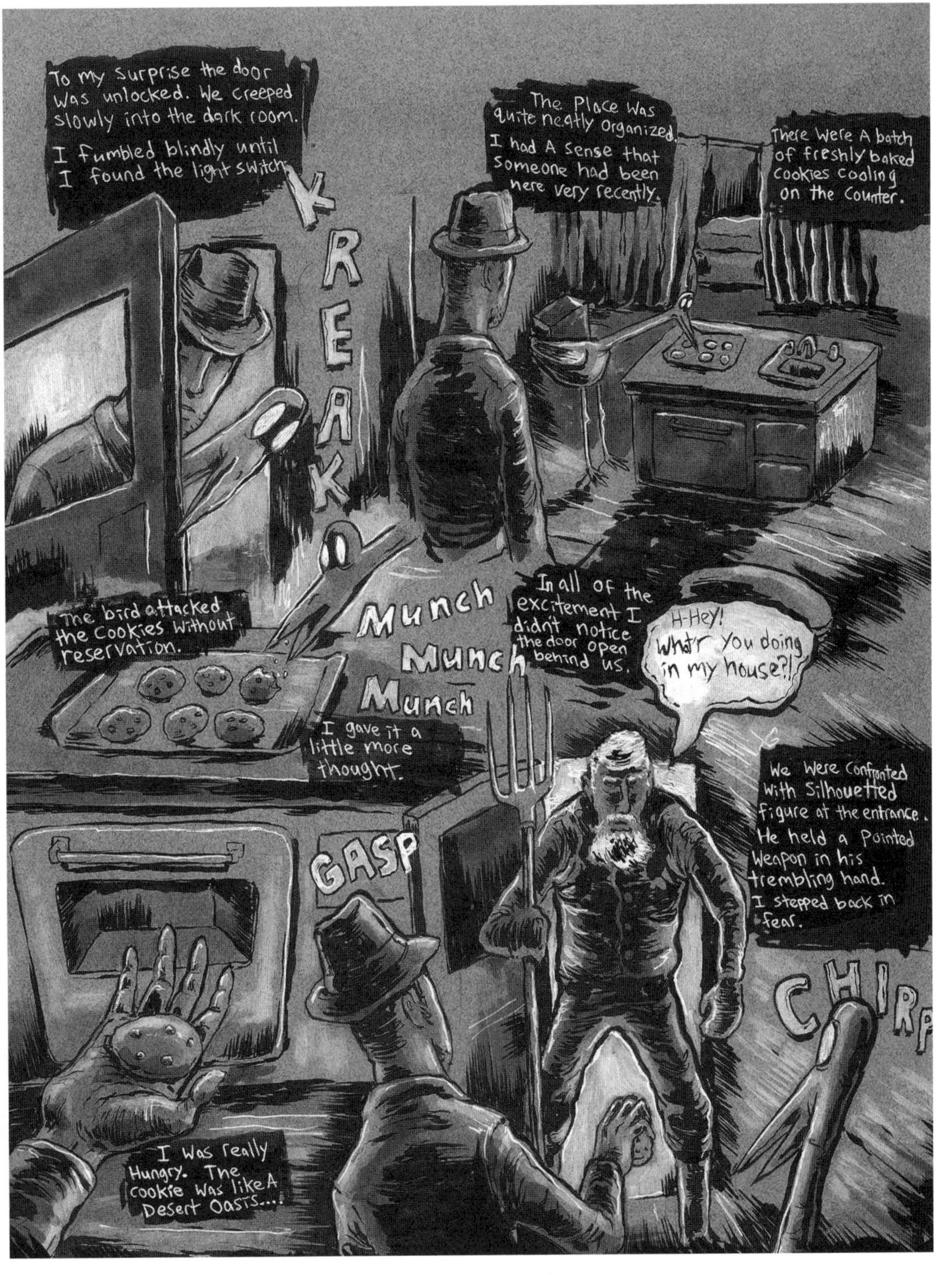
To my surprise the door was unlocked. We creeped slowly into the dark room.
I fumbled blindly until I found the light switch.
KREAK
The Place was quite neatly organized.
I had A sense that someone had been here very recently.
There were A batch of freshly baked cookies cooling on the counter.
The bird attacked the cookies without reservation.
Munch
Munch
Munch
I gave it a little more thought.
In all of the excitement I didn't notice the door open behind us.
H-Hey! What're you doing in my house?!
GASP
We were confronted with silhouetted figure at the entrance. He held a pointed weapon in his trembling hand. I stepped back in fear.
CHIRP
I was really Hungry. The cookie was like A Desert Oasis....

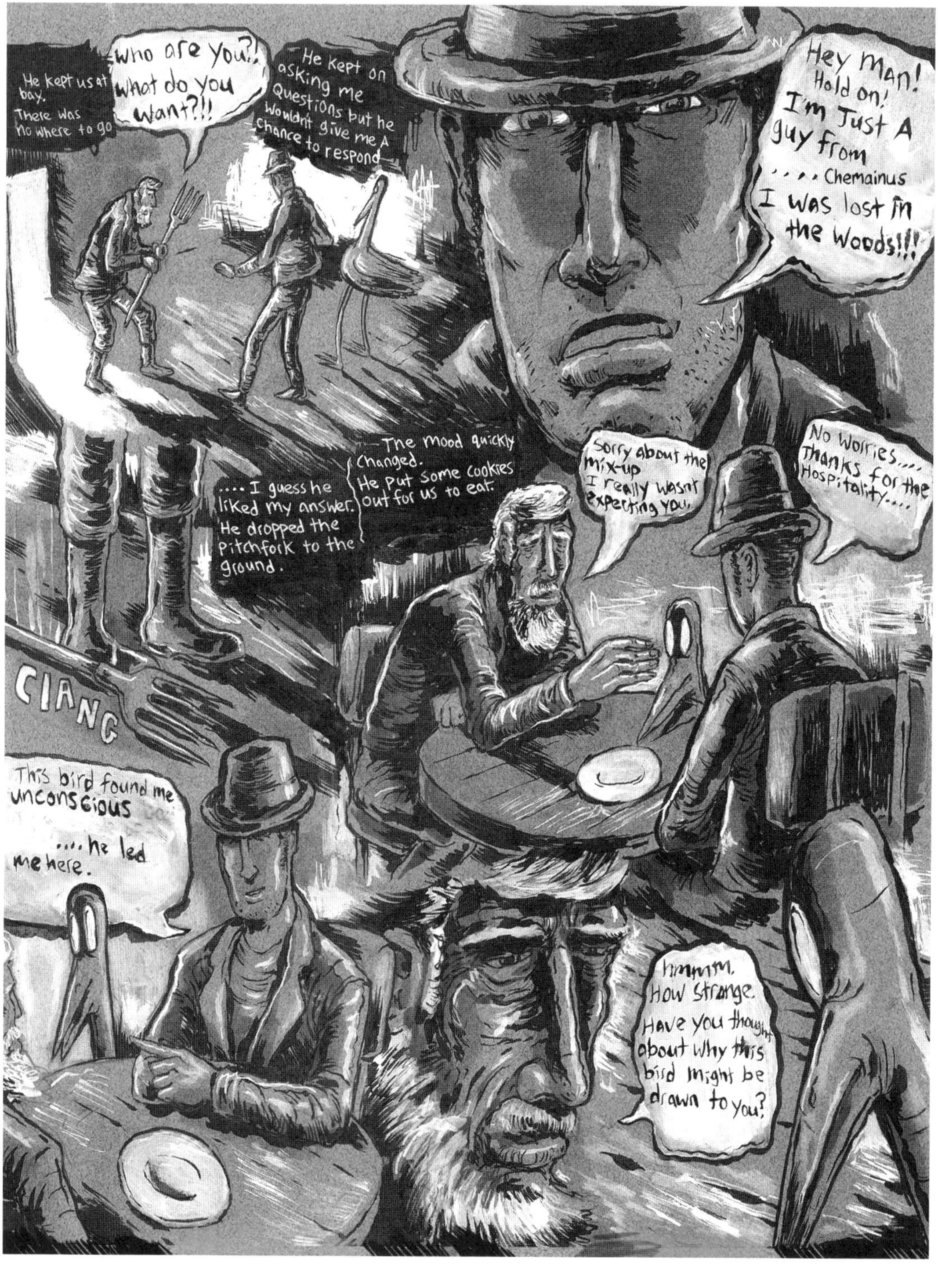
He kept us at bay. There was no where to go
Who are you?! What do you want?!!
He kept on asking me Questions but he wouldn't give me A chance to respond
Hey man! Hold on! I'm Just A guy from ....Chemainus I was lost in the woods!!!
.... I guess he liked my answer. He dropped the Pitchfork to the ground.
The mood quickly changed. He put some cookies out for us to eat.
Sorry about the mix-up I really wasn't expecting you.
No worries.... Thanks for the Hospitality....
CLANG
This bird found me unconscious ....he led me here.
hmmm. How Strange. Have you thought about why this bird might be drawn to you?

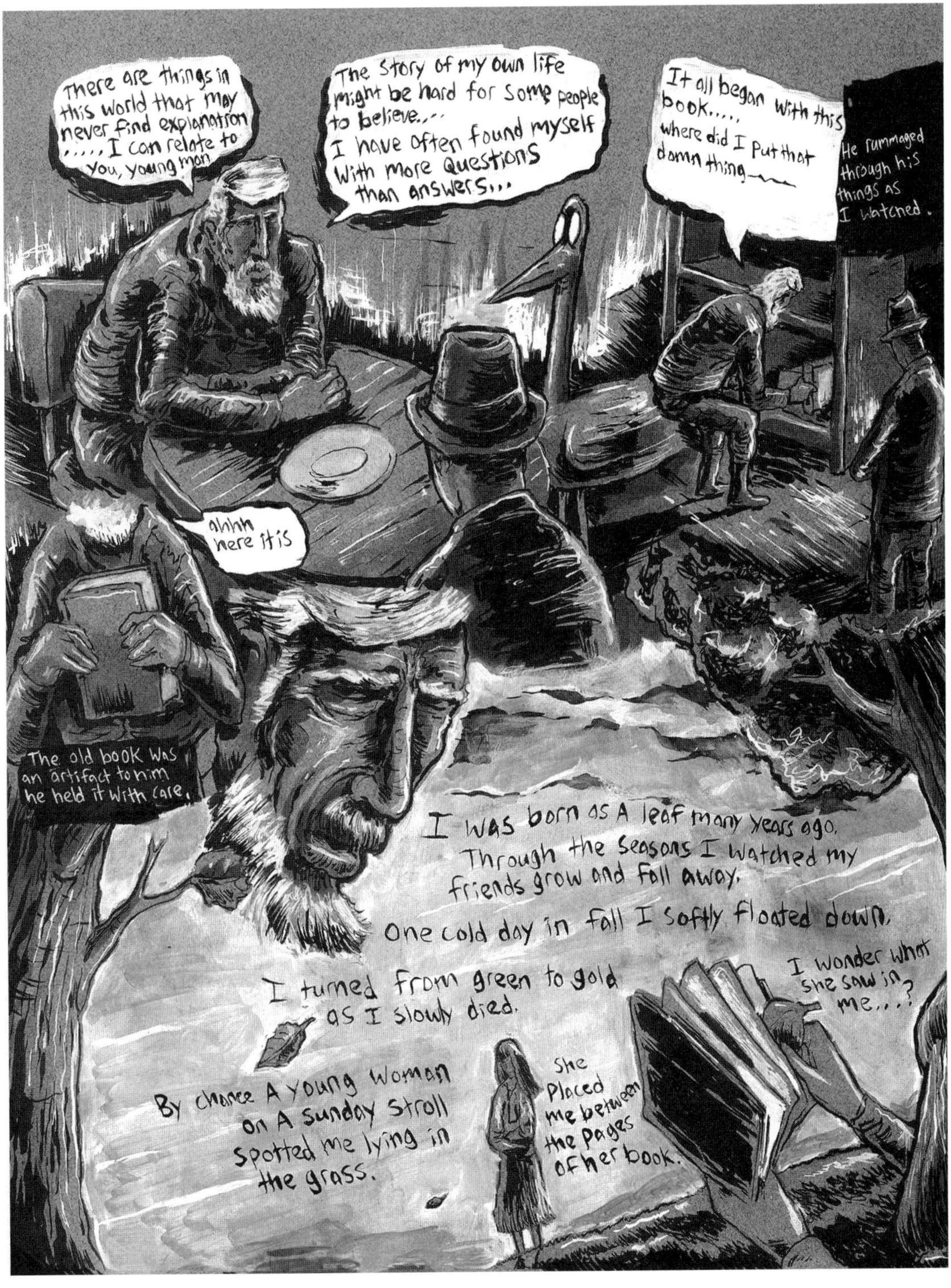
There are things in this world that may never find explanation ....., I can relate to you, young man
The story of my own life might be hard for some people to believe...
I have often found myself with more questions than answers...
It all began with this book.....,
where did I put that damn thing
He rummaged through his things as I watched.
ahhh here it is
The old book was an artifact to him he held it with care.
I was born as a leaf many years ago.
Through the seasons I watched my friends grow and fall away.
One cold day in fall I softly floated down.
I turned from green to gold as I slowly died.
I wonder what she saw in me...?
By chance a young woman on a Sunday stroll spotted me lying in the grass.
She placed me between the pages of her book.

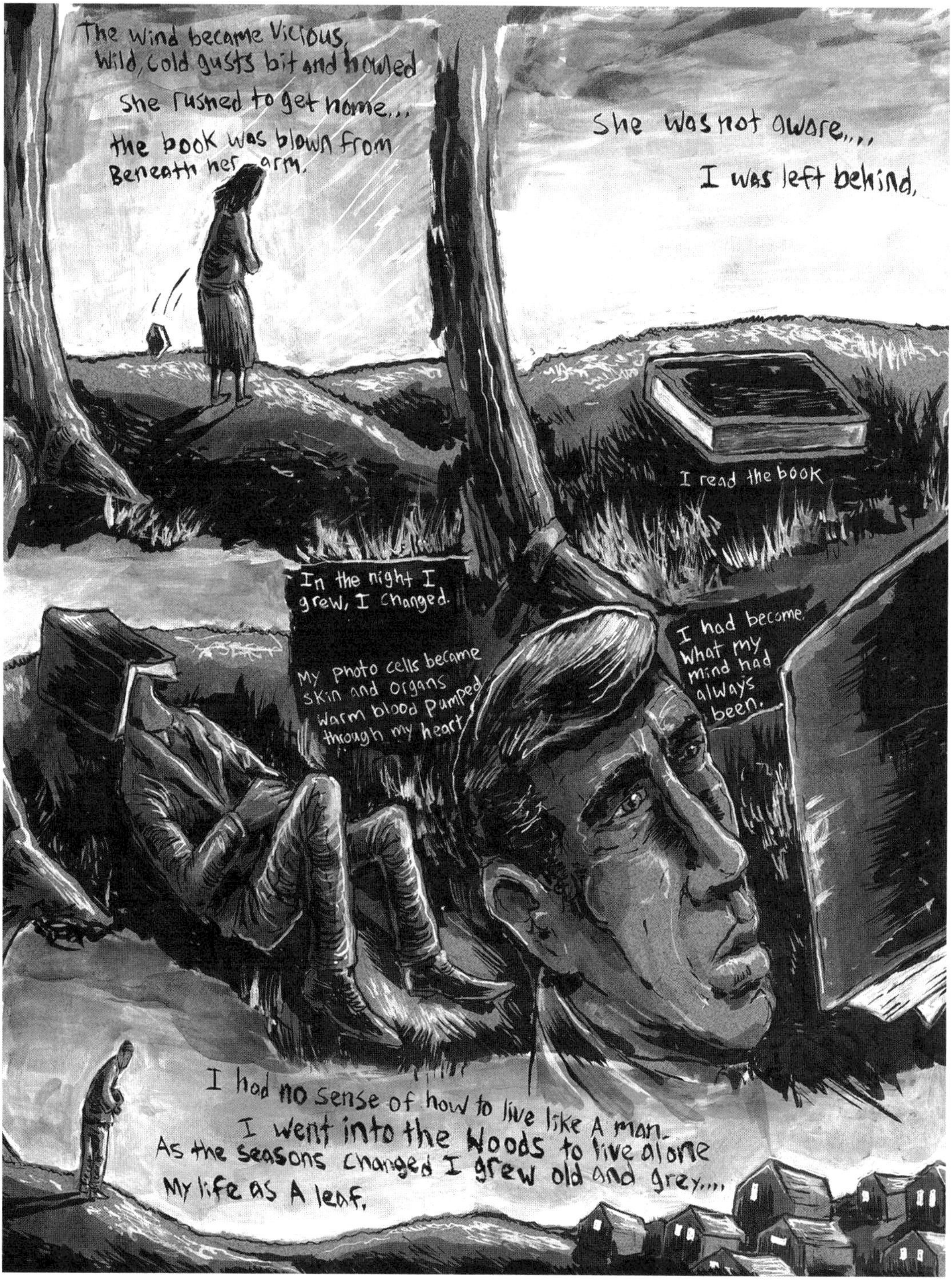
The wind became vicious,
Wild, cold gusts bit and howled
She rushed to get home...
the book was blown from
Beneath her arm.
She was not aware...
I was left behind.
I read the book
In the night I grew, I changed.
My photo cells became skin and organs
warm blood pumped through my heart
I had become what my mind had always been.
I had no sense of how to live like a man.
I went into the woods to live alone
As the seasons changed I grew old and grey....
My life as a leaf.

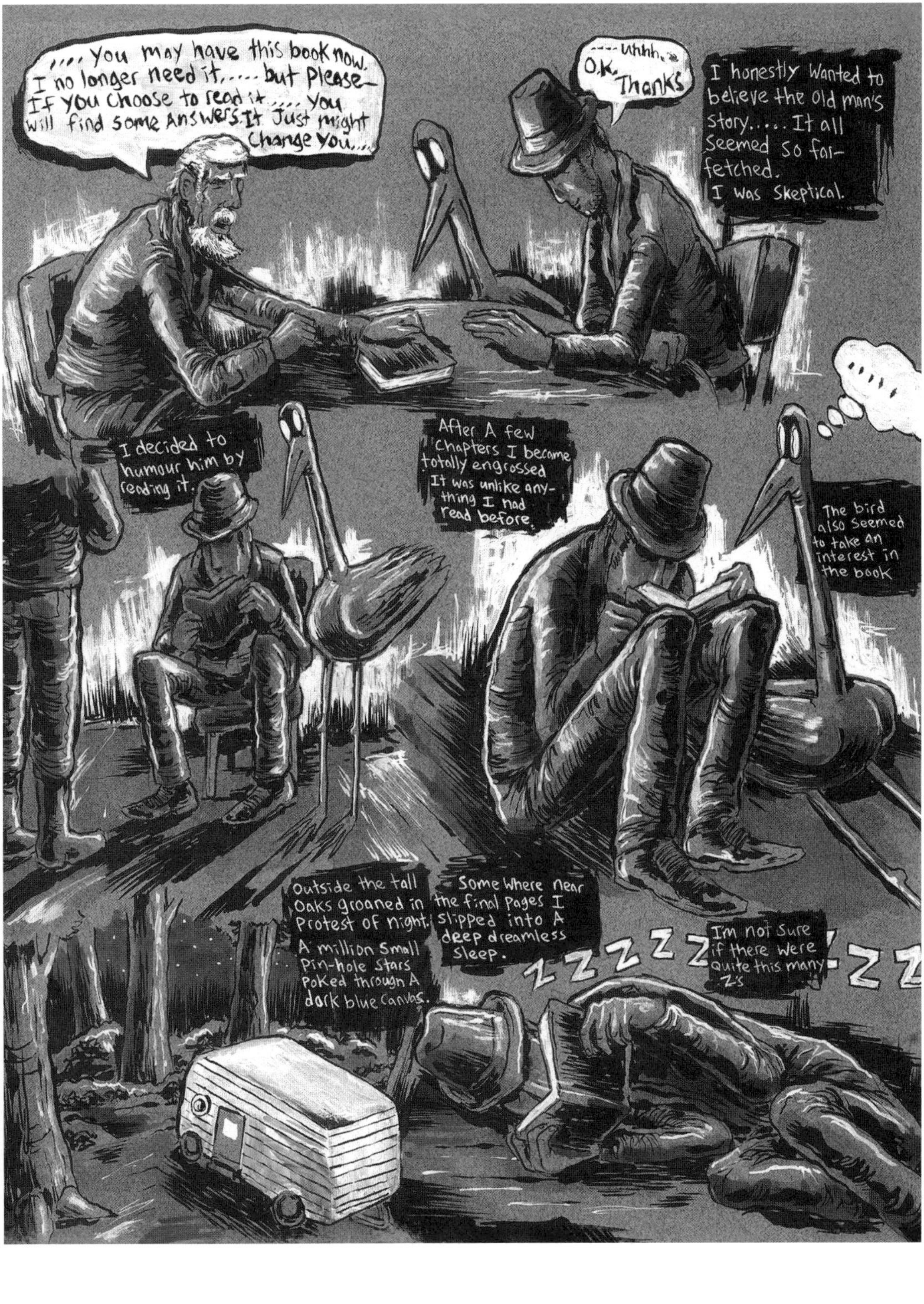

,,,, You may have this book now. I no longer need it,.... but please— If you choose to read it ,,,,, you will find some answers. It just might change you...
---- Uhhh,
O.K. Thanks
I honestly wanted to believe the old man's story..... It all seemed so far-fetched. I was skeptical.
I decided to humour him by reading it.
After A few chapters I became totally engrossed It was unlike any-thing I had read before.
The bird also seemed to take an interest in the book
....
Outside the tall Oaks groaned in Protest of night. A million Small Pin-hole Stars Poked through A dark blue Canvas.
Some Where near the final Pages I slipped into A deep dreamless sleep.
ZZZZZ
I'm not sure if there were quite this many Z's
ZZ

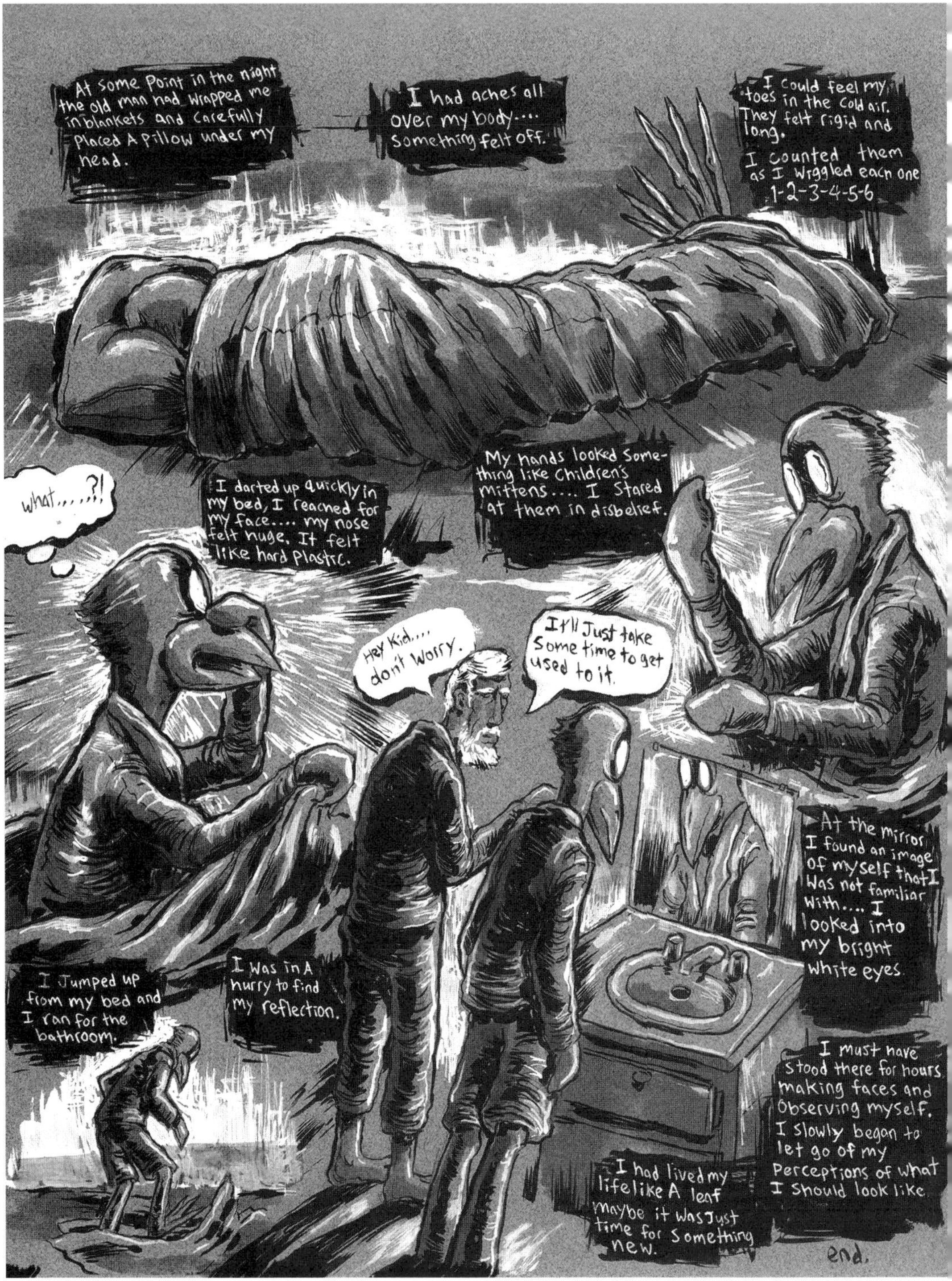
At some point in the night the old man had wrapped me in blankets and carefully placed a pillow under my head.
I had aches all over my body.... Something felt off.
I could feel my toes in the cold air. They felt rigid and long.
I counted them as I wiggled each one 1-2-3-4-5-6
what.....?!
I darted up quickly in my bed, I reached for my face.... my nose felt huge. It felt like hard plastic.
My hands looked something like children's mittens.... I stared at them in disbelief.
Hey Kid.... don't worry.
It'll just take some time to get used to it.
At the mirror I found an image of myself that I was not familiar with.... I looked into my bright white eyes.
I jumped up from my bed and I ran for the bathroom.
I was in A hurry to find my reflection.
I must have stood there for hours making faces and observing myself. I slowly began to let go of my perceptions of what I should look like.
I had lived my life like A leaf maybe it was just time for something new.
end.

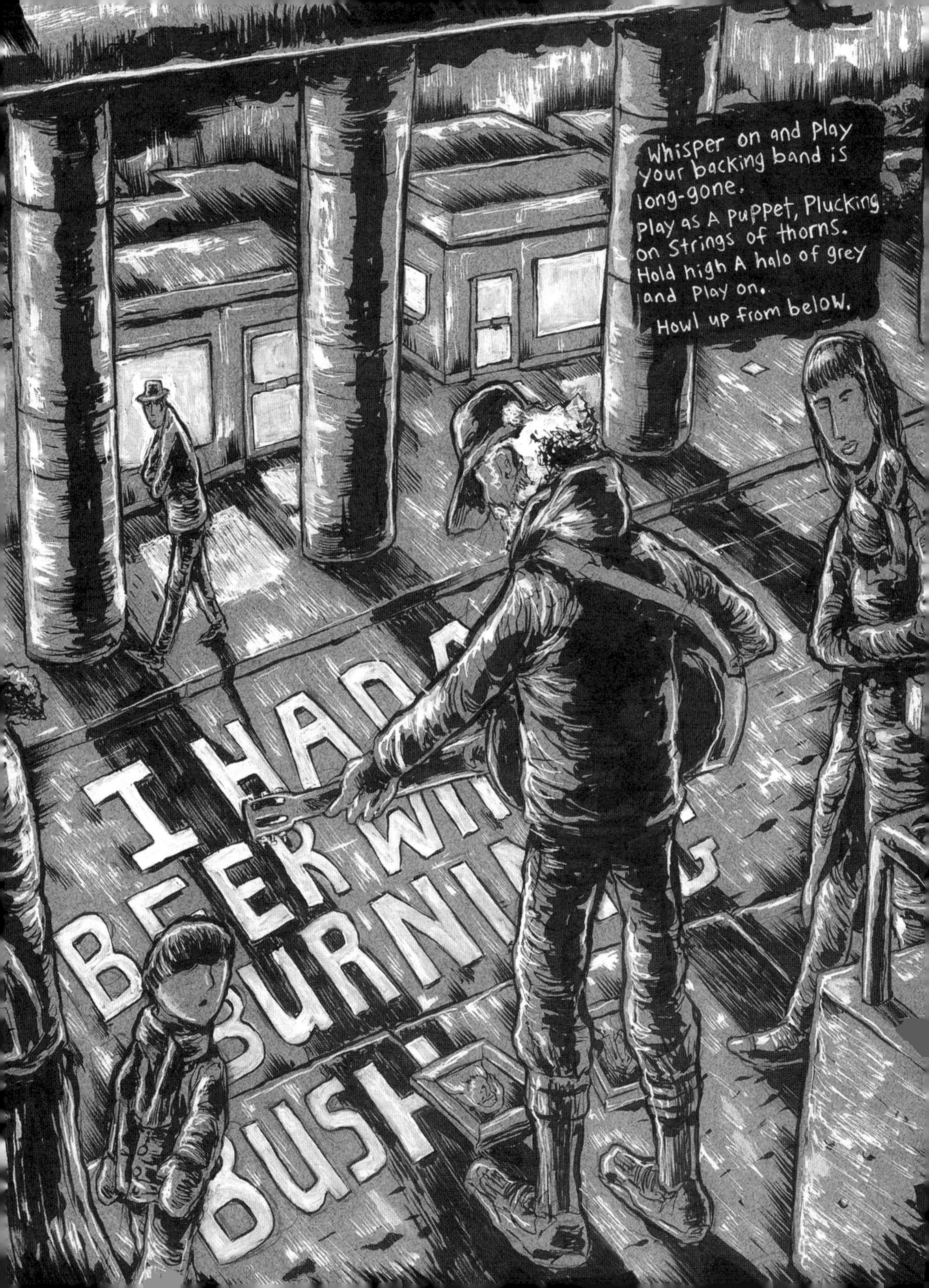
Whisper on and play
your backing band is
long-gone.
Play as A Puppet, Plucking
on Strings of thorns.
Hold high A halo of grey
and Play on.
Howl up from below.
I HAD
ER WI
BURNI
BUSH

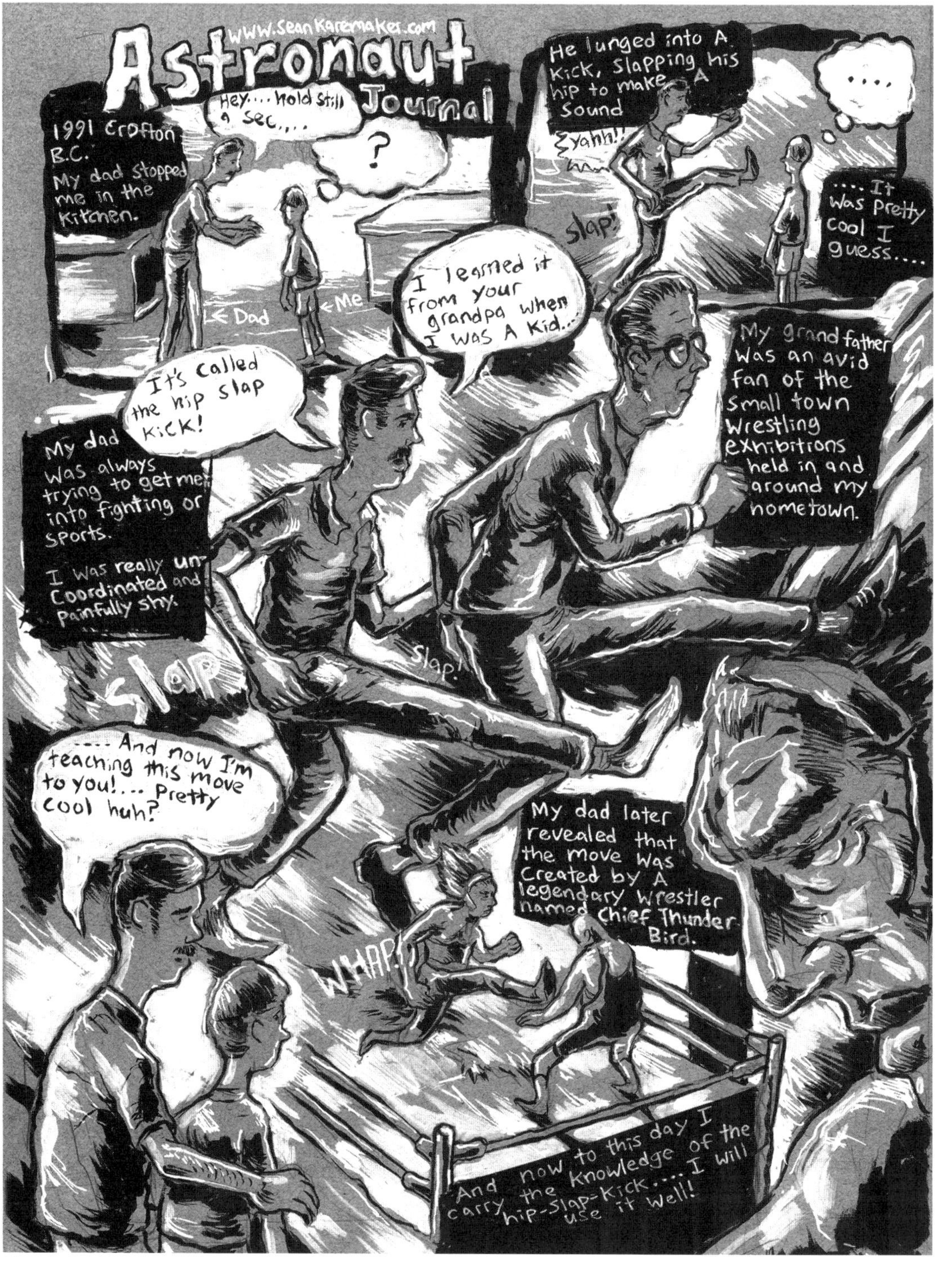
www.SeanKaremaker.com
Astronaut Journal
1991 Crofton B.C. My dad stopped me in the Kitchen.
Hey.... hold still a sec,...
?
Dad
Me
He lunged into A Kick, Slapping his hip to make A Sound
Yahh!!
Slap!
....
.... It was pretty cool I guess....
It's called the hip slap kick!
I learned it from your grandpa when I was A Kid...
My dad was always trying to get me into fighting or sports.
I was really un-coordinated and painfully shy.
My grand father was an avid fan of the small town Wrestling exhibitions held in and around my hometown.
Slap
Slap!
.... And now I'm teaching this move to you!... Pretty cool huh?
My dad later revealed that the move was Created by A legendary Wrestler named Chief Thunder Bird.
WHAP!
And now to this day I carry the Knowledge of the hip-slap-kick.... I will use it well!

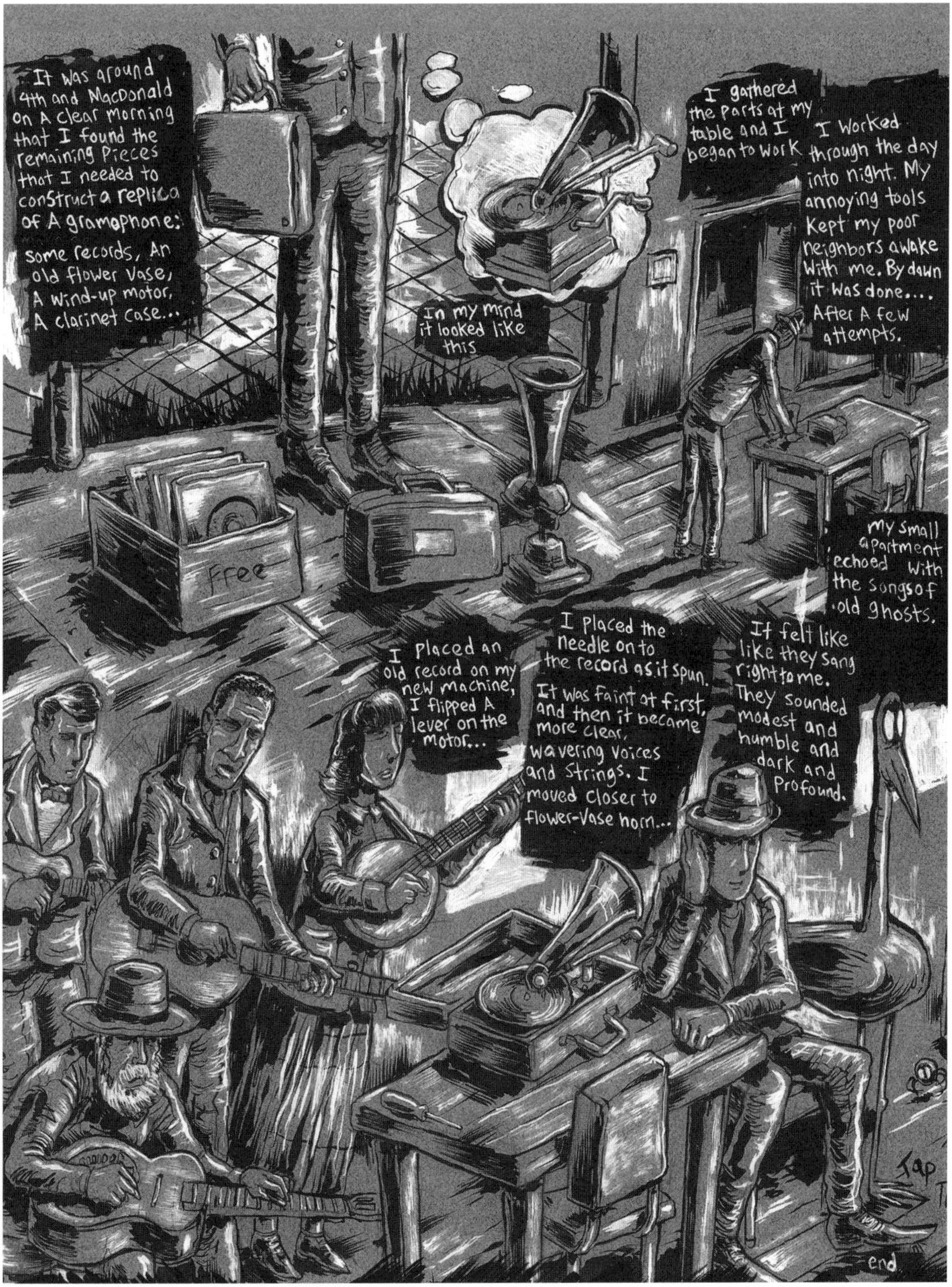
It was around 4th and MacDonald on A clear morning that I found the remaining Pieces that I needed to construct a replica of A gramophone:
some records, An old flower vase, A wind-up motor, A clarinet case...
In my mind it looked like this
I gathered the parts at my table and I began to work
I worked through the day into night. My annoying tools kept my poor neighbors awake with me. By dawn it was done.... After A few attempts.
Free
My small apartment echoed with the songs of old ghosts.
I placed an old record on my new machine, I flipped A lever on the motor...
I placed the needle on to the record as it spun.
It was faint at first, and then it became more clear, wavering voices and strings. I moved closer to flower-vase horn...
It felt like like they sang right to me.
They sounded modest and humble and dark and profound.
Jap
end.

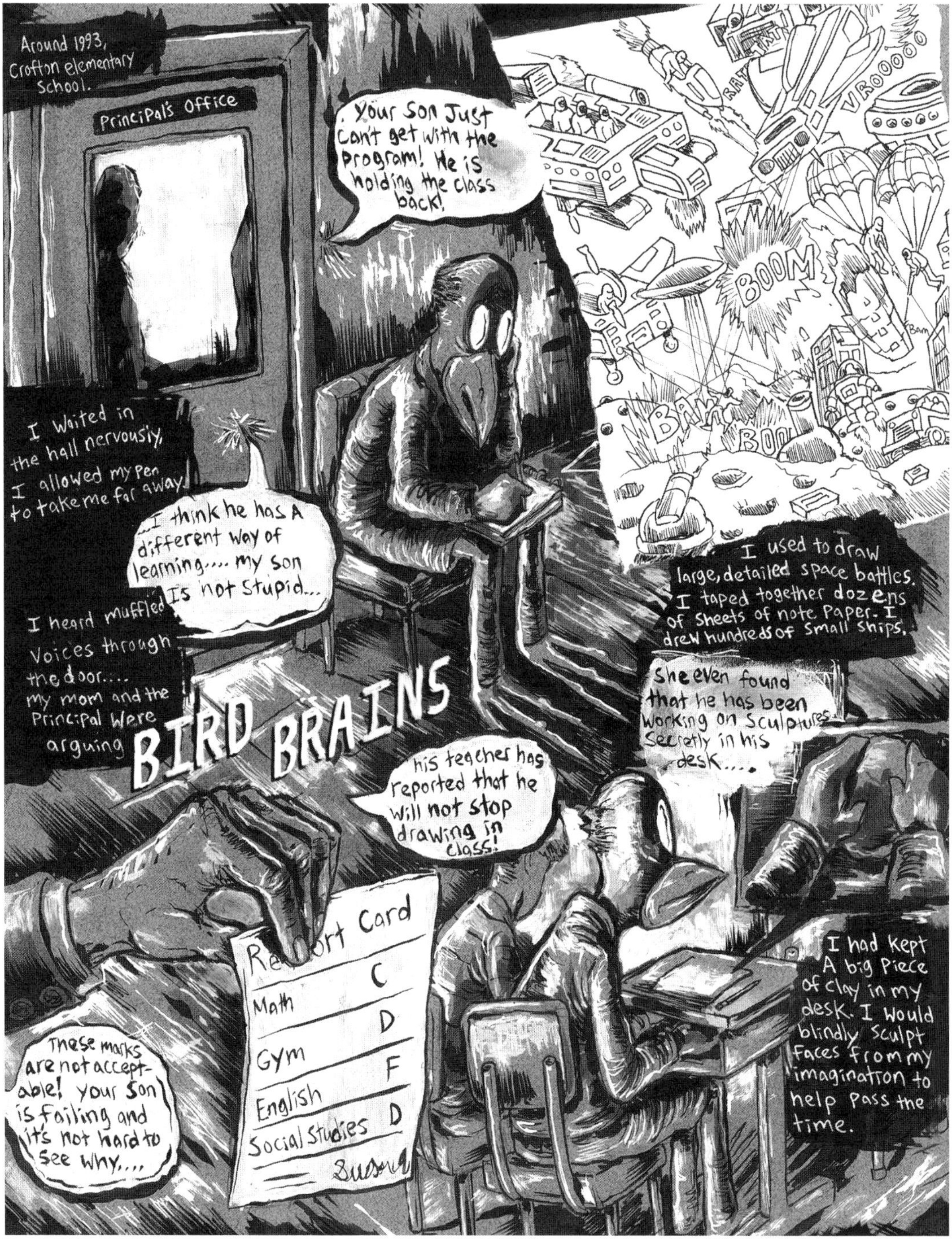
Around 1993, Crofton elementary School.
Principal's Office
Your Son Just can't get with the program! He is holding the class back!
RAT
VROOOOO
BOOM
Bam
BAM
BOO
I waited in the hall nervously, I allowed my pen to take me far away.
...I think he has A different way of learning.... my son Is not Stupid...
I used to draw large, detailed space battles. I taped together dozens of Sheets of note Paper. I drew hundreds of Small Ships.
I heard muffled Voices through the door.... my mom and the Principal were arguing
BIRD BRAINS
She even found that he has been working on Sculptures Secretly in his desk....
his teacher has reported that he will not stop drawing in class!
Report Card
Math C
Gym D
English F
Social Studies D
These marks are not acceptable! your Son is failing and it's not hard to See why...
I had kept A big Piece of clay in my desk. I would blindly Sculpt Faces from my imagination to help Pass the time.

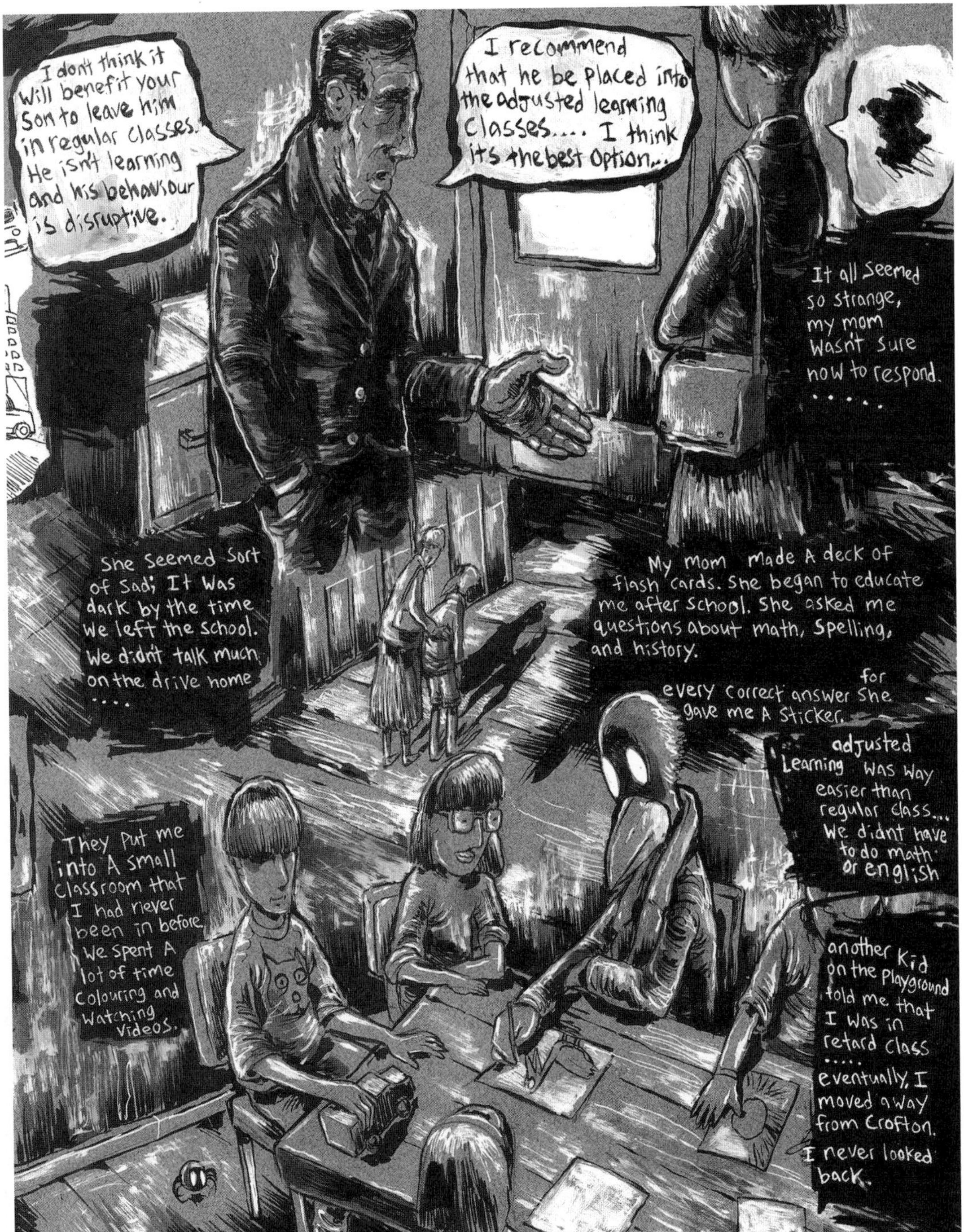
I don't think it will benefit your son to leave him in regular classes. He isn't learning and his behaviour is disruptive.
I recommend that he be placed into the adjusted learning classes.... I think its the best option...
It all seemed so strange, my mom wasn't sure how to respond. . . . . .
She seemed sort of sad; It was dark by the time we left the school. We didn't talk much on the drive home . . . .
My mom made a deck of flash cards. She began to educate me after school. She asked me questions about math, spelling, and history.
for every correct answer she gave me a sticker.
adjusted Learning was way easier than regular class... We didnt have to do math or english
They put me into a small classroom that I had never been in before. We spent a lot of time colouring and watching videos.
another kid on the playground told me that I was in retard class . . . . .
eventually, I moved away from Crofton. I never looked back.

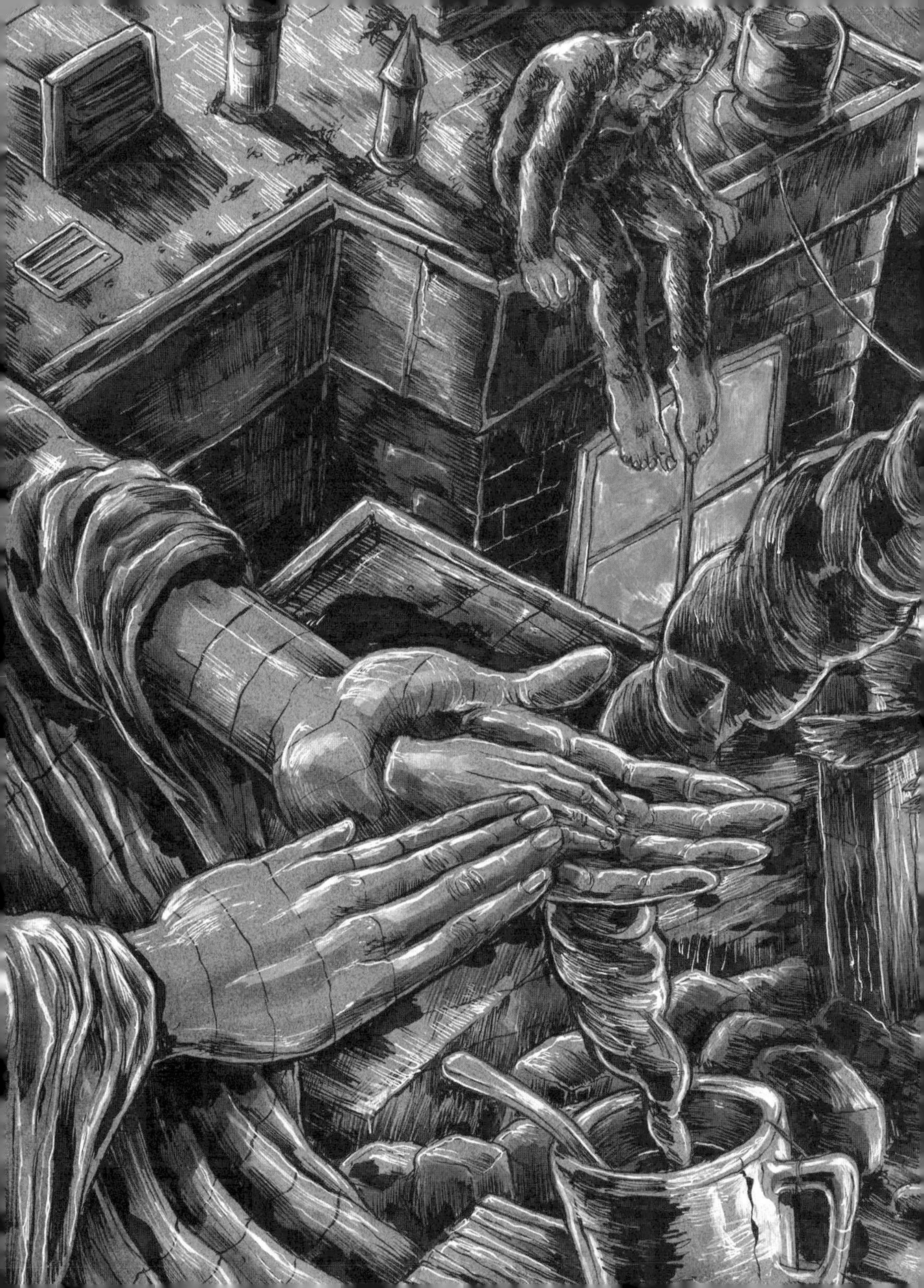

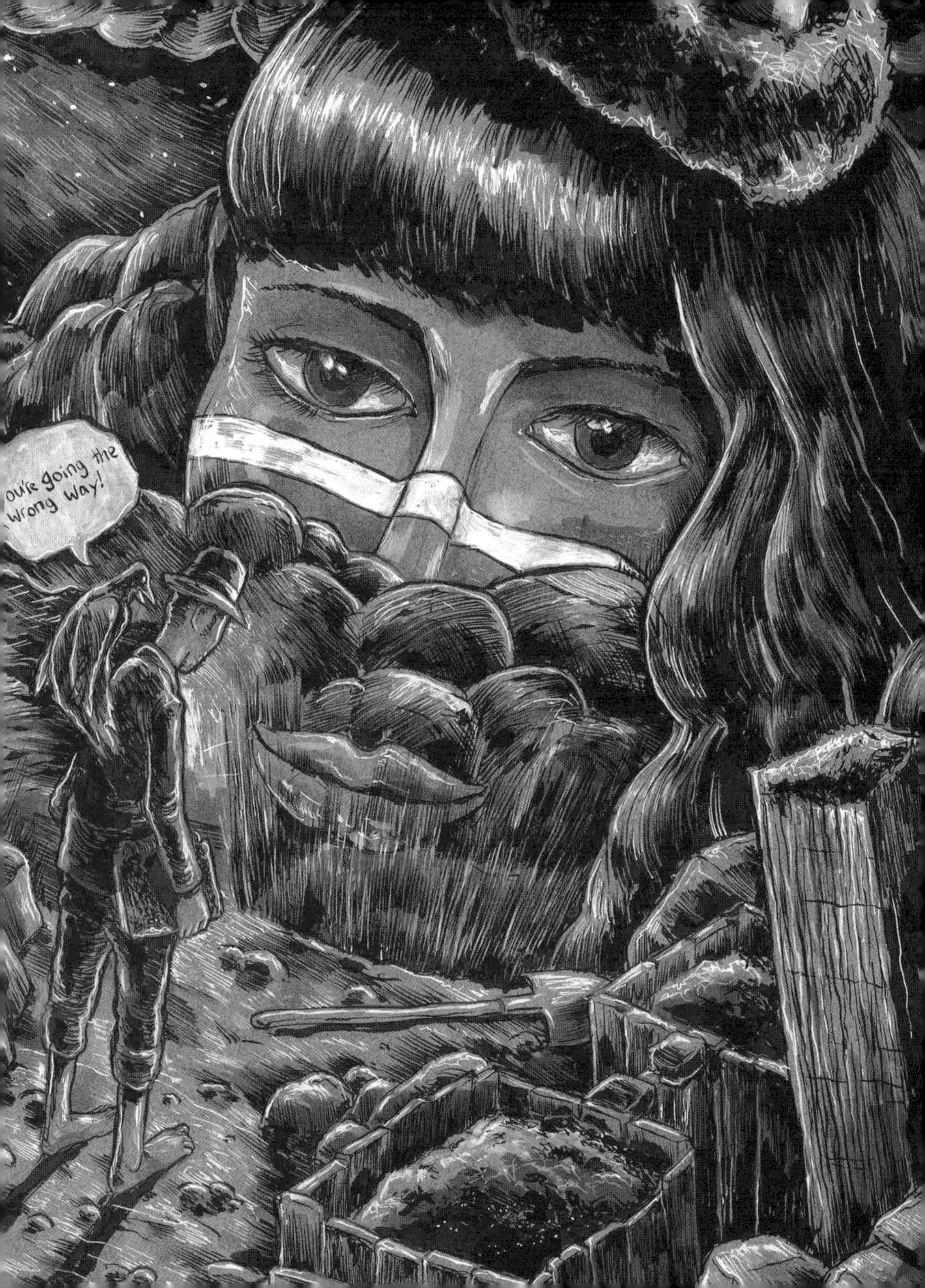
ou're going the wrong way!

Collecting Letters

I left that old car burning on the highway near Nanaimo. I wandered from the country to the big city with my broken hands and Beverly Hillbilly dreams. I had learned to wear false confidence by drinking and fighting and staying up late.

A friend introduced me to her at a party; We were both awkward, I made her nervous and she did the same for me. I did my best to hide it. We talked for a while and wandered around the gallery. I took the long bus ride out to see her in South Surrey. She held my hand and talked about political subjects that I would never understand.

I got to know the beauty of her and she knew my weakness.
She told me that she loved me, so sudden, so lucky, so real.
I decided to leave. I was a damned coward. She handed me an envelope.

I got a place at Larch and Second where I began collecting things....
Papers, letters, books and comics in boxes, book shelves and cases. It was a big place.... lots of room to collect, to expand, to work. I kept the lights on as I went out each night to guide me back home as the city slept.

I felt uneasy and pined over her. I began to focus more on art and self expression. I spent my evenings drawing harmless pictures based on romance. I ran my fingertips over that unopened letter. The paper was full of age, torn at the edges. I found momentary validation from temporary lovers at one night shows. I found a secondary spot in the back of a cafe on Broadway where I would feast on weed balanced by coffee and hidden rum.
I try to live the life of a stereotype. It's fun for a while.

For five long years.
Each evening she finds me there and secretly carries me home. I awoke each night as the mosquitoes circled and collided with the warm, orange glow of my room. The after-image of her, resting softly on my eyelids.
I looked like shit. I stayed focused on my romantic ideal.
She became a myth to me, I began to doubt myself.

Was she ever real?
Still in the pocket of that old, worn jacket I found an envelope. Carefully I tore away the edge of the thing to reveal an artifact in blue pen on yellowed paper. The letter is simple, it's an invitation. It was always there.
I submit to her and she carries me home. In the morning I collect the letters and take out the trash.

Somewhere near Nanaimo a fire continues to burn...

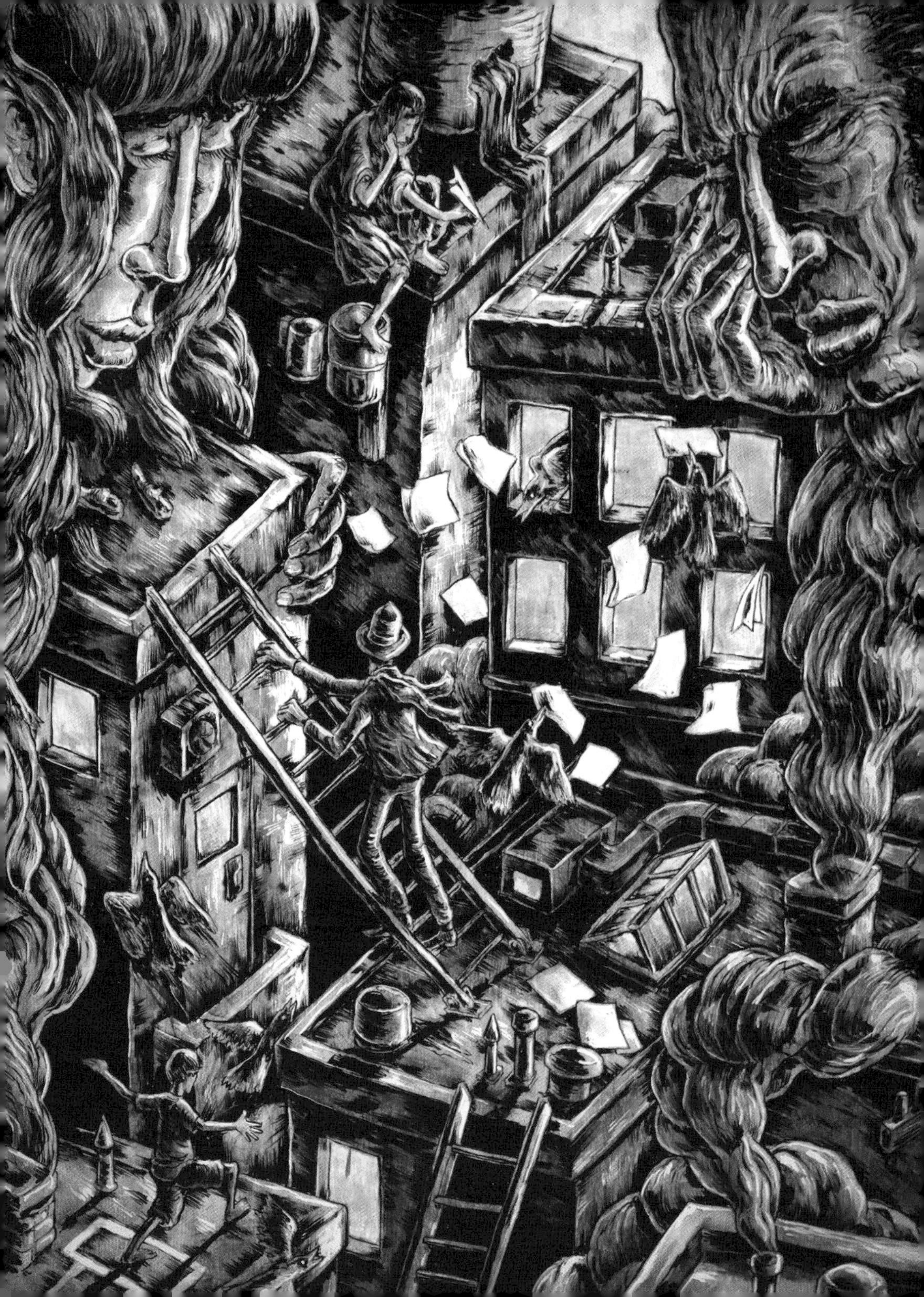

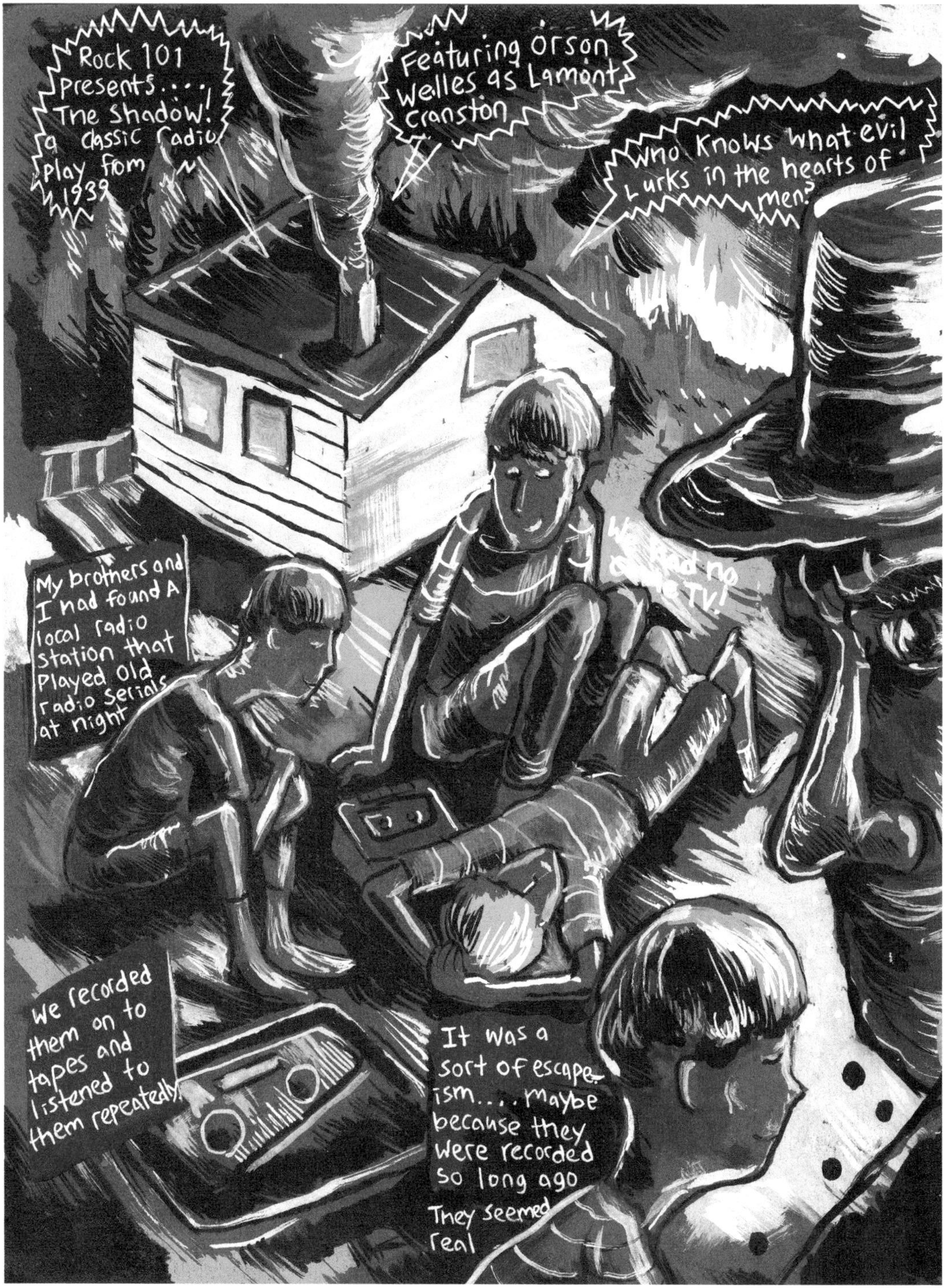
Rock 101 Presents.... The Shadow! a classic radio play from 1939
Featuring Orson Welles as Lamont Cranston
Who knows what evil lurks in the hearts of men?
My brothers and I had found A local radio station that played old radio serials at night
We recorded them on to tapes and listened to them repeatedly
It was a sort of escape-ism.... maybe because they were recorded so long ago They seemed real

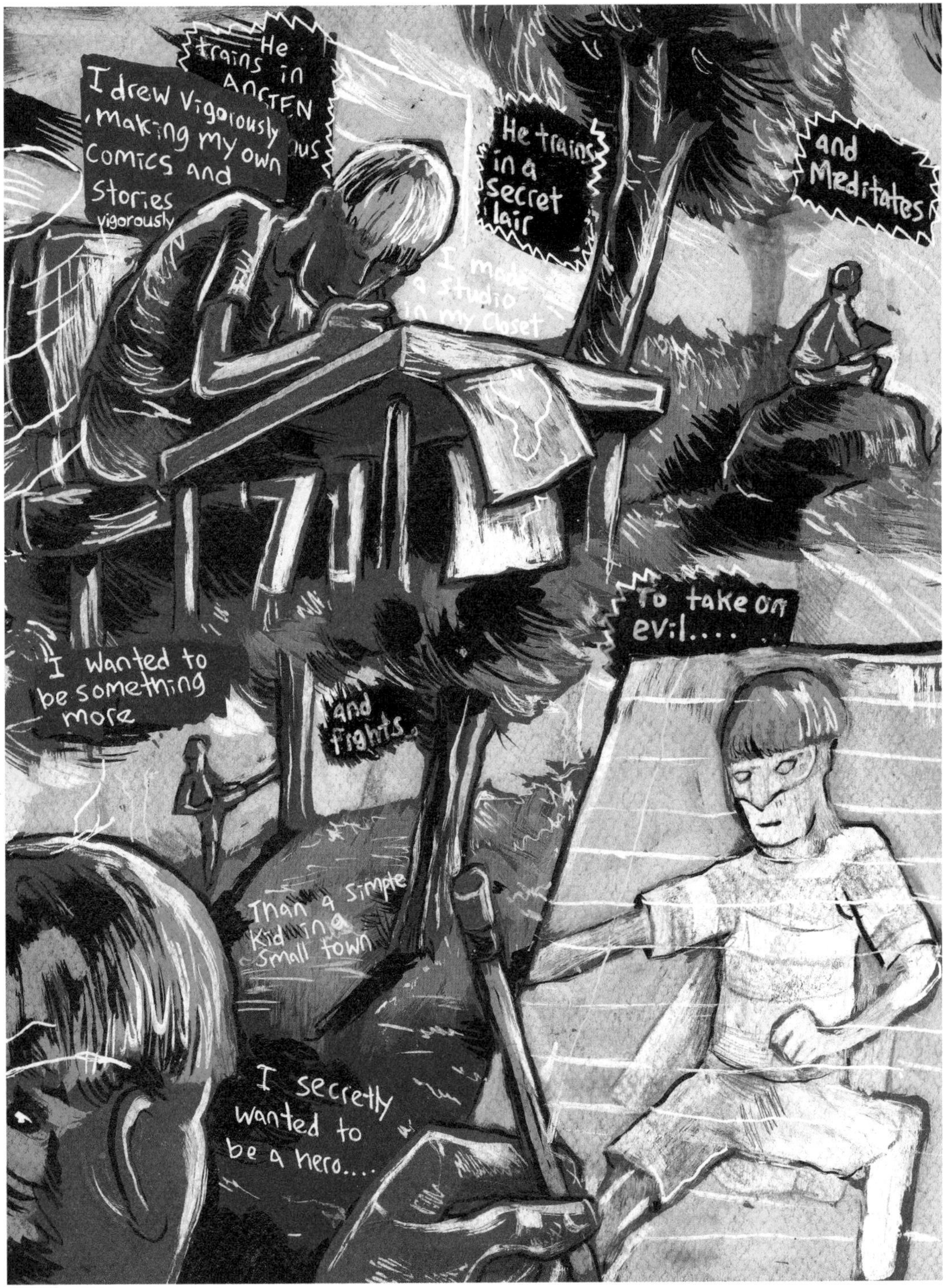
He trains in ANCIEN
ous
I drew Vigorously, making my own comics and stories vigorously
He trains in a secret lair
and Meditates
I made a studio in my closet
To take on evil....
I wanted to be something more
and fights.
Than a simple kid in a small town
I secretly wanted to be a hero....

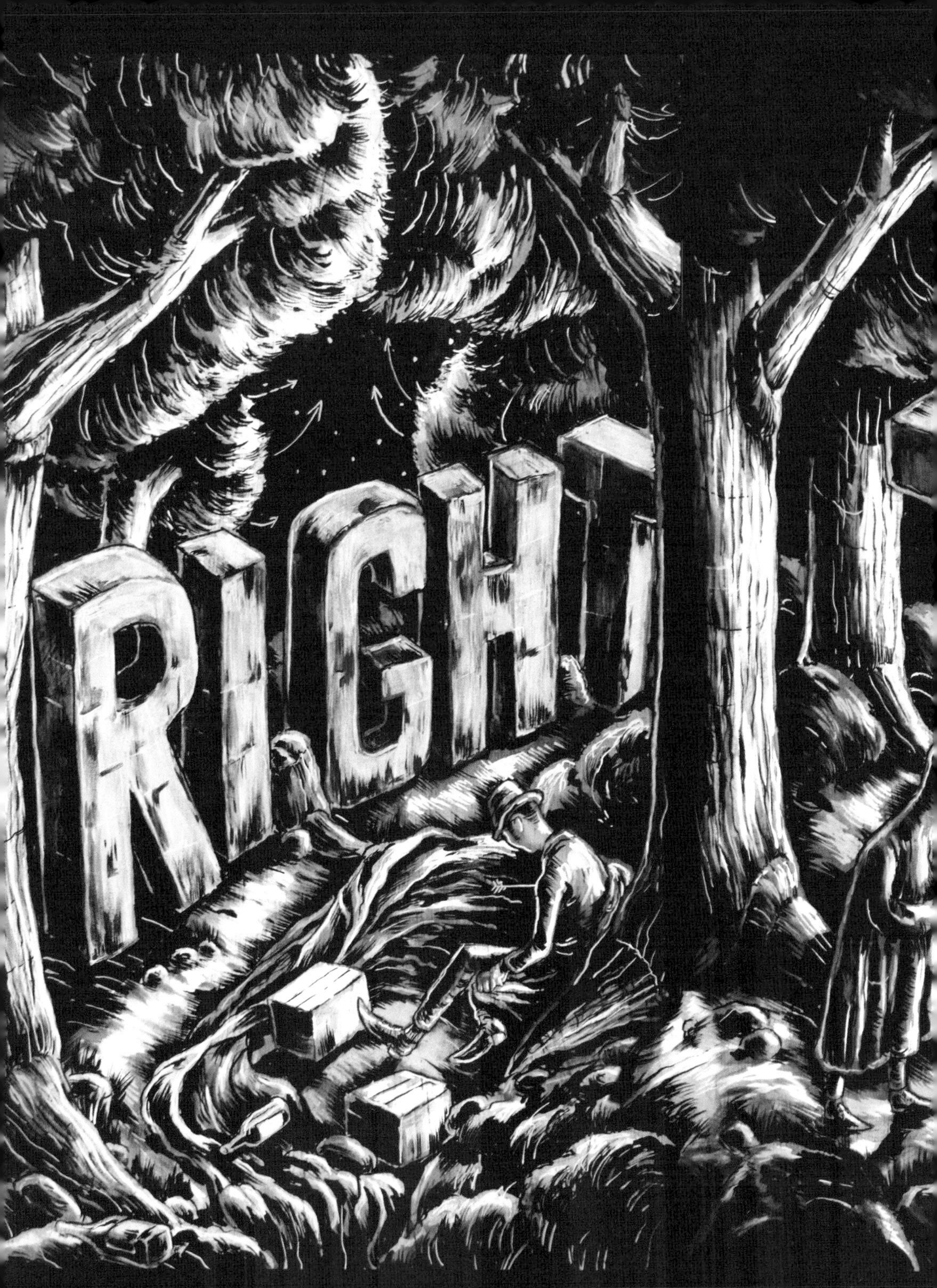
RIGHT

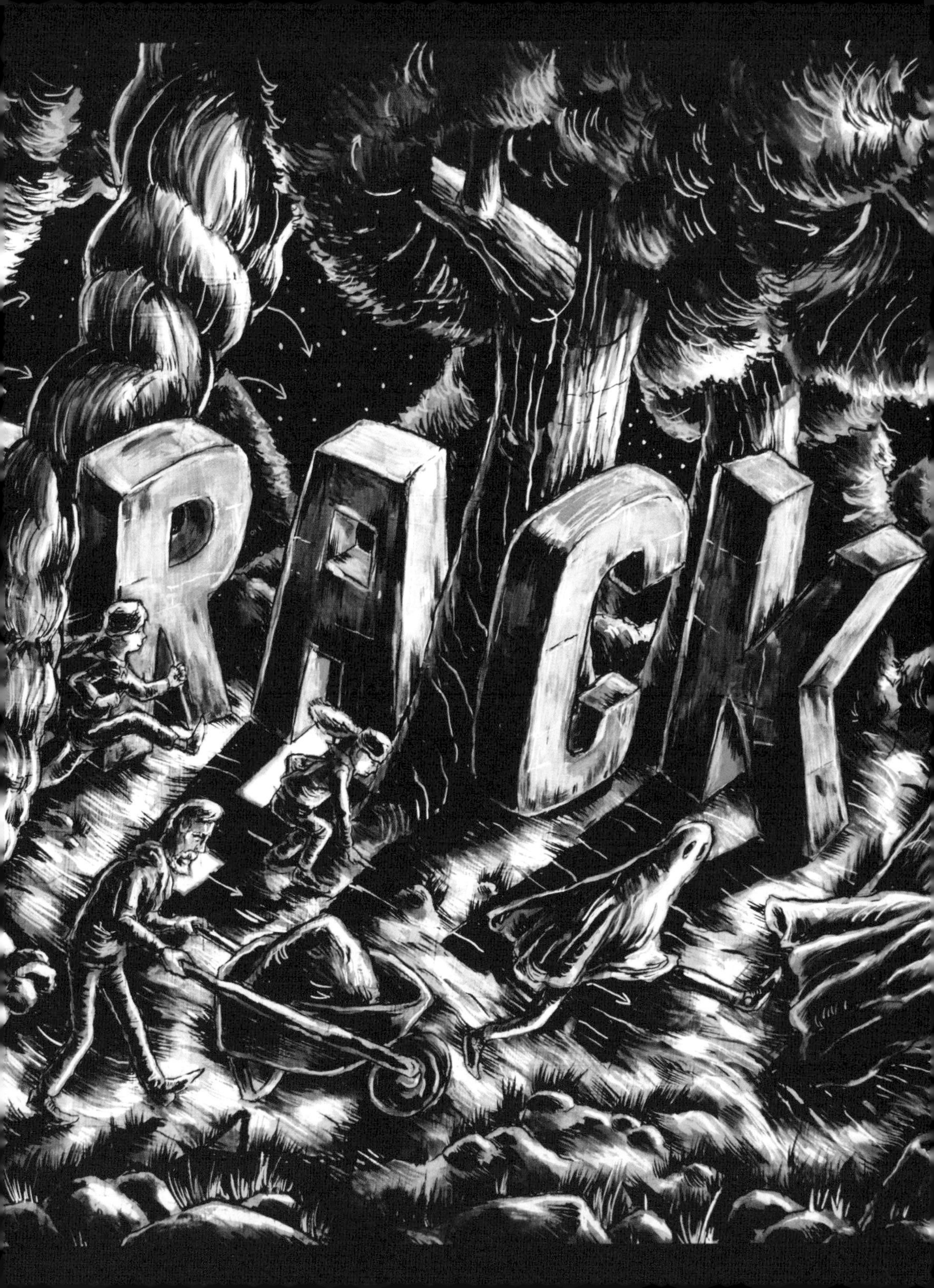

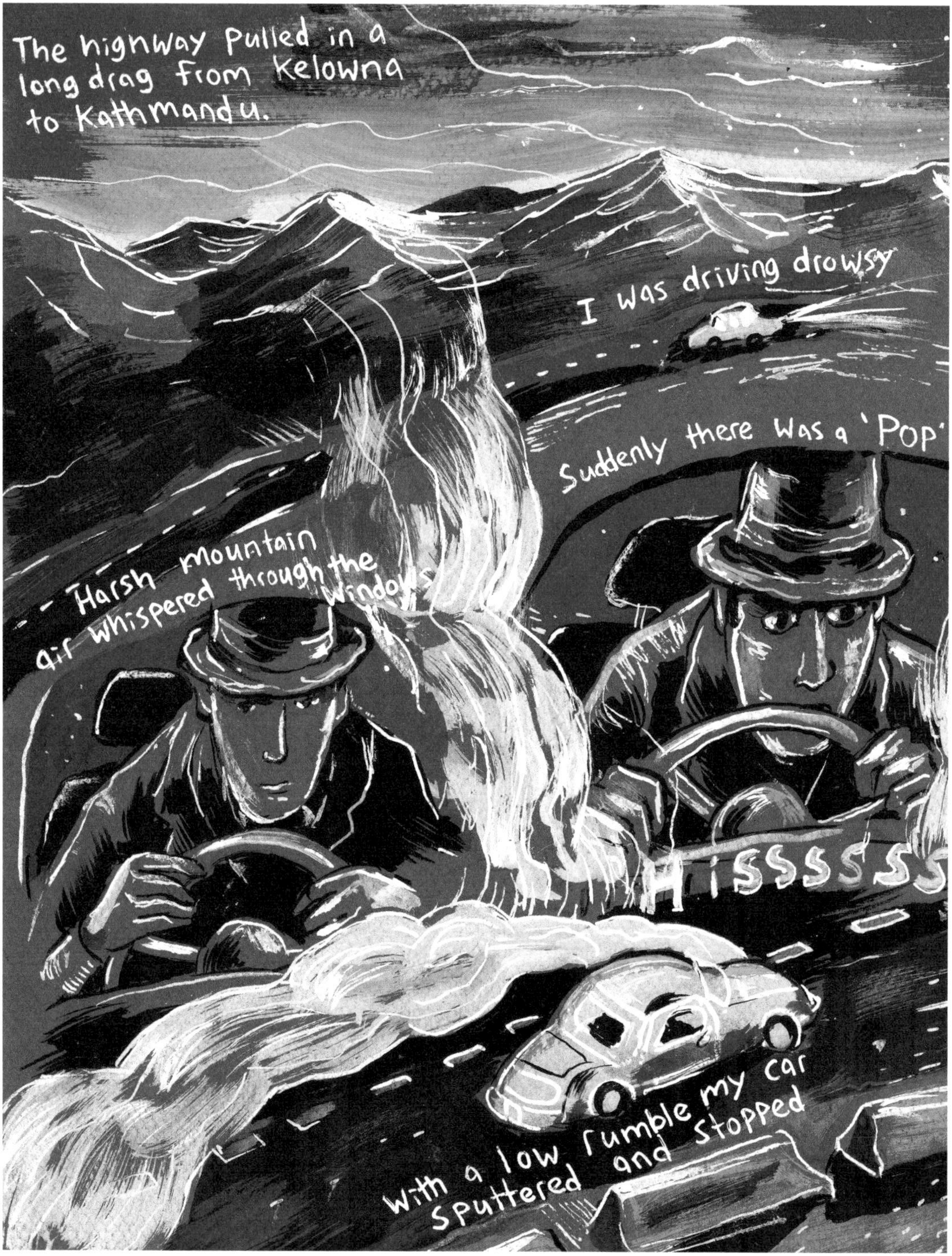
The highway pulled in a long drag from Kelowna to Kathmandu.
I was driving drowsy
Suddenly there was a 'POP'
Harsh mountain air whispered through the windows
HISSSSSS
With a low rumble my car sputtered and stopped

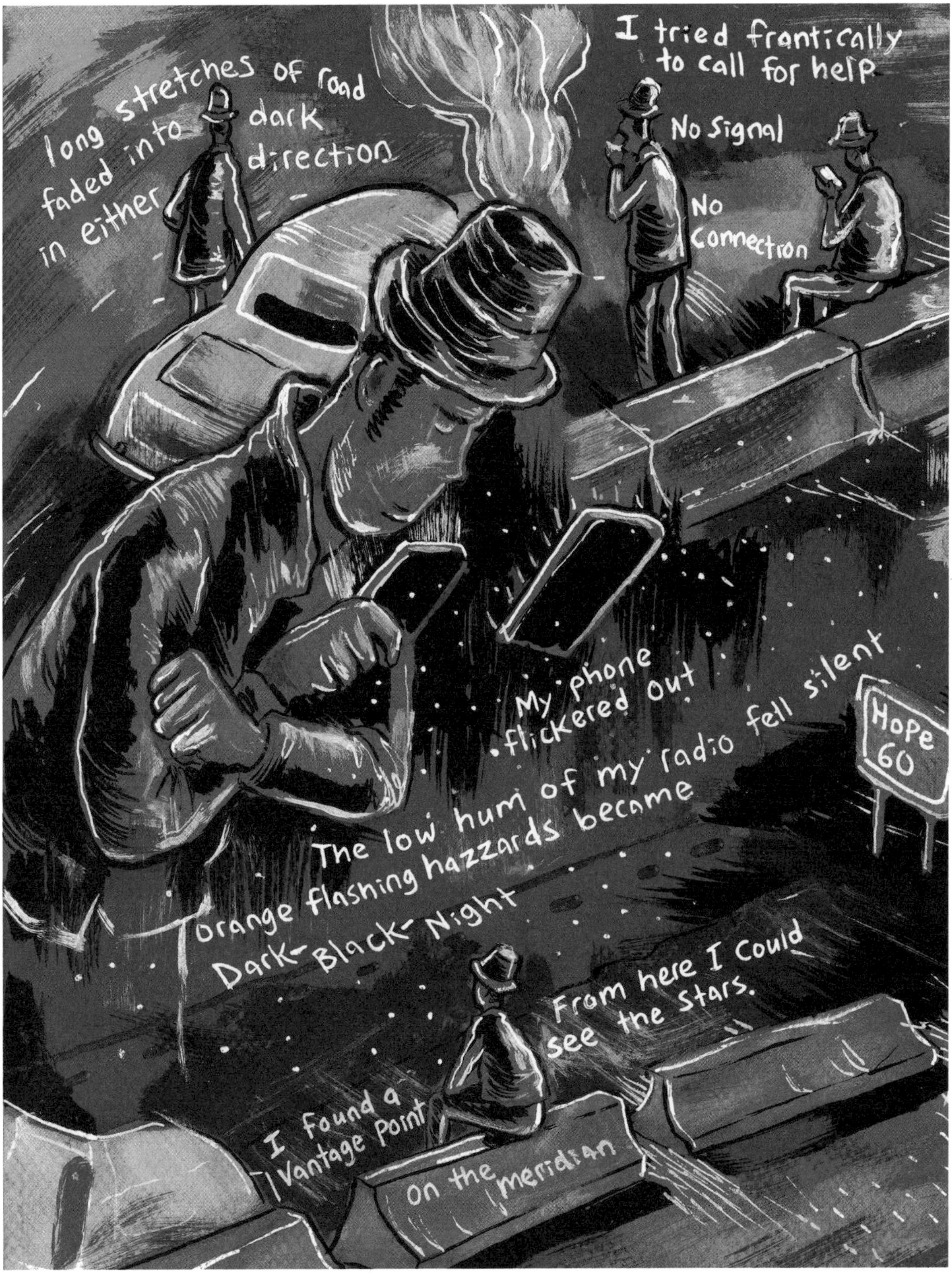
long stretches of road faded into dark in either direction
I tried frantically to call for help
No Signal
No Connection
My phone flickered out
The low hum of my radio fell silent
Hope 60
Orange flashing hazzards became
Dark- Black- Night
From here I could see the stars.
I found a vantage point
on the meridian

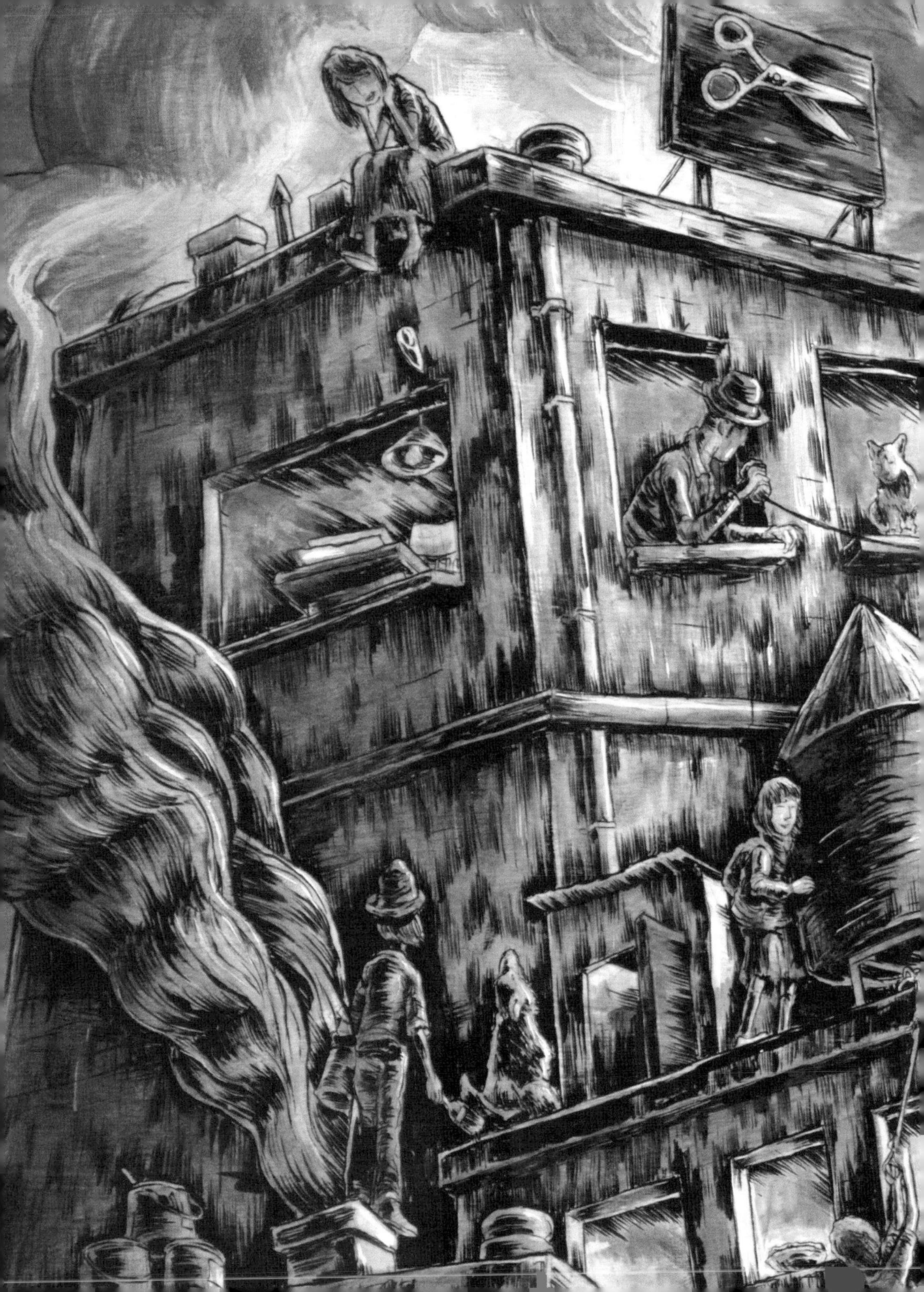

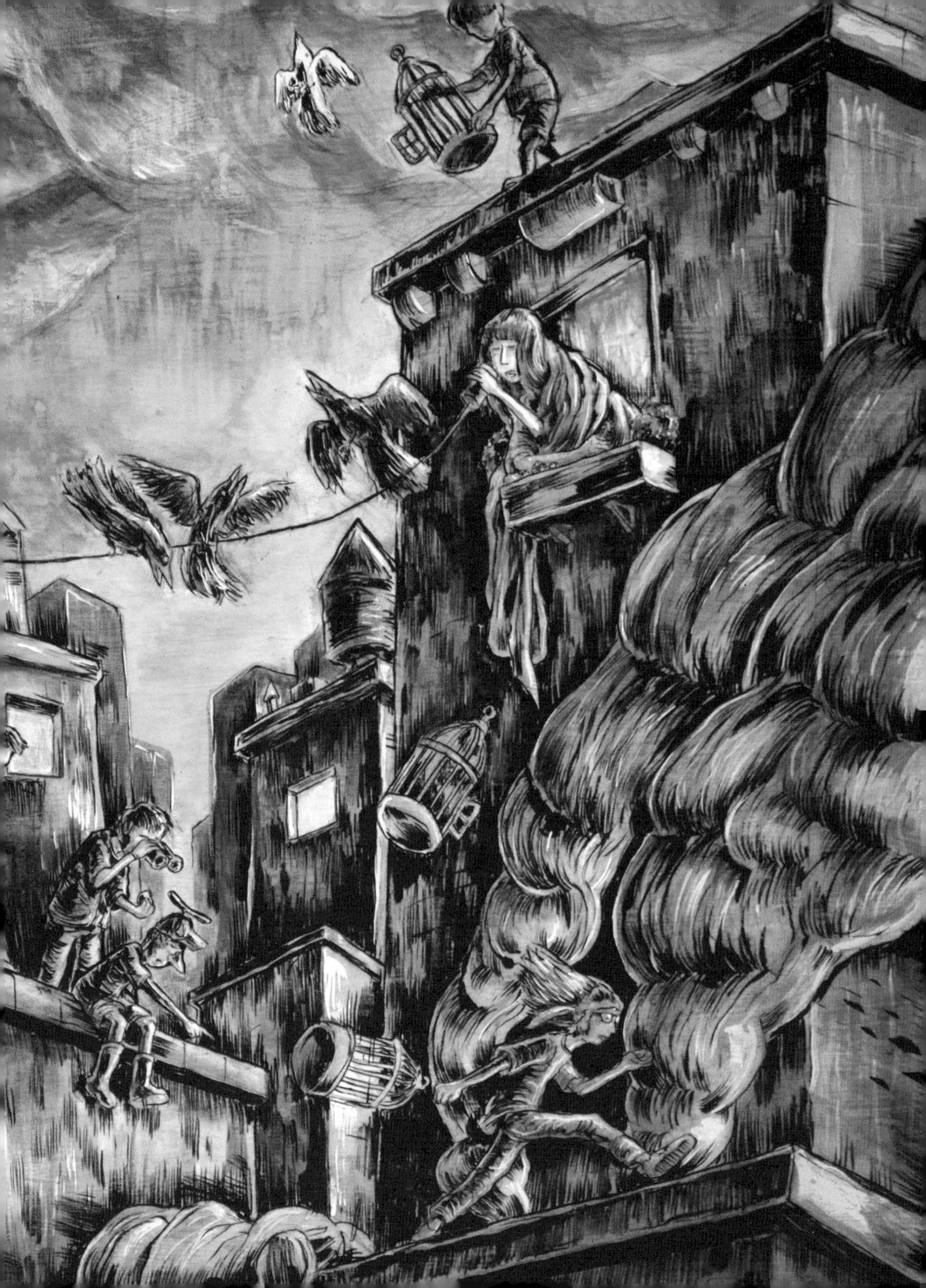

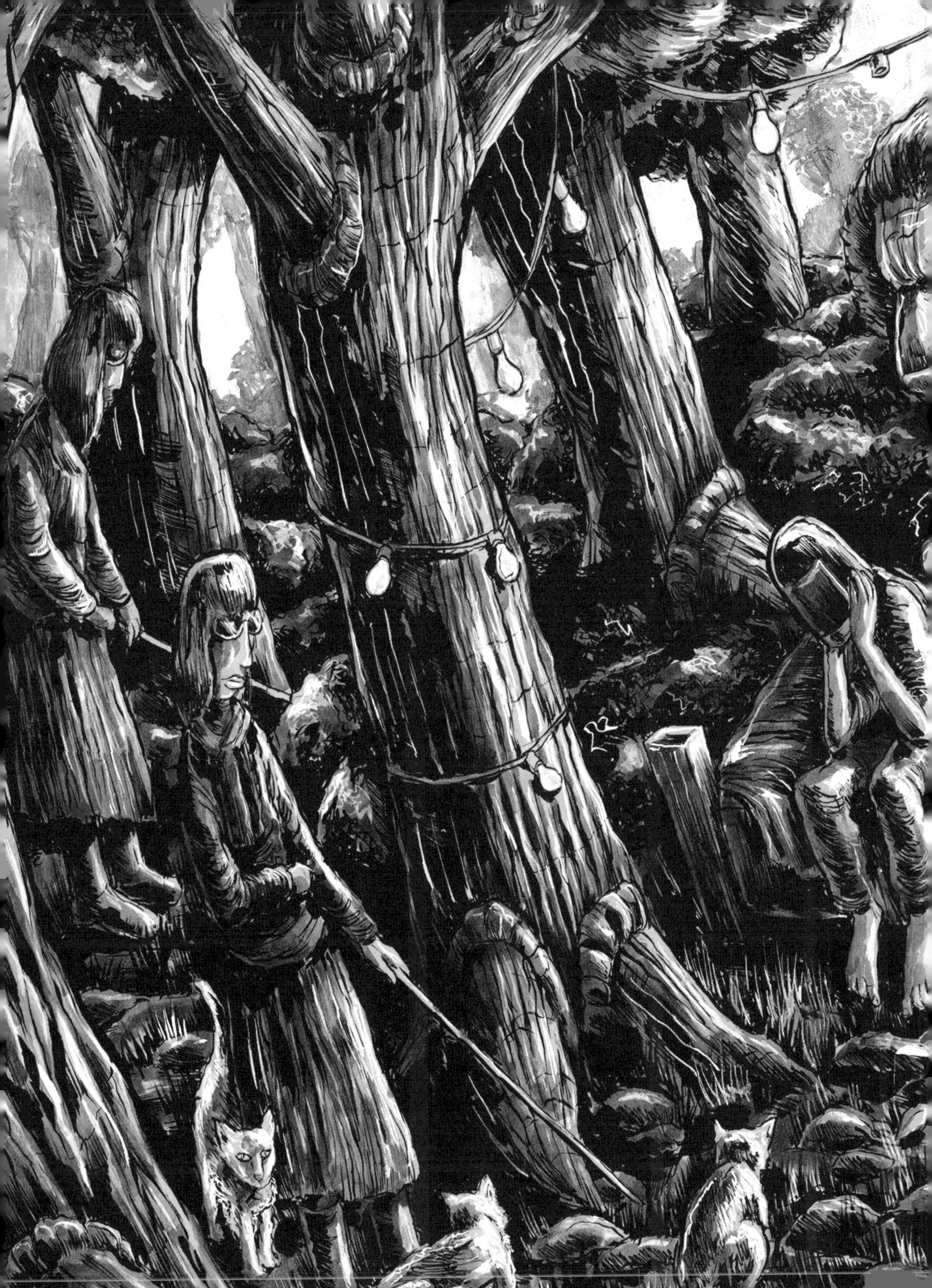

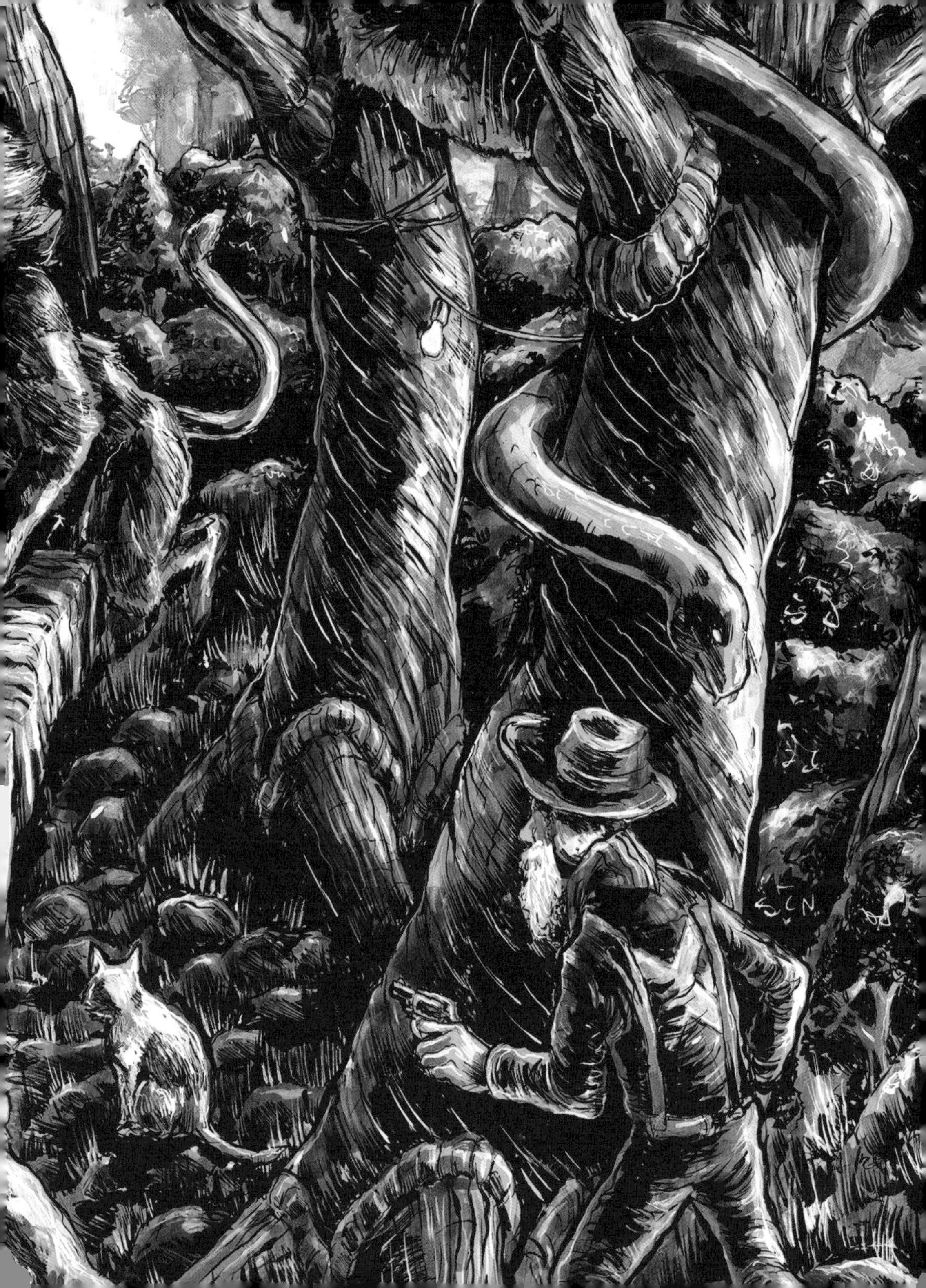

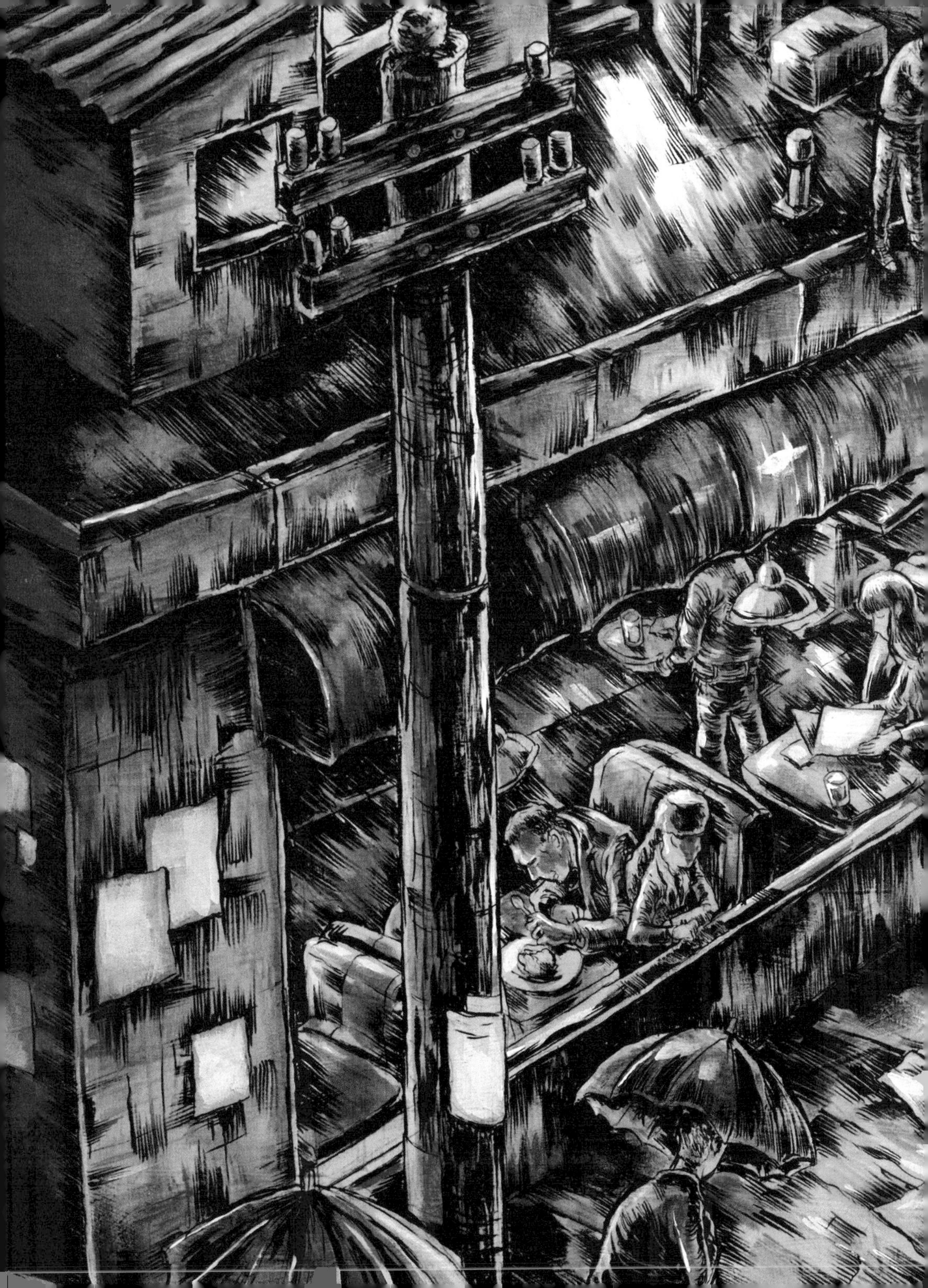

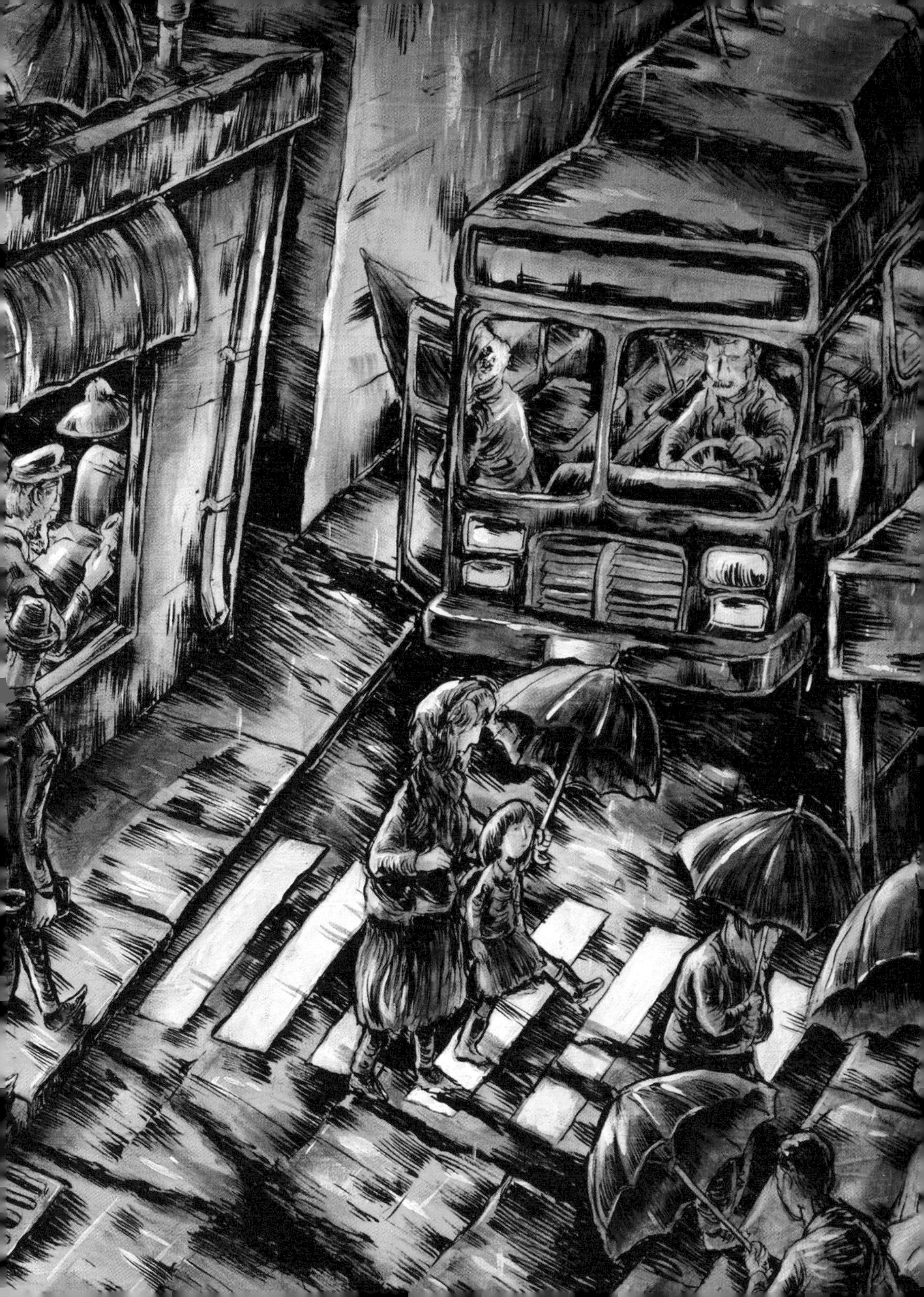

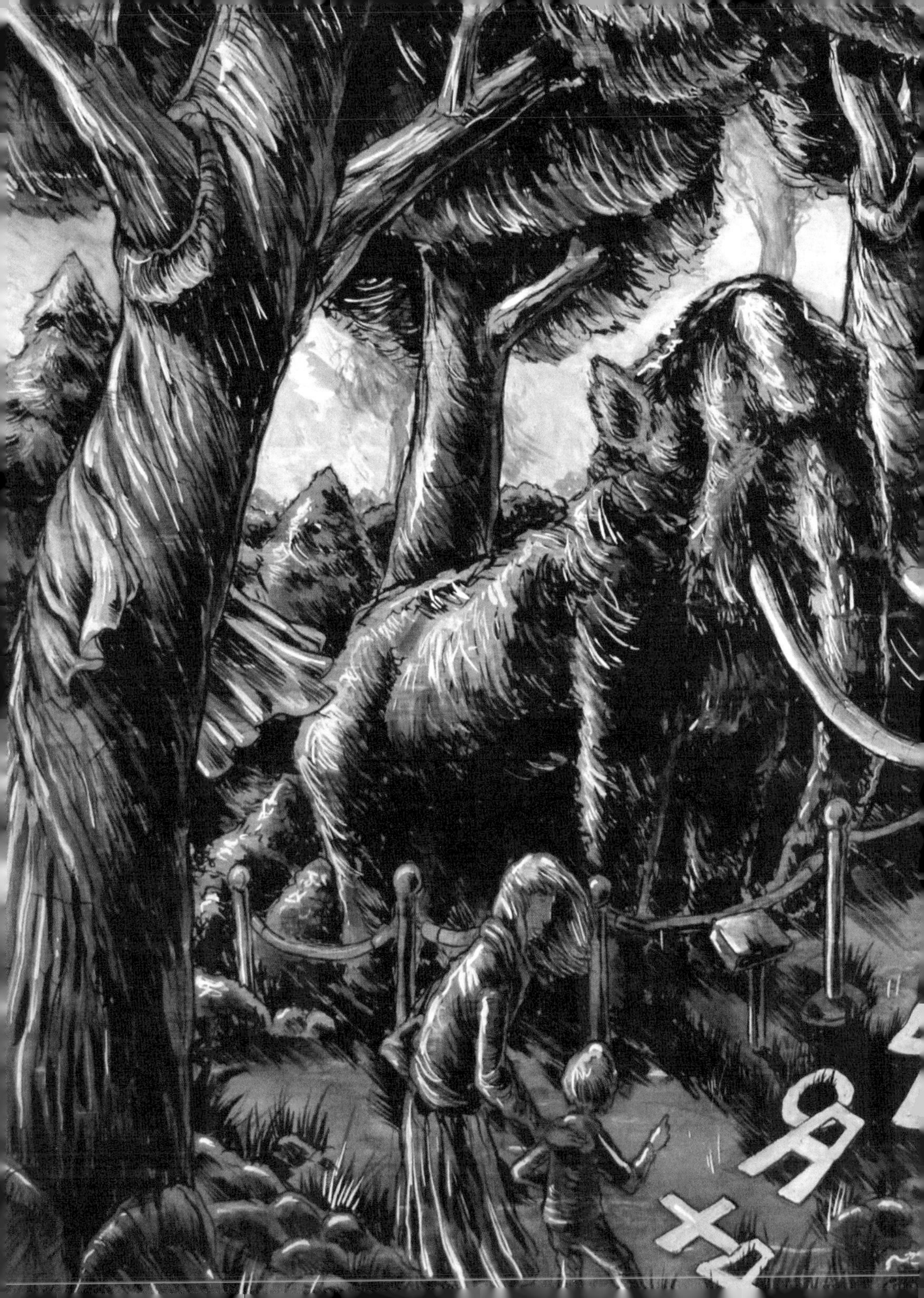

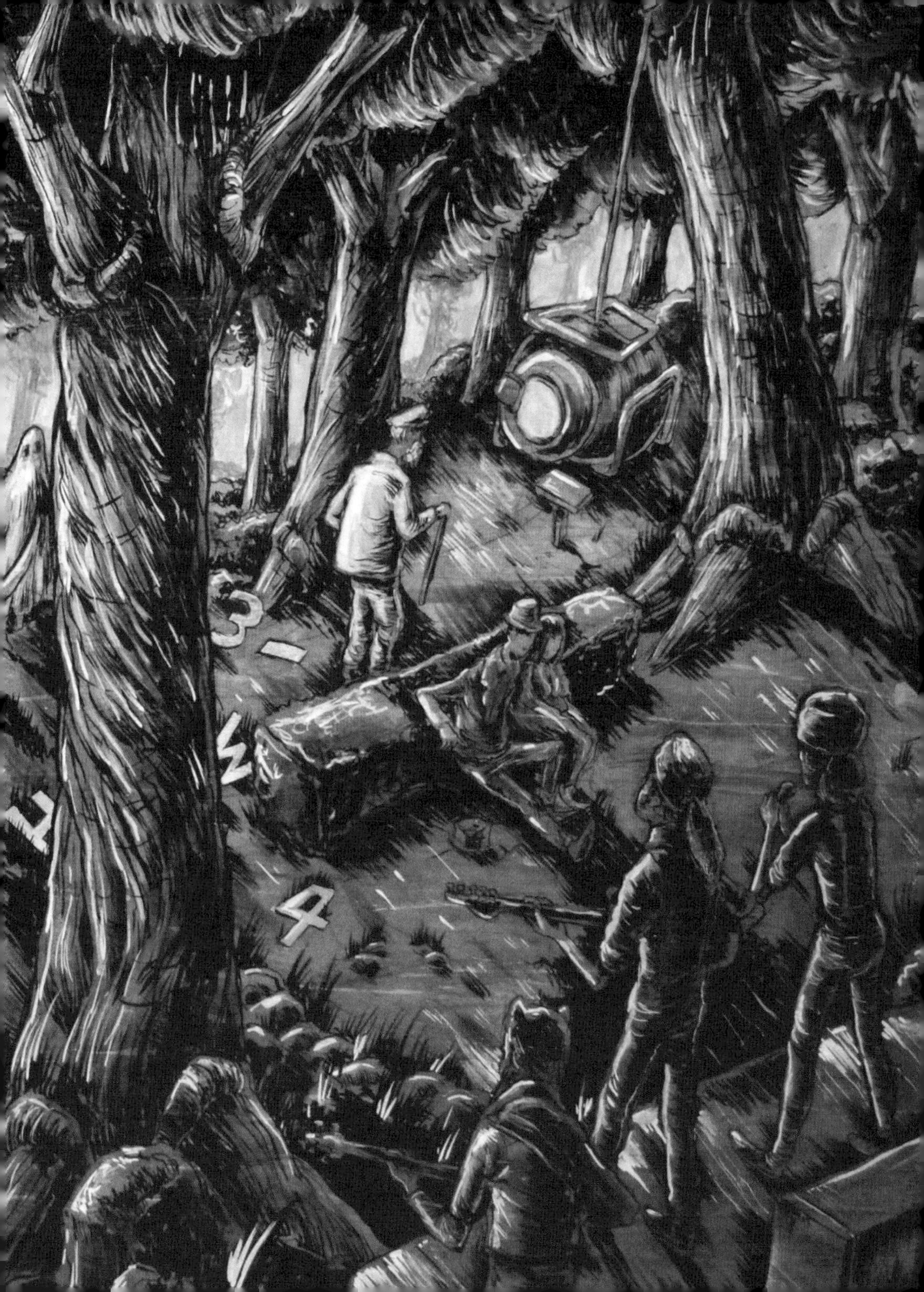
3
W
4

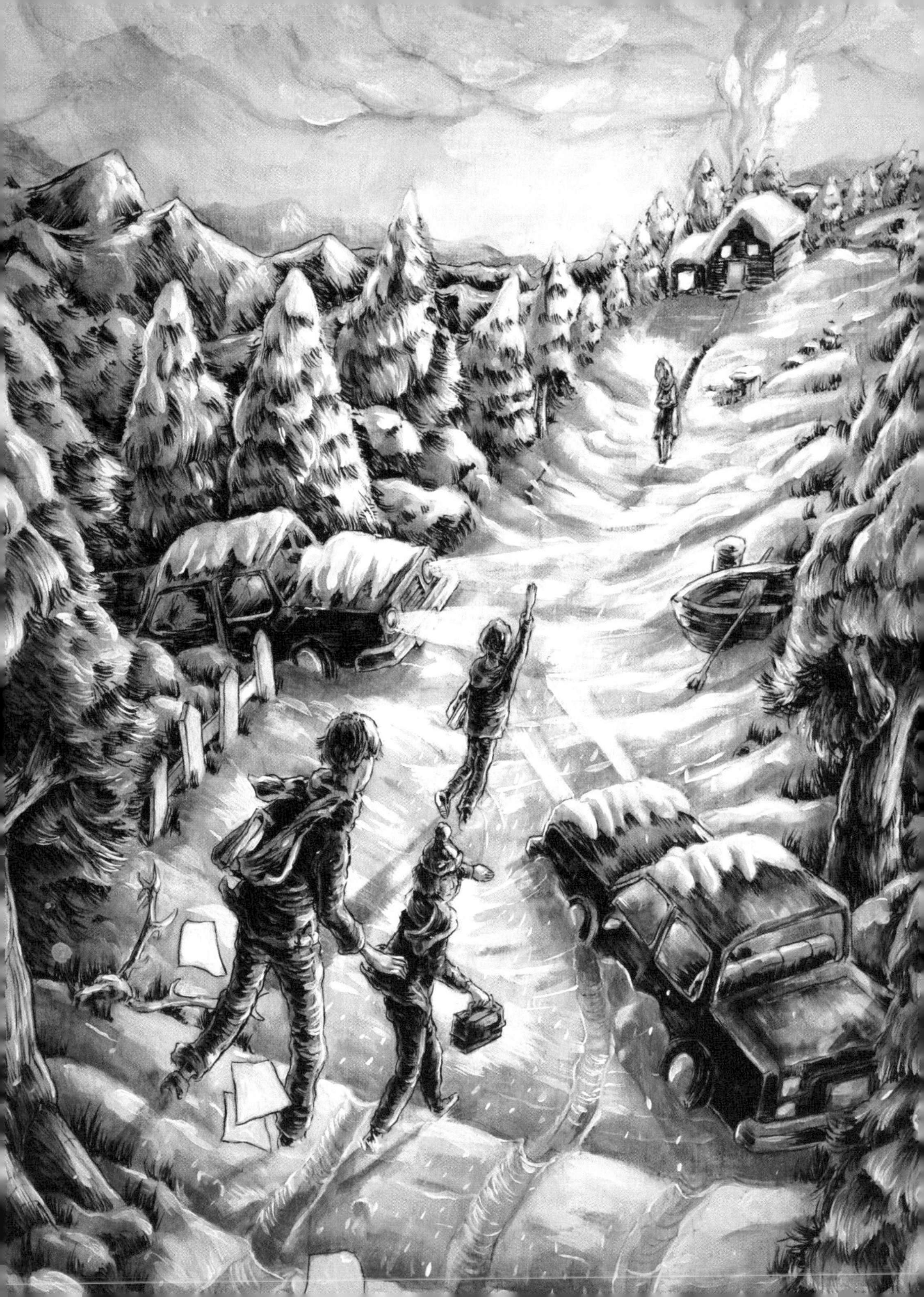

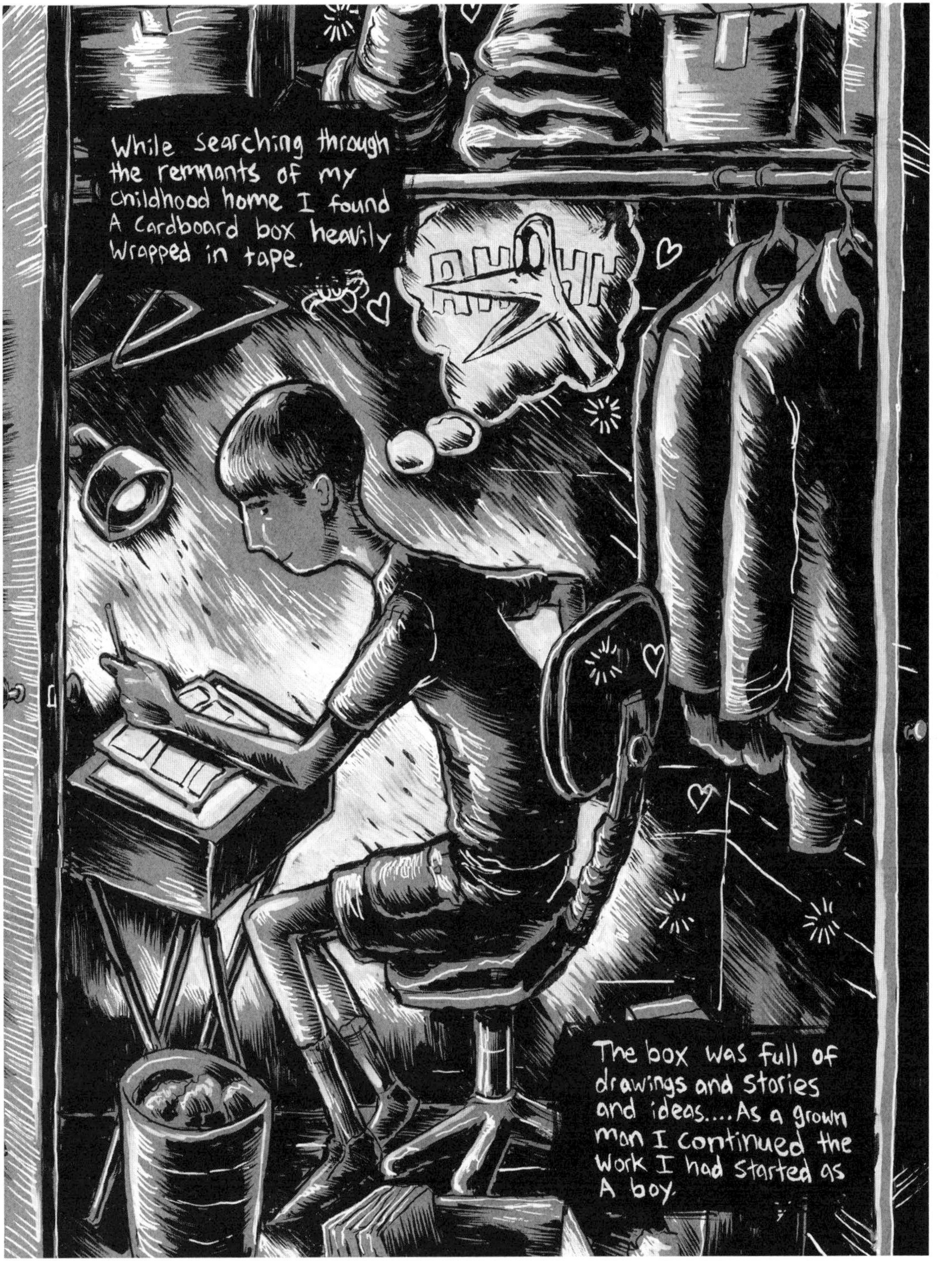
While searching through the remnants of my childhood home I found A cardboard box heavily wrapped in tape.
The box was full of drawings and stories and ideas.... As a grown man I continued the work I had started as A boy.

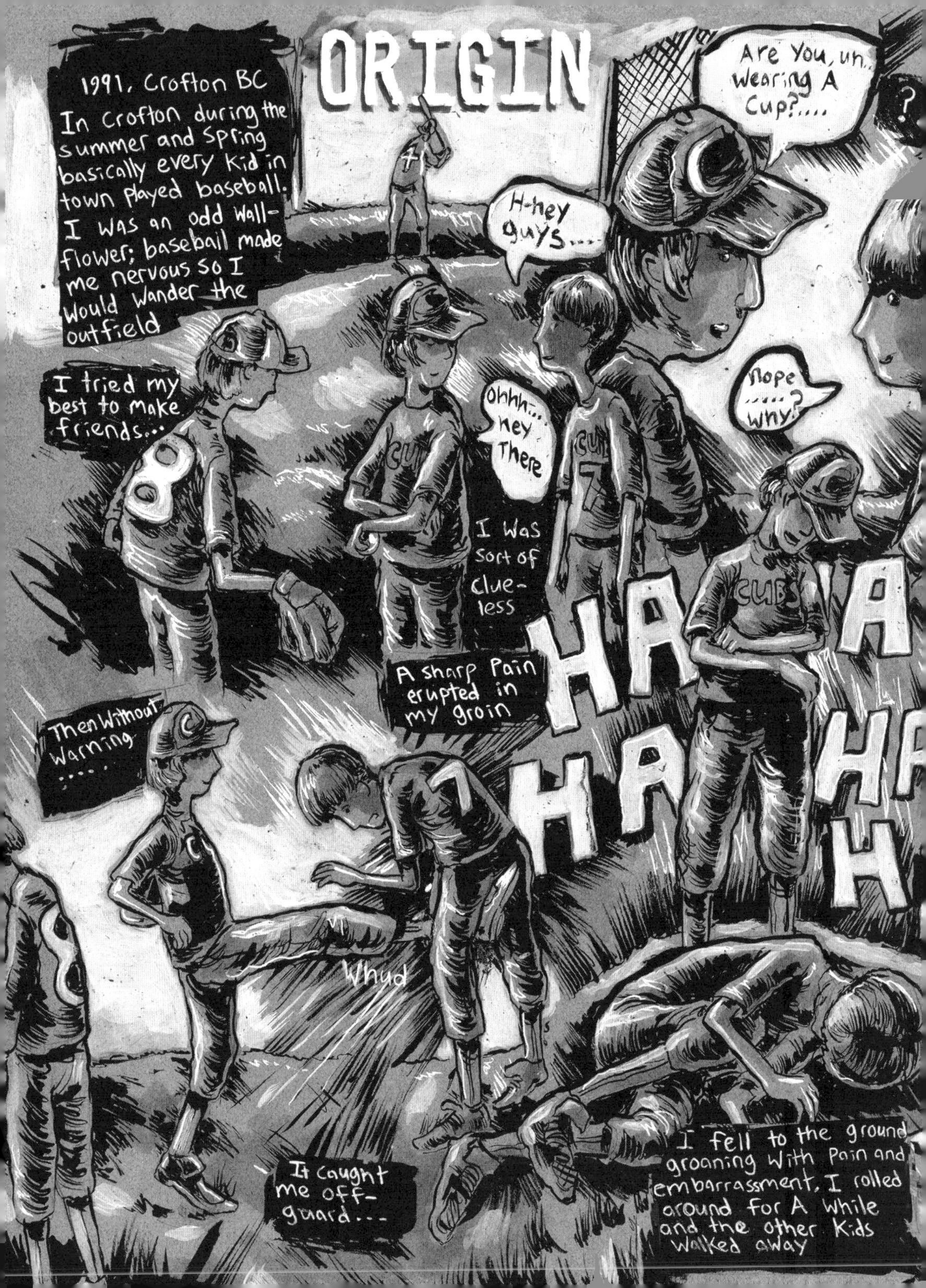
ORIGIN
1991, Crofton BC
In Crofton during the summer and Spring basically every Kid in town played baseball. I was an odd Wall-flower; baseball made me nervous so I would Wander the outfield
Are you, uh.. Wearing A Cup?.....
?
H-hey guys....
I tried my best to make friends...
Ohhh... hey There
Nope ..... why?
I Was Sort of Clue-less
A sharp Pain erupted in my groin
HA HA HA HA HA
Then Without Warning ....
Whud
It caught me off-guard...
I fell to the ground groaning with Pain and embarrassment. I rolled around for A while and the other Kids Walked away

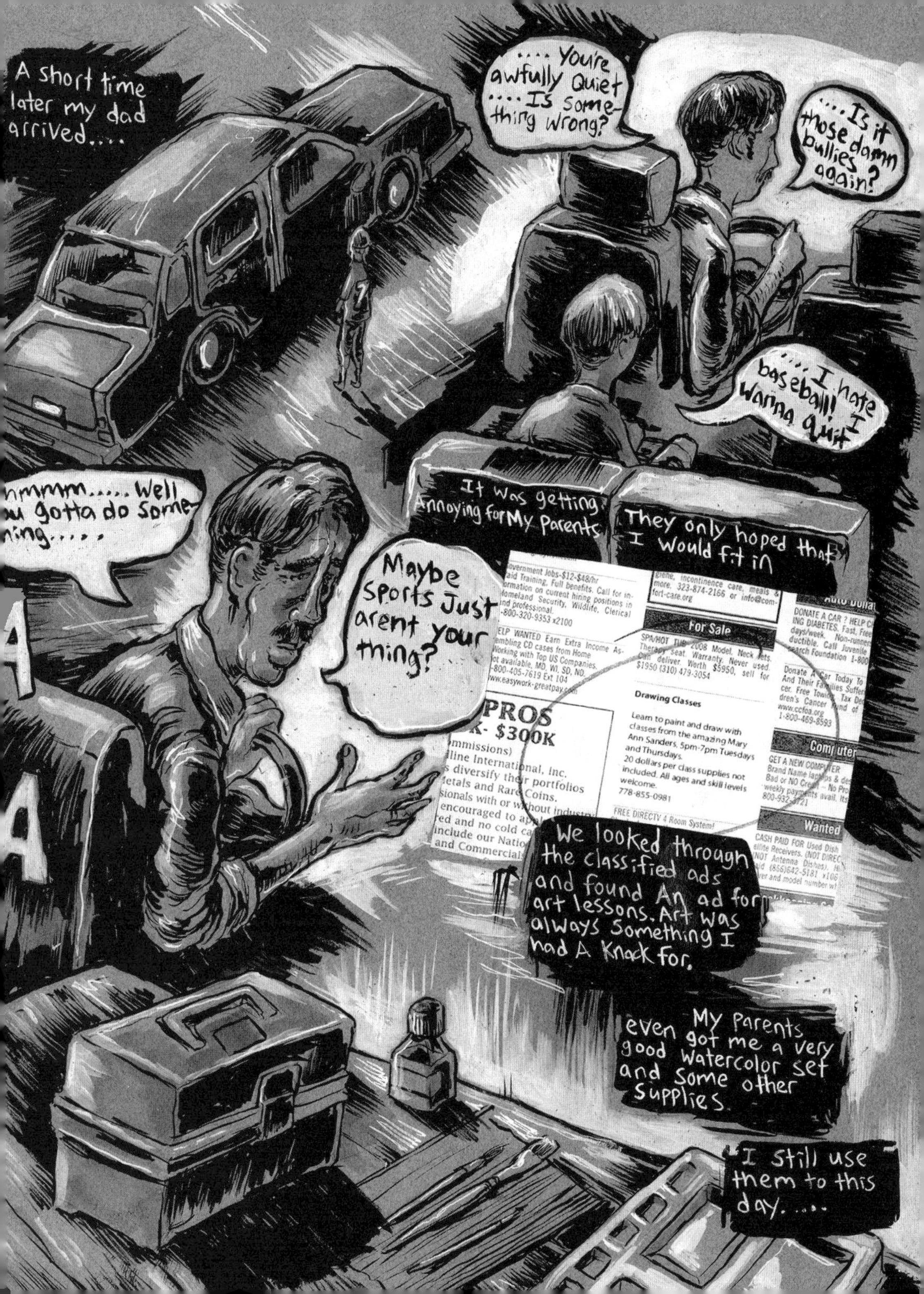

A short time later my dad arrived....
.... You're awfully Quiet .... Is something wrong?
....Is it those damn bullies again?
....I hate baseball! I wanna quit
It was getting Annoying for My Parents
They only hoped that I would fit in
hmmm.....Well you gotta do something.....
Maybe Sports Just arent your thing?
For Sale
Drawing Classes
Learn to paint and draw with classes from the amazing Mary Ann Sanders, 5pm-7pm Tuesdays and Thursdays.
20 dollars per class supplies not included. All ages and skill levels welcome.
778-855-0981
We looked through the classified ads and found An ad for art lessons. Art was always Something I had A Knack for.
My Parents even got me a very good watercolor set and Some other Supplies.
I still use them to this day.....

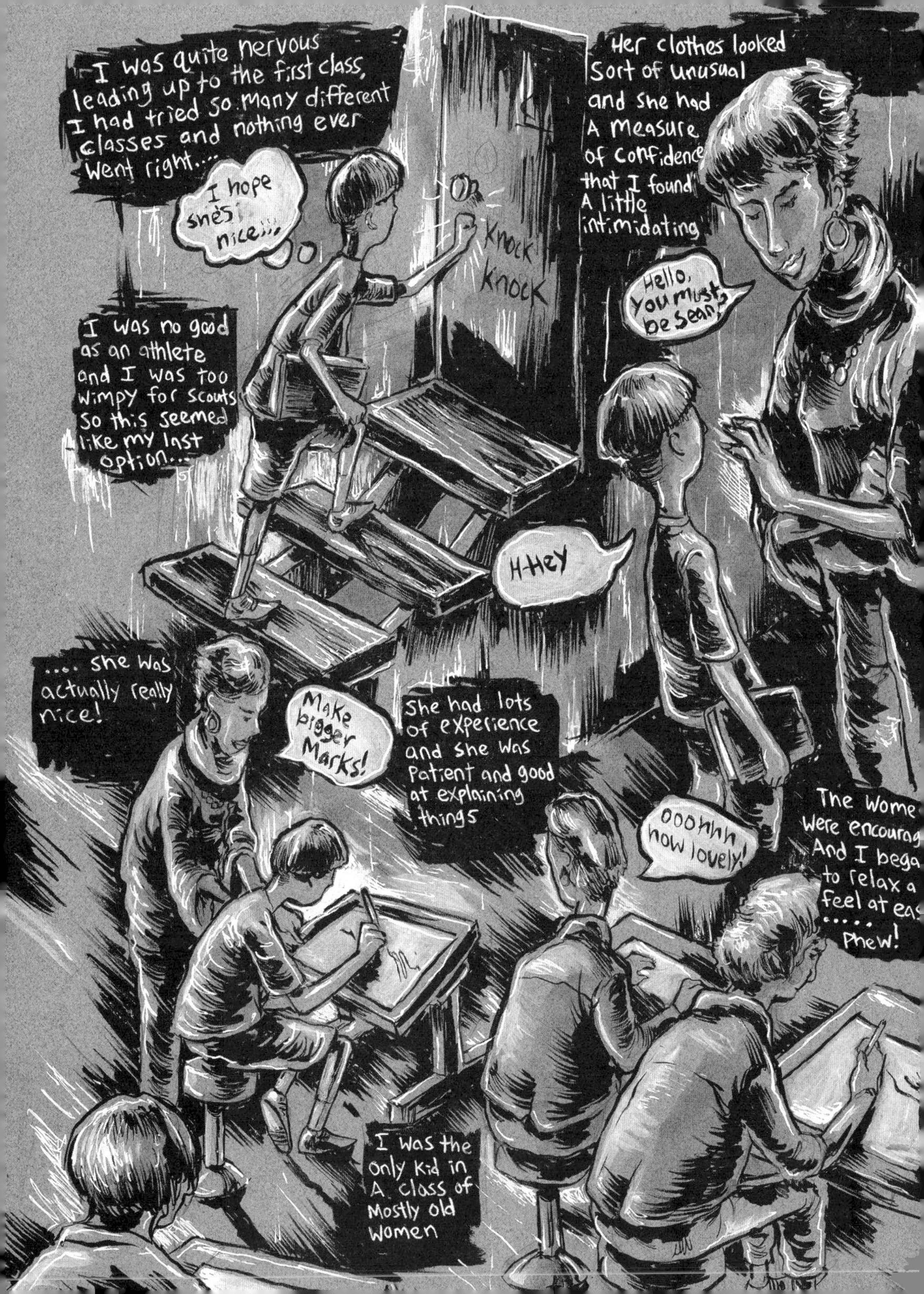
I was quite nervous leading up to the first class, I had tried so many different classes and nothing ever went right....
I hope she's nice...
Knock knock
I was no good as an athlete and I was too wimpy for Scouts so this seemed like my last option...
Her clothes looked sort of unusual and she had a measure of confidence that I found a little intimidating
Hello, you must be Sean?
H-Hey
.... she was actually really nice!
Make bigger marks!
She had lots of experience and she was patient and good at explaining things
ooohhh how lovely!
The wome were encourag And I bega to relax a feel at eas ..... Phew!
I was the only kid in a class of mostly old women

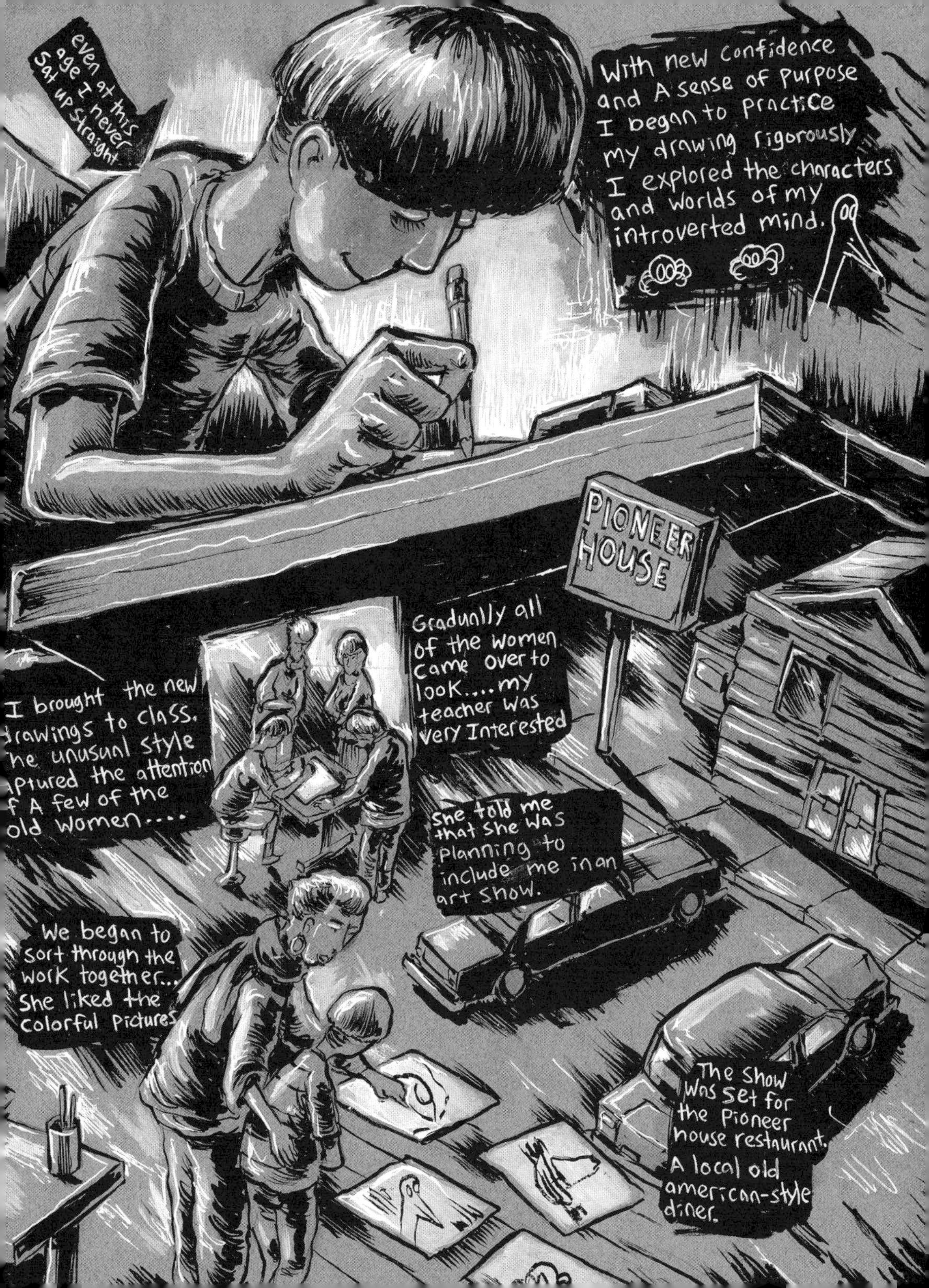

even at this age I never sat up straight
With new confidence and A sense of Purpose I began to practice my drawing rigorously I explored the characters and worlds of my introverted mind.
PIONEER HOUSE
I brought the new rawings to class. he unusual style ptured the attention f A few of the old women....
Gradually all of the women came over to look....my teacher was very Interested
She told me that she was planning to include me in an art show.
We began to sort through the work together... She liked the colorful Pictures
The show was set for the Pioneer house restaurant.
A local old american-style diner.

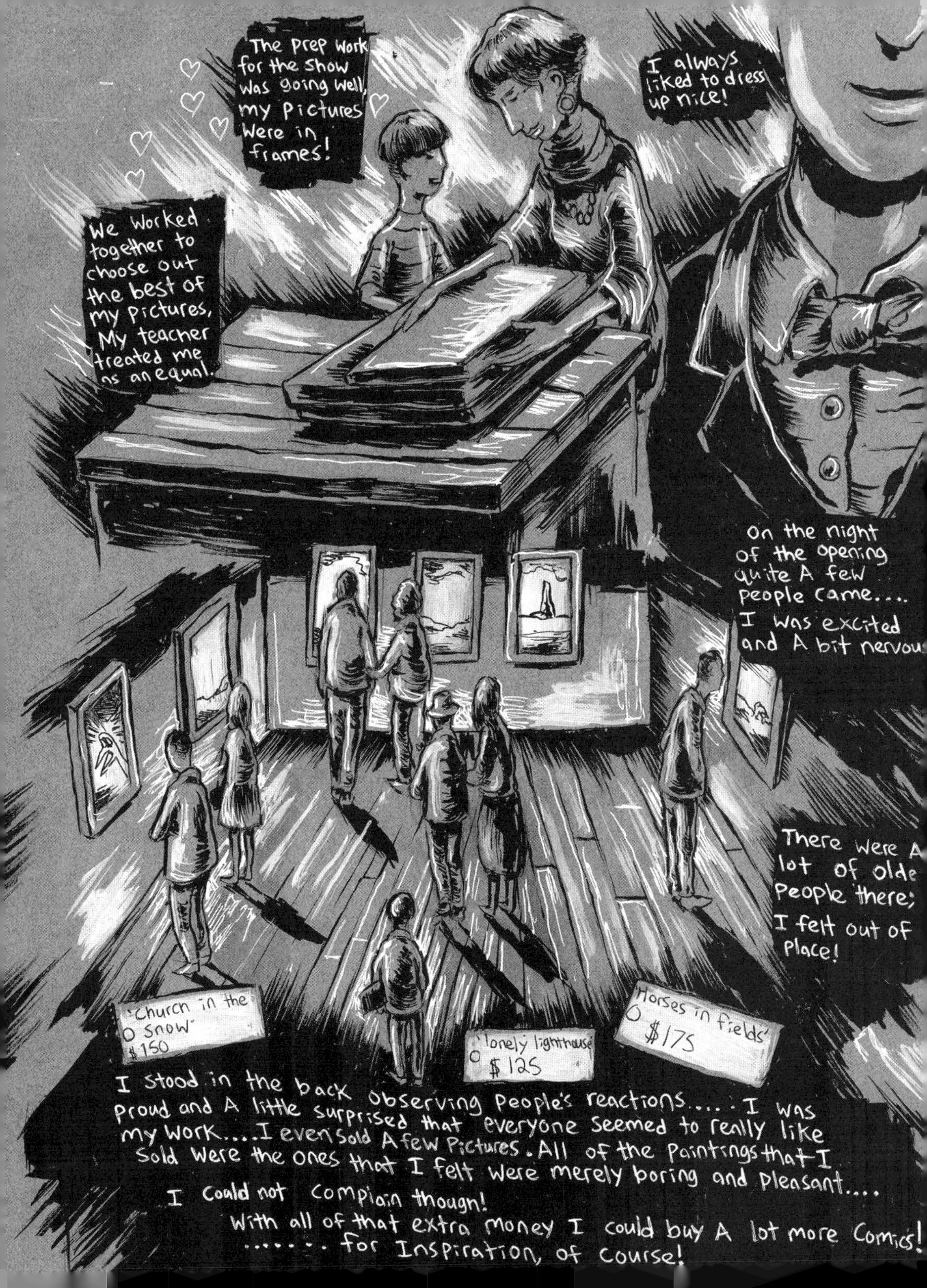

The prep work for the show was going well, my pictures were in frames!
I always liked to dress up nice!
We worked together to choose out the best of my pictures, My teacher treated me as an equal.
On the night of the opening quite A few people came.... I was excited and A bit nervou
There were A lot of olde People there; I felt out of Place!
'Church in the snow' $150
'lonely lighthouse' $125
'Horses in fields' $175
I stood in the back observing people's reactions.... I was proud and A little surprised that everyone seemed to really like my work....I even sold A few pictures. All of the paintings that I sold were the ones that I felt were merely boring and pleasant....
I could not complain though!
With all of that extra money I could buy A lot more Comics!
...... for Inspiration, of course!

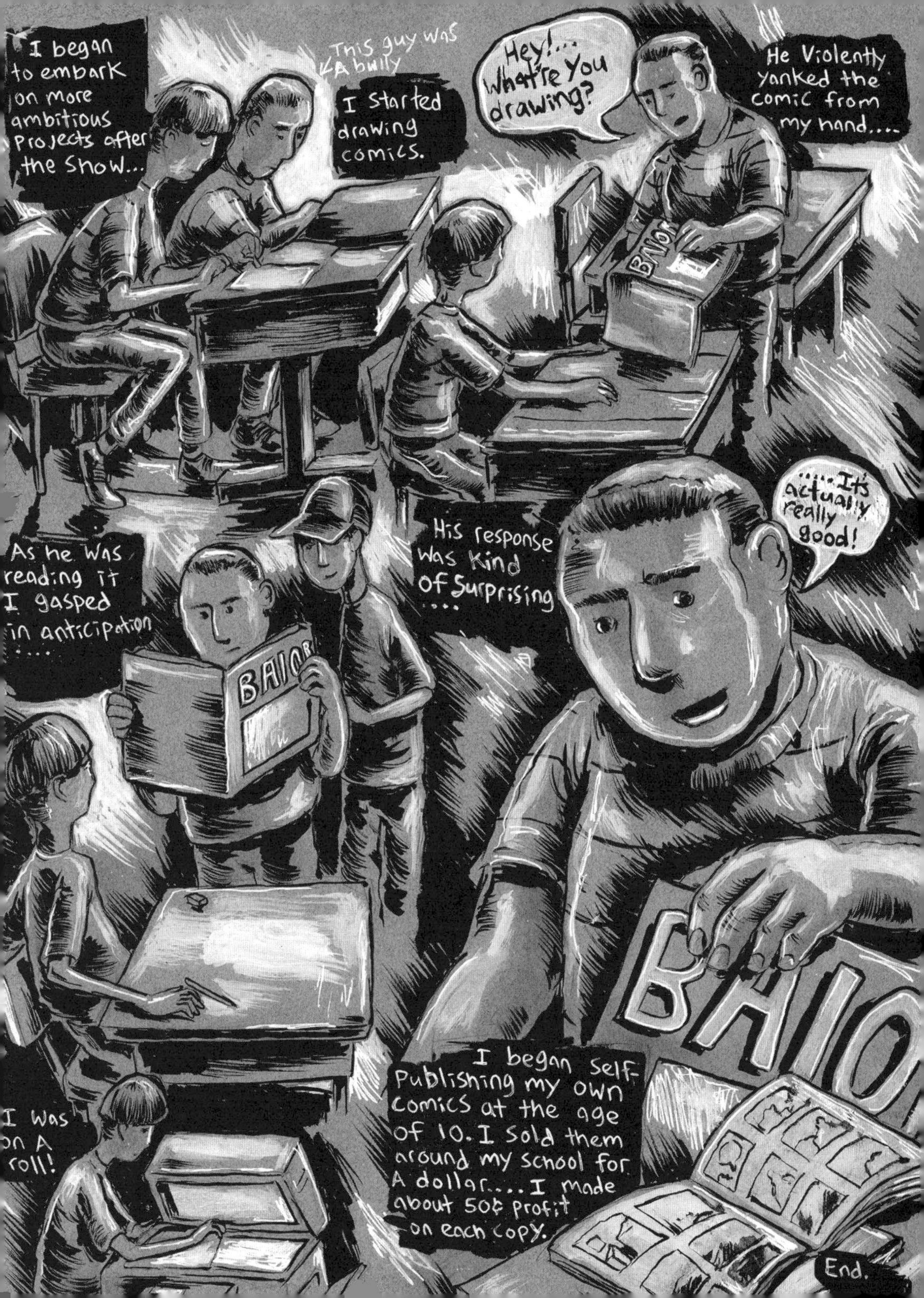
I began to embark on more ambitious Projects after the Show...
This guy was A bully
I started drawing comics.
Hey!... What're you drawing?
He Violently yanked the comic from my hand....
BAIO
As he was reading it I gasped in anticipation....
BAIO
His response was kind of Surprising....
....It's actually really good!
I was on A roll!
I began self-Publishing my own comics at the age of 10. I sold them around my school for A dollar.... I made about 50¢ profit on each copy.
BAIO
End.

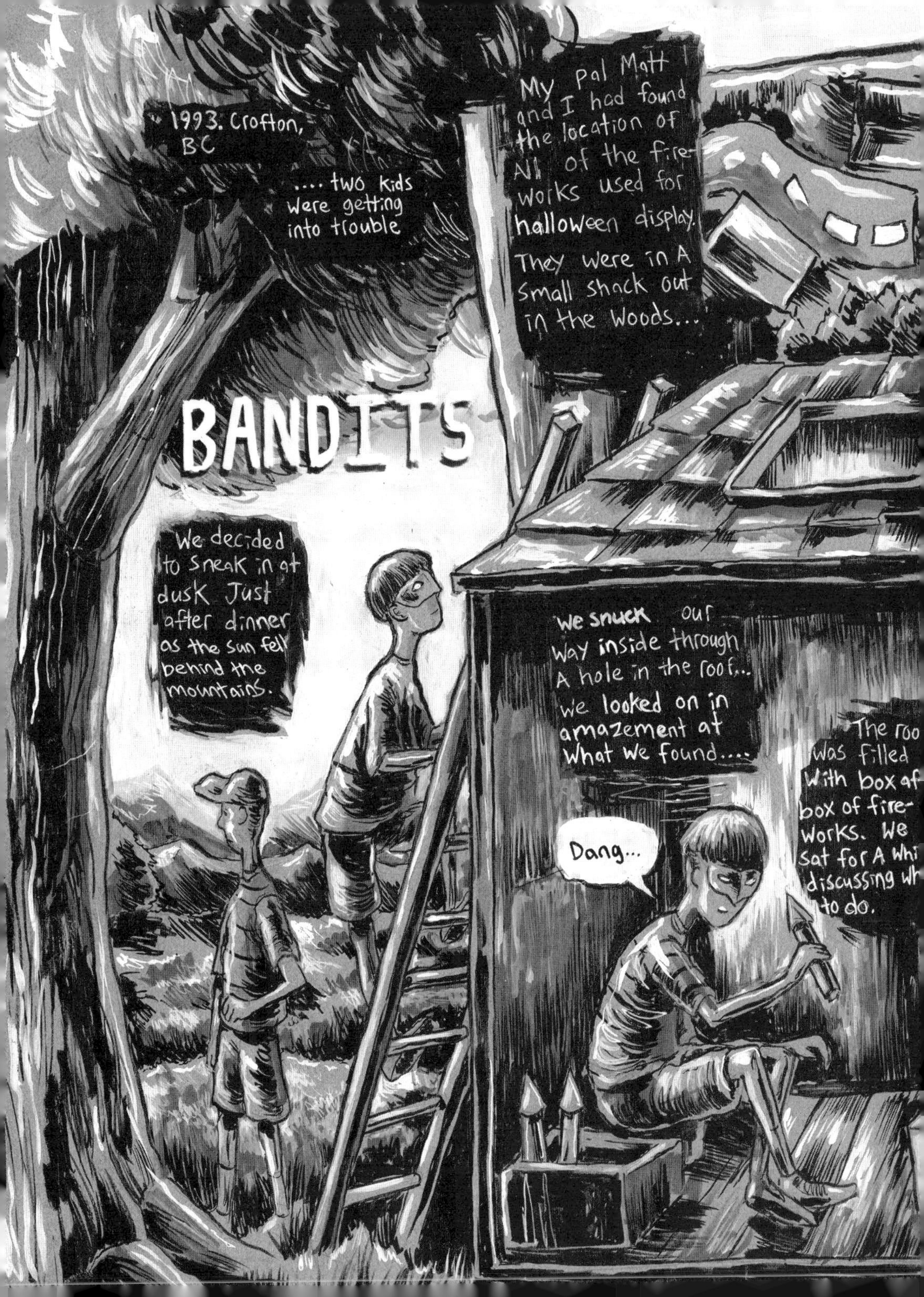

1993. Crofton, BC
.... two kids were getting into trouble
My Pal Matt and I had found the location of All of the fireworks used for halloween display. They were in A Small shack out in the woods...
BANDITS
We decided to sneak in at dusk Just after dinner as the sun fell behind the mountains.
We snuck our way inside through A hole in the roof... we looked on in amazement at What we found....
Dang...

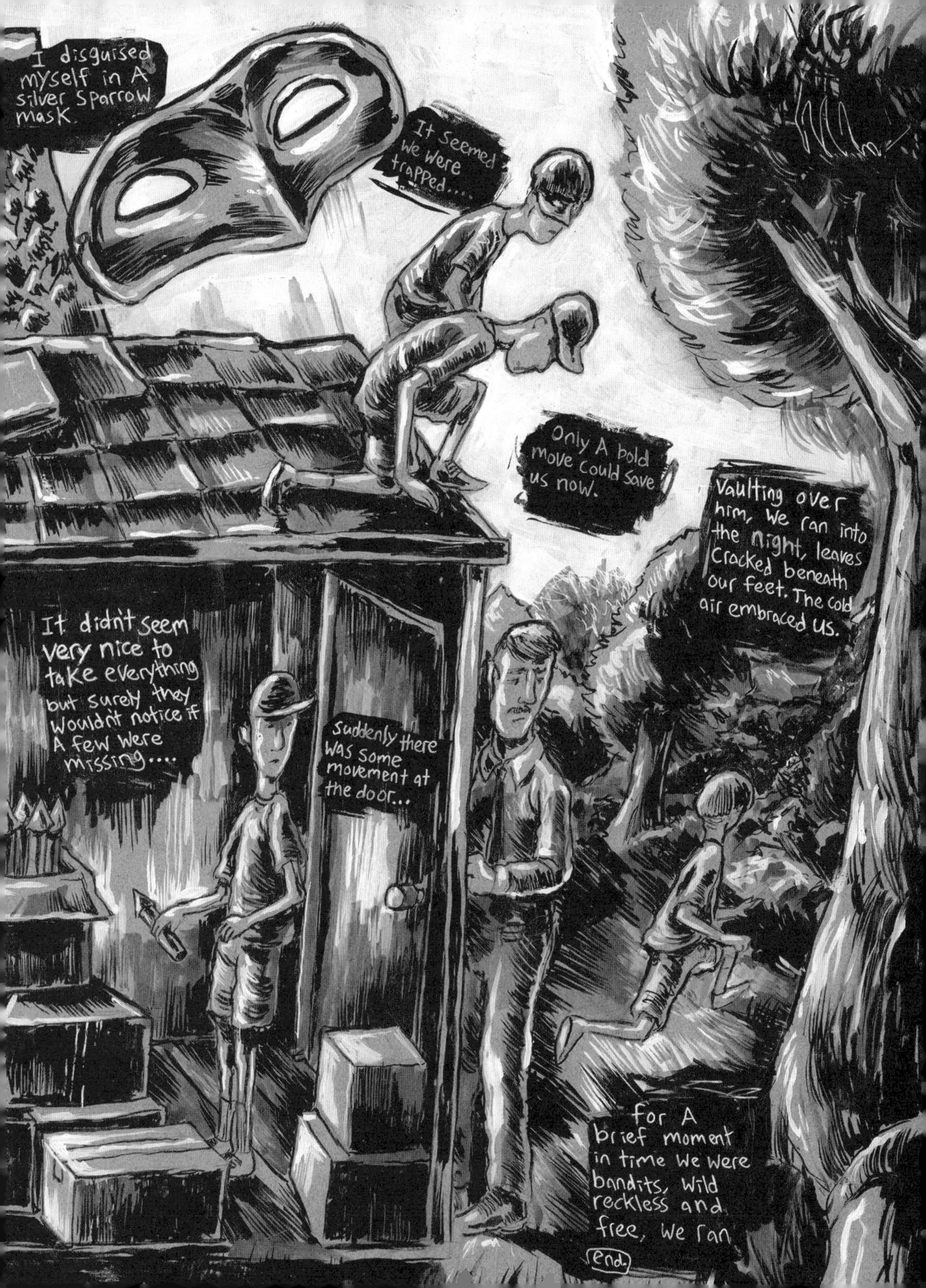
I disguised myself in A silver Sparrow mask.
It Seemed we were trapped....
Only A bold move could save us now.
Vaulting over him, we ran into the night, leaves Cracked beneath our feet. The cold air embraced us.
It didn't seem very nice to take everything but surely they wouldn't notice if A few were missing....
Suddenly there was some movement at the door...
For A brief moment in time we were bandits, wild reckless and free, we ran
end.

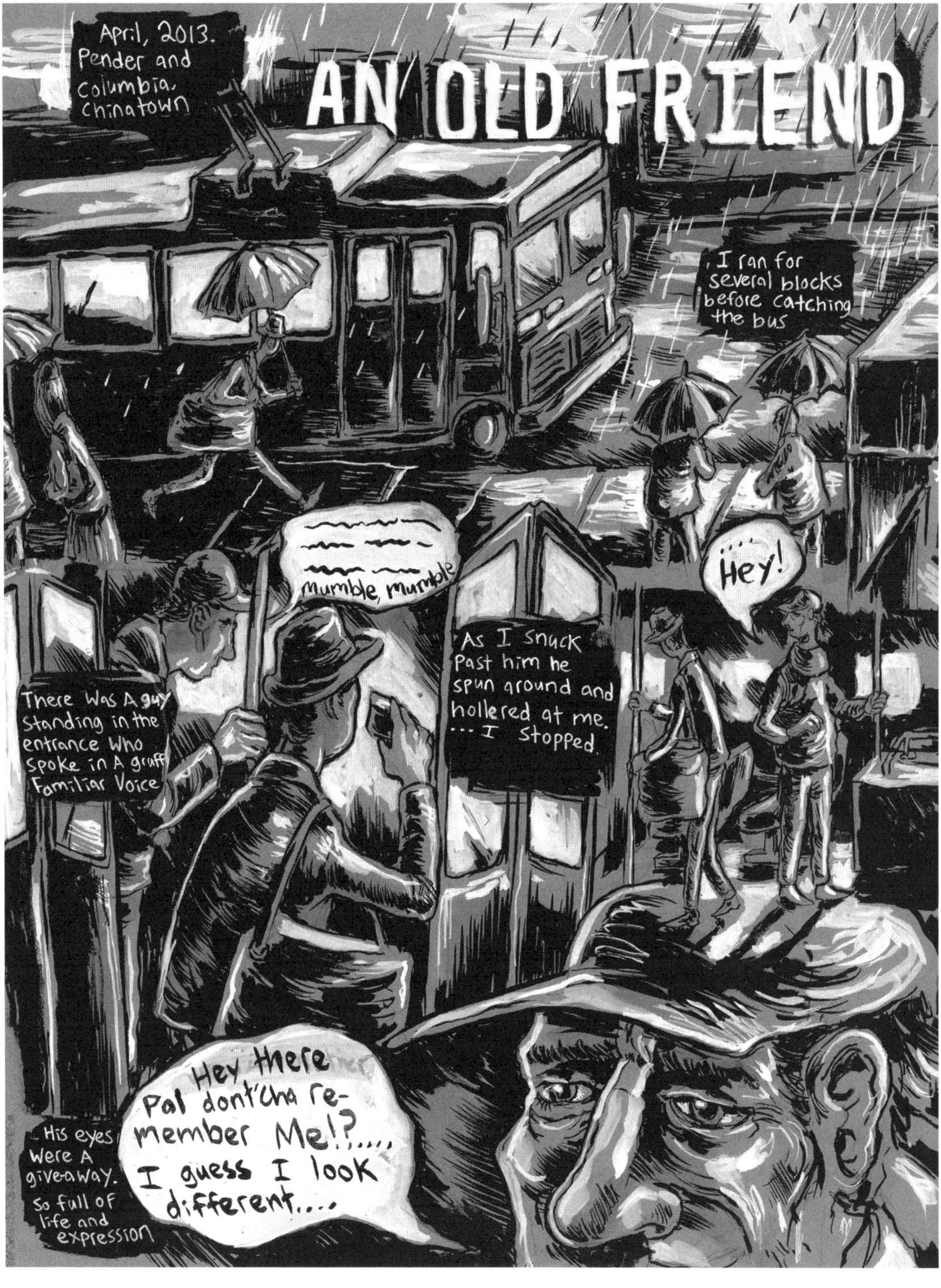
April, 2013.
Pender and Columbia, Chinatown
AN OLD FRIEND
I ran for several blocks before catching the bus
mumble, mumble
There was a guy standing in the entrance who spoke in a gruff familiar voice
As I snuck past him he spun around and hollered at me. ... I stopped.
.... Hey!
His eyes were a giveaway. So full of life and expression
Hey there Pal dont'cha re-member Me!?.... I guess I look different....

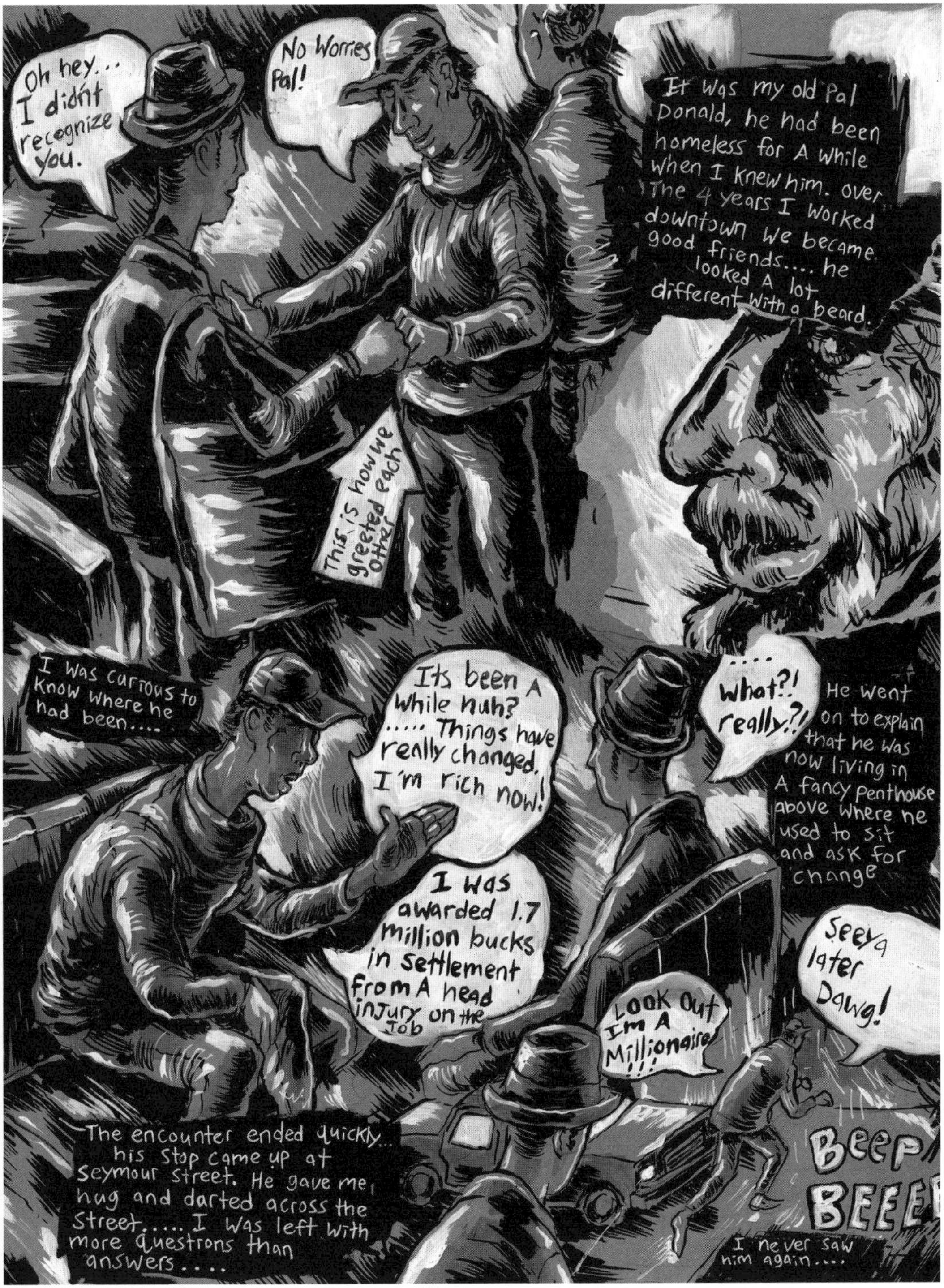
Oh hey... I didn't recognize you.
No Worries Pal!
It was my old Pal Donald, he had been homeless for A while when I knew him. over The 4 years I worked downtown we became good friends.... he looked A lot different with a beard.
This is how we greeted each other
I was curious to know where he had been....
Its been A while huh? ..... Things have really changed, I'm rich now!
I was awarded 1.7 million bucks in settlement from A head injury on the Job
.... what?! really?!
He went on to explain that he was now living in A fancy penthouse above where he used to sit and ask for change
Seeya later Dawg!
LOOK Out I'M A Millionaire!!!
The encounter ended quickly... his stop came up at Seymour Street. He gave me hug and darted across the Street..... I was left with more questions than answers....
Beep
BEEE
I never saw him again....

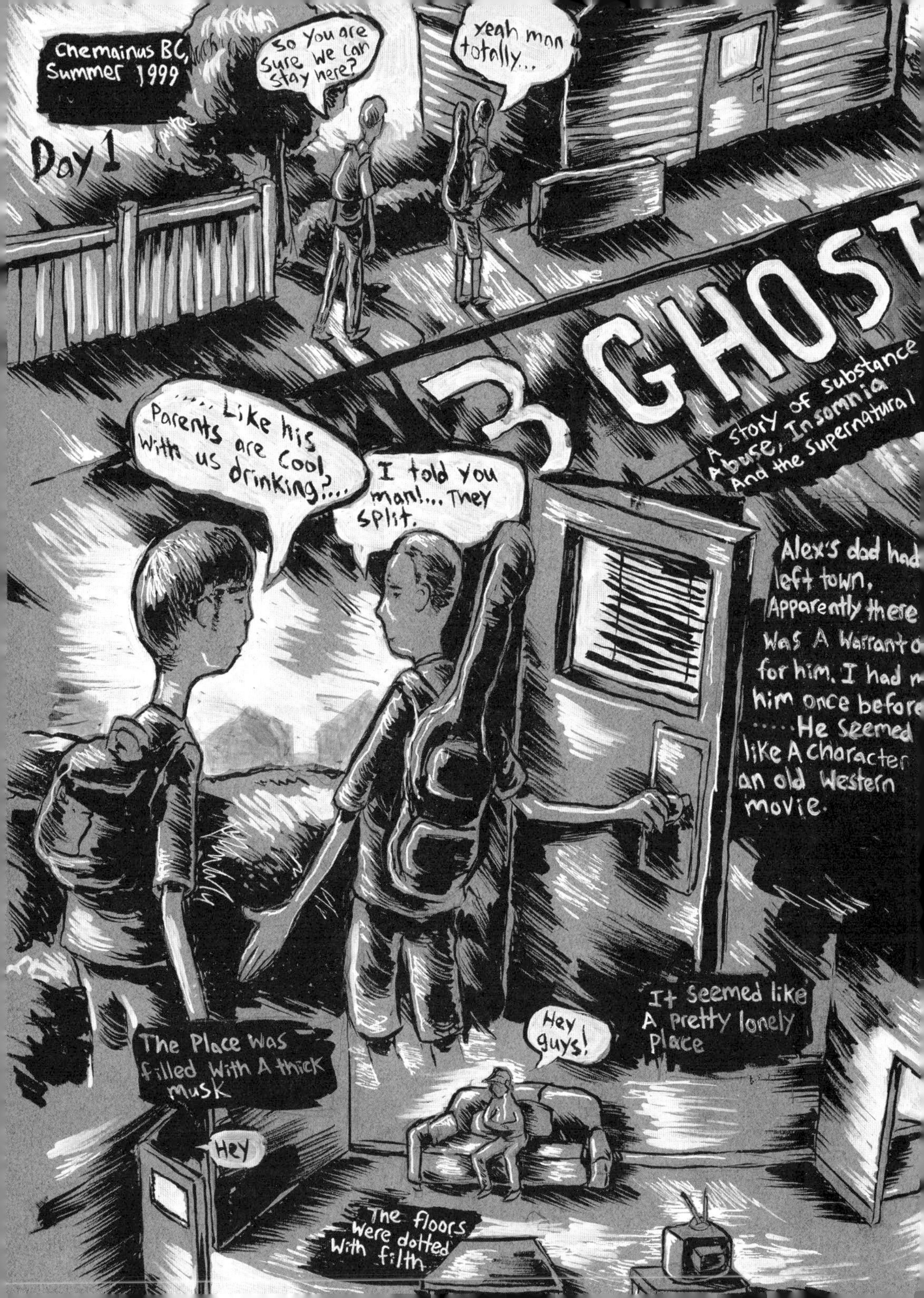
Chemainus BC, Summer 1999
Day 1
So you are sure we can stay here?
yeah man totally...
3 GHOST
A story of Substance Abuse, Insomnia And the Supernatural
.....Like his Parents are Cool with us drinking?....
I told you man!... They split.
Alex's dad had left town, Apparently there was A warrant o for him. I had m him once before .....He Seemed like A character an old Western movie.
It seemed like A pretty lonely place
Hey guys!
The Place was filled with A thick musk
Hey
The floors were dotted with filth

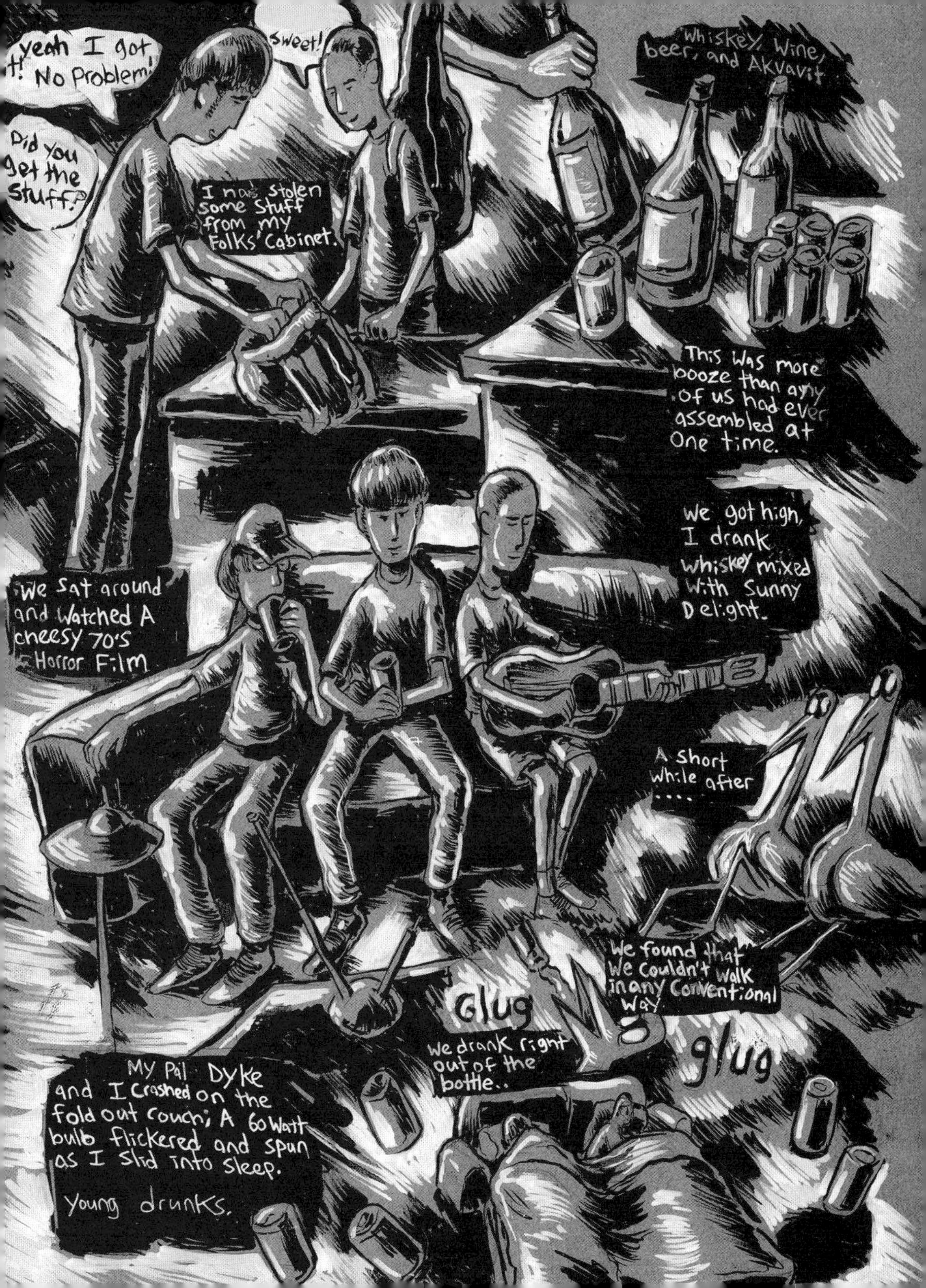
Did you get the stuff?
yeah I got it! No Problem!
Sweet!
I had stolen some stuff from my Folks' Cabinet.
Whiskey, Wine, beer, and Akvavit
This Was more booze than any of us had ever assembled at One time.
We sat around and Watched A cheesy 70's Horror Film
We got high, I drank whiskey mixed With Sunny Delight.
A Short while after ....
We found that We couldn't walk in any Conventional way.
Glug
glug
We drank right out of the bottle..
My Pal Dyke and I Crashed on the fold out couch; A 60 Watt bulb flickered and spun as I slid into sleep.
young drunks.

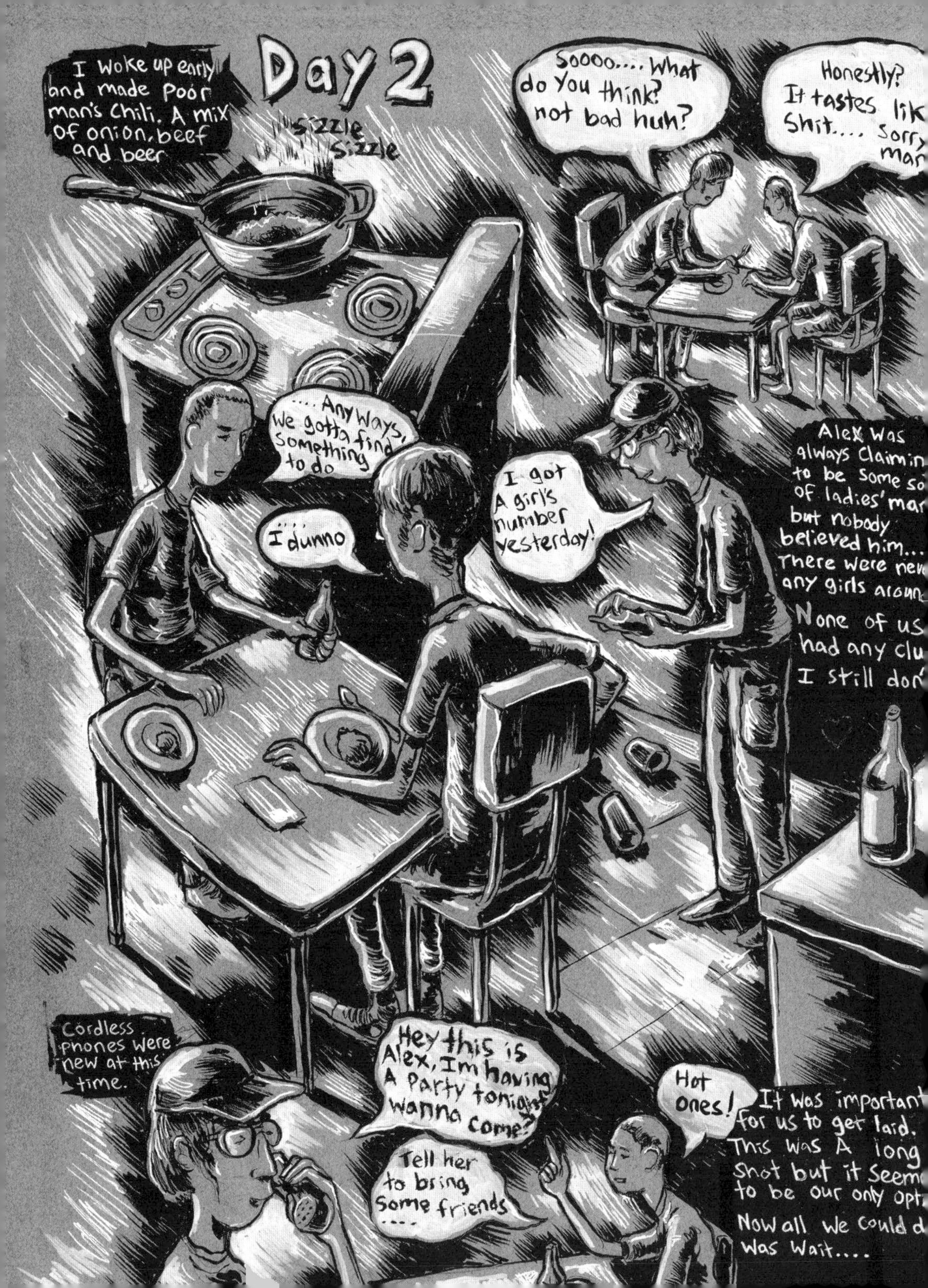
I woke up early and made poor man's Chili. A mix of onion, beef and beer
Day 2
sizzle sizzle
Soooo.... What do You think? not bad huh?
Honestly? It tastes lik Shit.... Sorry mar
....Any ways, we gotta find something to do
...I dunno
I got A girl's number yesterday!
Alex was always Claimin to be some so of ladies' mar but nobody believed him... There were neve any girls aroun
None of us had any clu
I still don'
Cordless phones were new at this time.
Hey this is Alex, I'm having A Party tonight wanna come?
Tell her to bring some friends ....
Hot ones!
It was important for us to get laid. This was A long shot but it seem to be our only opt
Now all we could d was wait....

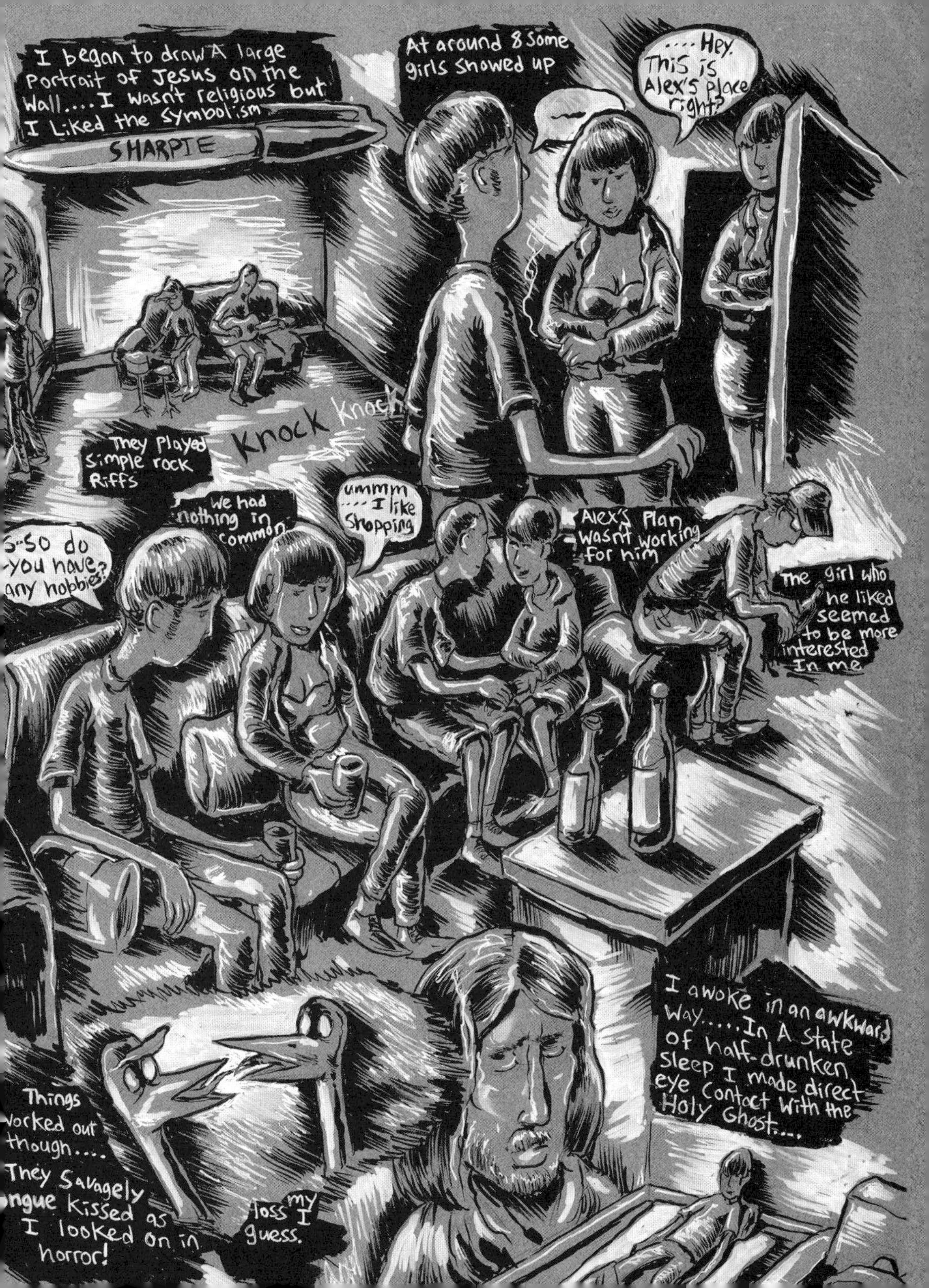
I began to draw A large Portrait of Jesus on the Wall.... I wasn't religious but I Liked the symbolism
SHARPIE
At around 8 Some girls showed up
....Hey. This is Alex's place right?
Knock Knock
They Played simple rock Riffs
We had nothing in common
S-So do you have any hobbies?
ummm ....I like Shopping
Alex's Plan wasn't working for him
The girl who he liked seemed to be more interested In me
I awoke in an awkward Way.....In A State of half-drunken Sleep I made direct eye contact with the Holy Ghost....
Things worked out though....
They Savagely ngue kissed as I looked on in horror!
my loss I guess.

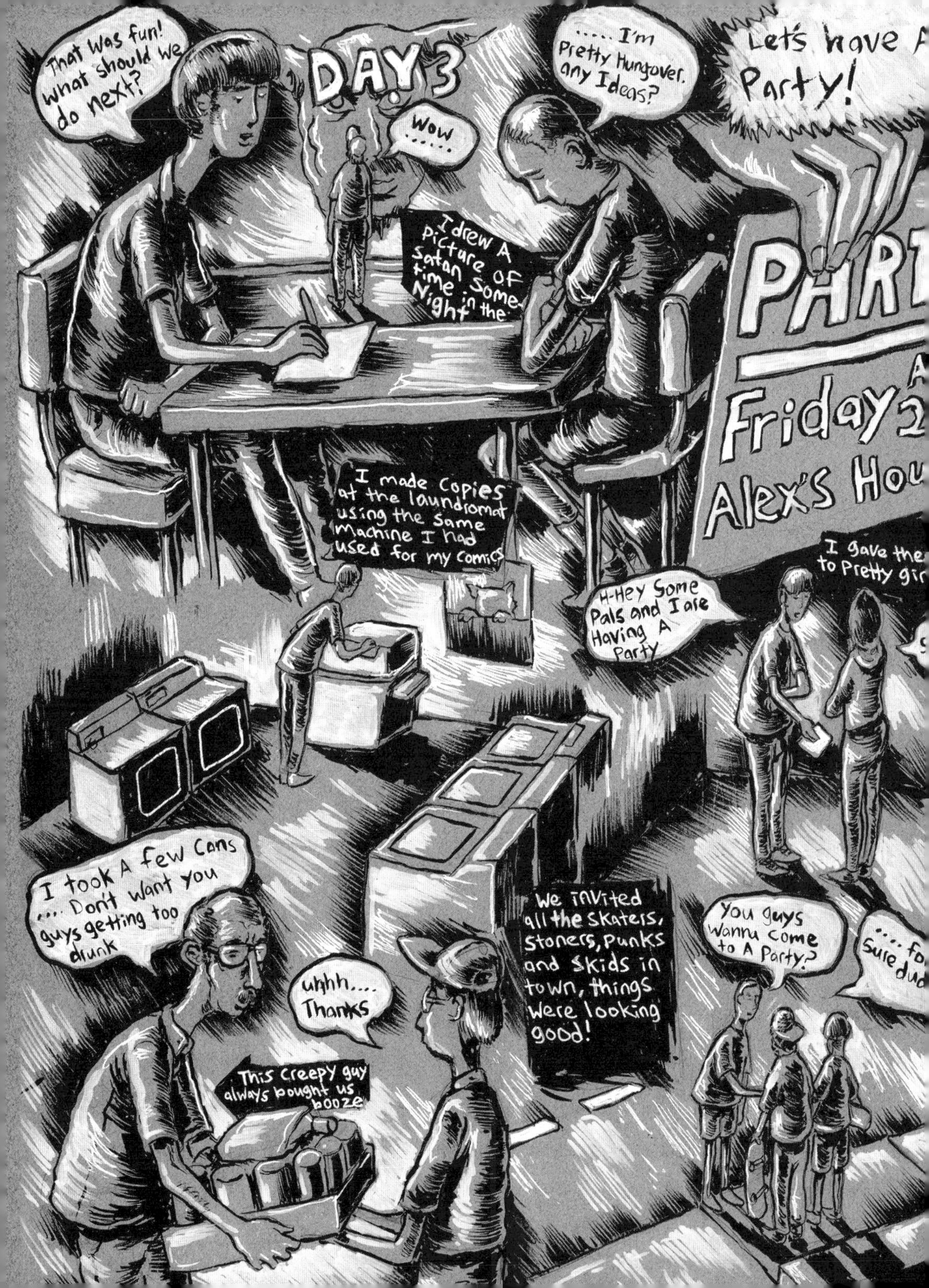

That was fun! what should we do next?
DAY 3
Wow ......
..... I'm Pretty Hungover. any Ideas?
Let's have
Party!
I drew A Picture of Satan Some-time in the Night
Friday
Alex's
I made copies at the laundromat using the same machine I had used for my comics
H-Hey Some Pals and I are Having A Party
I gave
to Pretty
I took A few Cans .... Don't want you guys getting too drunk
uhhh.... Thanks
This creepy guy always bought us booze
We invited all the skaters, stoners, punks and skids in town, things were looking good!
You guys wanna come to A Party?

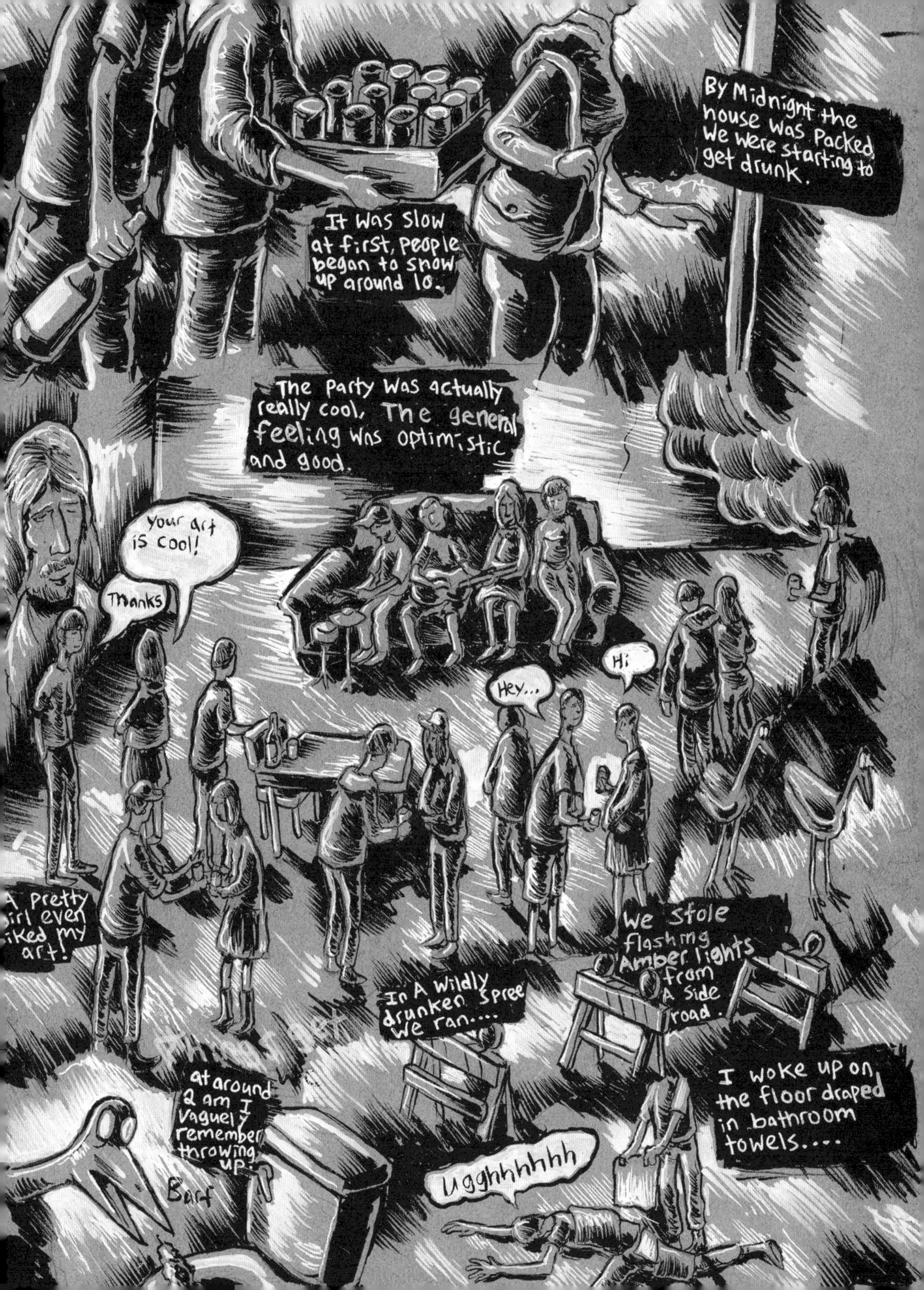
It was slow at first, people began to show up around 10.
By Midnight the house was Packed We were starting to get drunk.
The Party was actually really cool. The general feeling was optimistic and good.
Your art is cool!
Thanks
Hey...
Hi
A pretty girl even liked my art!
We stole flashing Amber lights from A side road.
In A wildly drunken spree we ran....
at around 2 am I vaguely remember throwing up.
Barf
Ugghhhhhh
I woke up on the floor draped in bathroom towels....

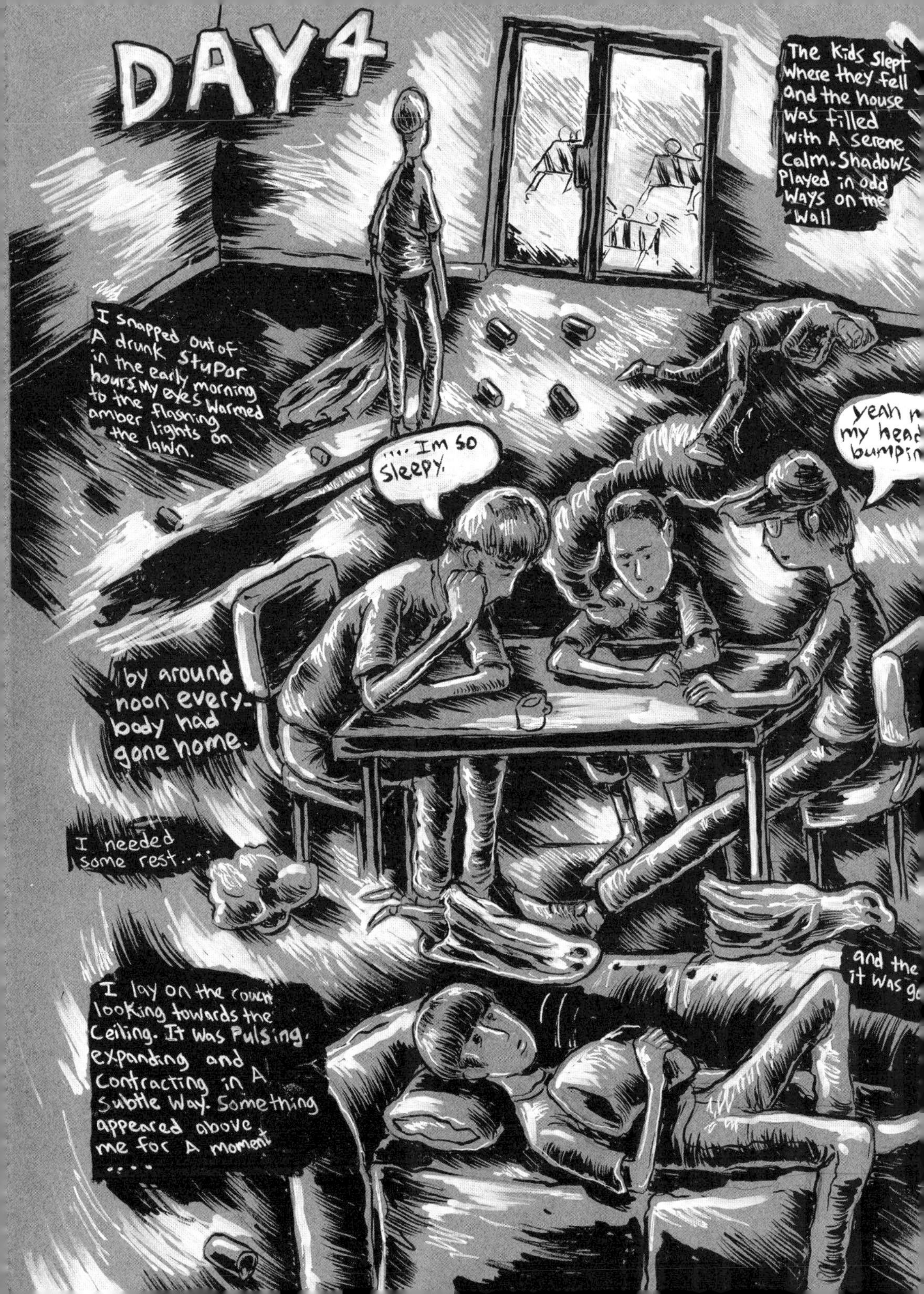
DAY 4
The Kids Slept where they fell and the house was filled with A serene calm. Shadows Played in odd ways on the wall
I snapped out of A drunk stupor in the early morning hours. My eyes warmed to the flashing amber lights on the lawn.
... Im so sleepy.
yeah m my head bumpin
by around noon every-body had gone home.
I needed some rest....
and the it was go
I lay on the couch looking towards the Ceiling. It was Pulsing, expanding and contracting in A subtle way. Something appeared above me for A moment ....

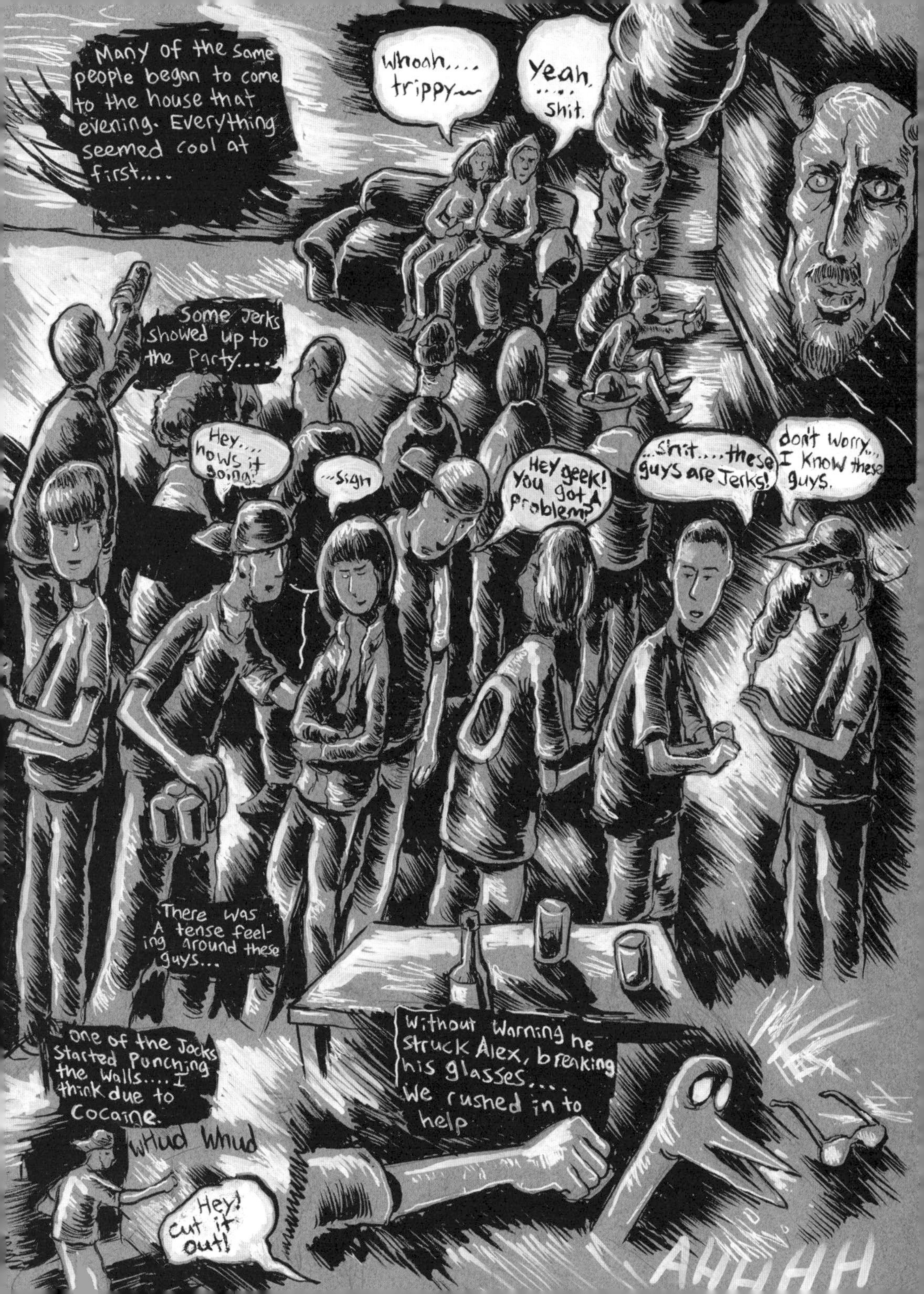
Many of the same people began to come to the house that evening. Everything seemed cool at first....
Whoah.... trippy...
Yeah.... shit.
Some Jerks showed up to the Party....
Hey.... hows it going!
...Sigh
Hey geek! You got A problem?
...Shit.... these guys are Jerks!
don't worry... I know these guys.
There was A tense feeling around these guys...
one of the Jocks Started Punching the walls.... I think due to Cocaine.
Without Warning he struck Alex, breaking his glasses.... We rushed in to help
WHud Whud
Hey! cut it out!
AHHHH

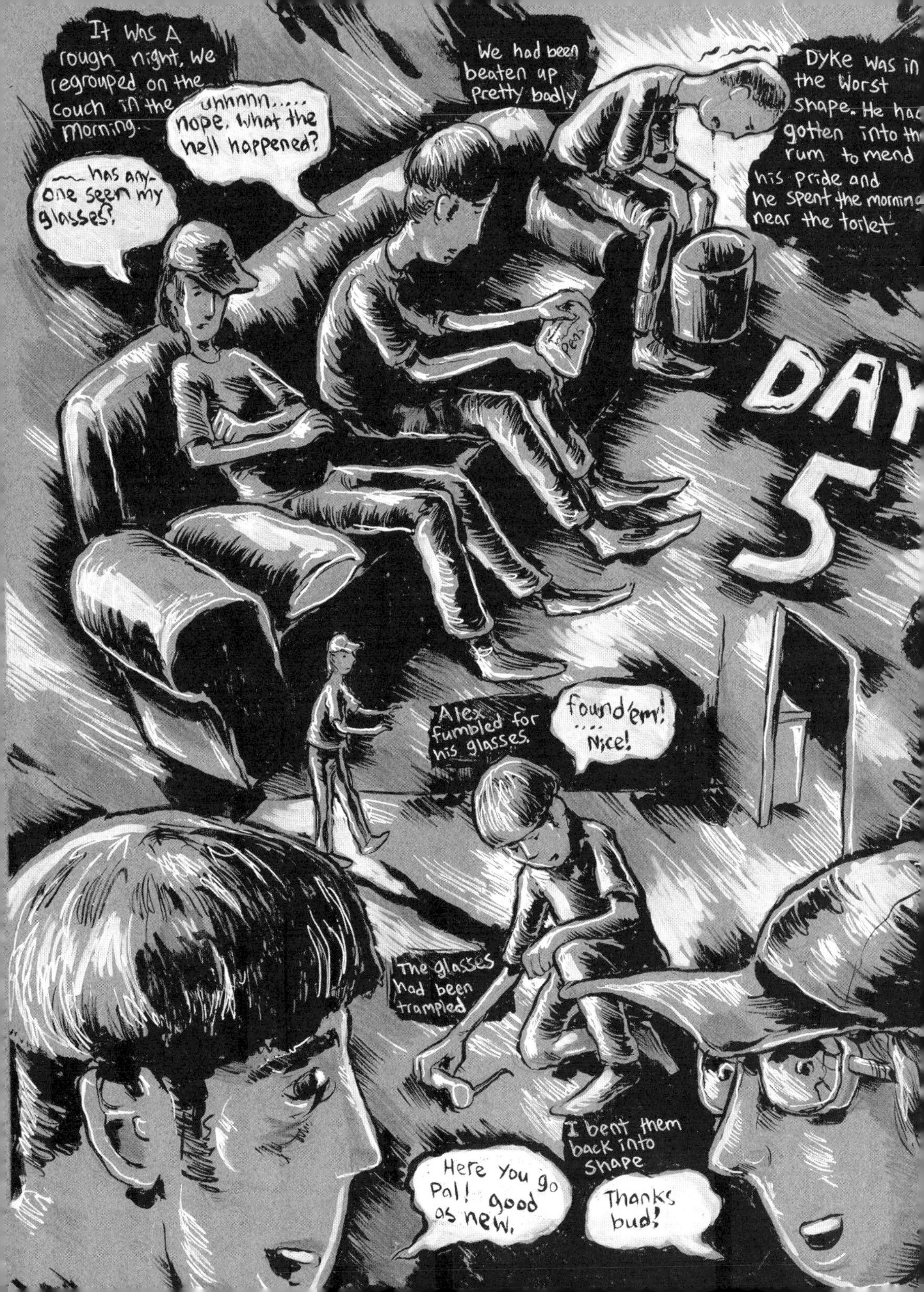
It was A rough night, we regrouped on the couch in the morning.
uhhnnn..... nope. What the hell happened?
We had been beaten up pretty badly
Dyke was in the worst shape. He had gotten into the rum to mend his pride and he spent the morning near the toilet.
— has any-one seen my glasses?
DAY 5
Alex fumbled for his glasses.
found 'em! .... Nice!
The glasses had been trampled
I bent them back into shape
Here you go Pal! good as new.
Thanks bud!

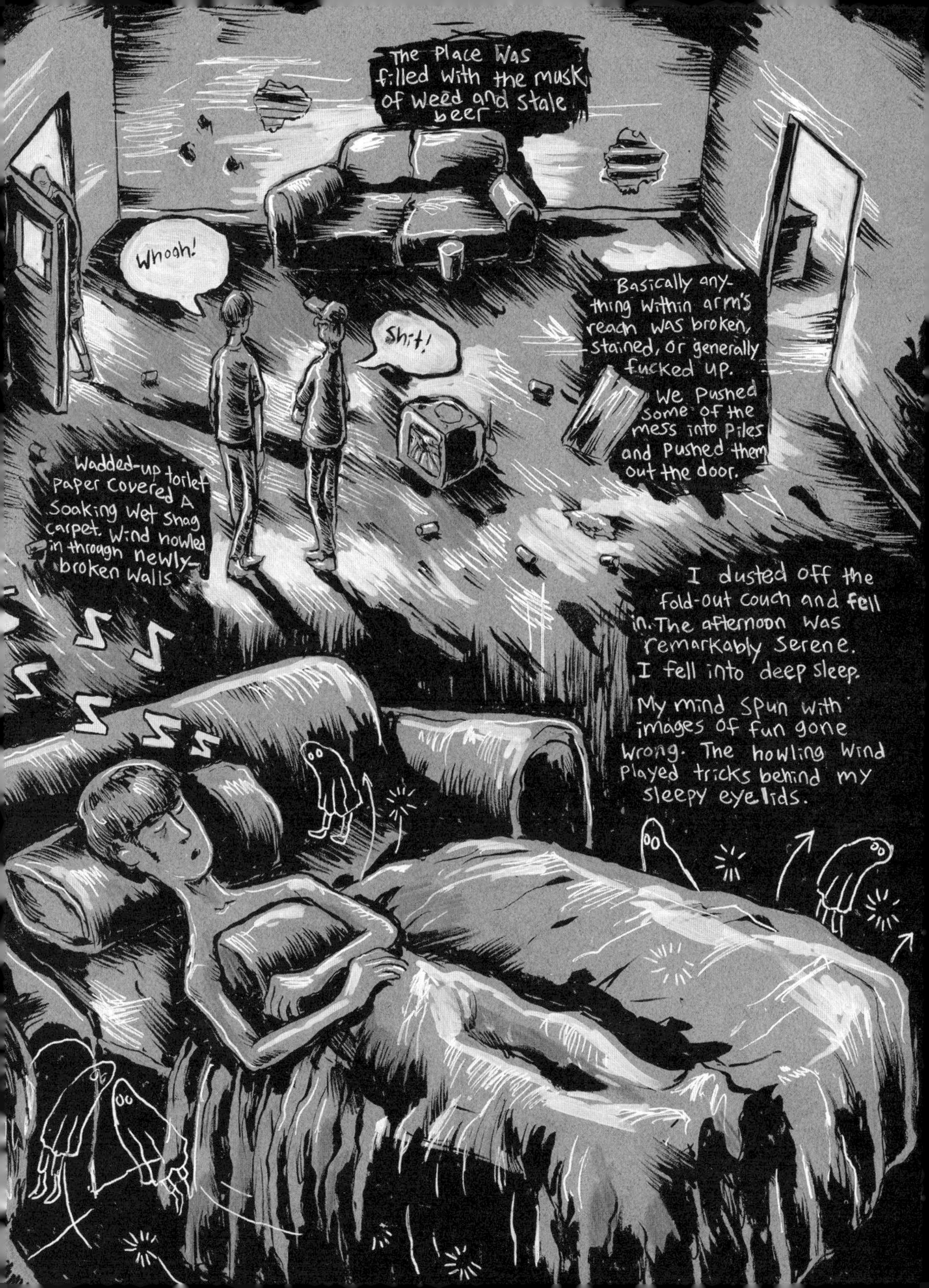
The Place Was filled with the musk of weed and stale beer
Whoah!
Shit!
Basically anything within arm's reach was broken, stained, or generally fucked up.
We Pushed some of the mess into Piles and Pushed them out the door.
Wadded-up toilet Paper Covered A Soaking Wet Shag carpet. Wind howled in through newly-broken Walls
I dusted off the fold-out couch and fell in. The afternoon was remarkably Serene. I fell into deep sleep.
My mind Spun with images of fun gone wrong. The howling wind Played tricks behind my sleepy eyelids.

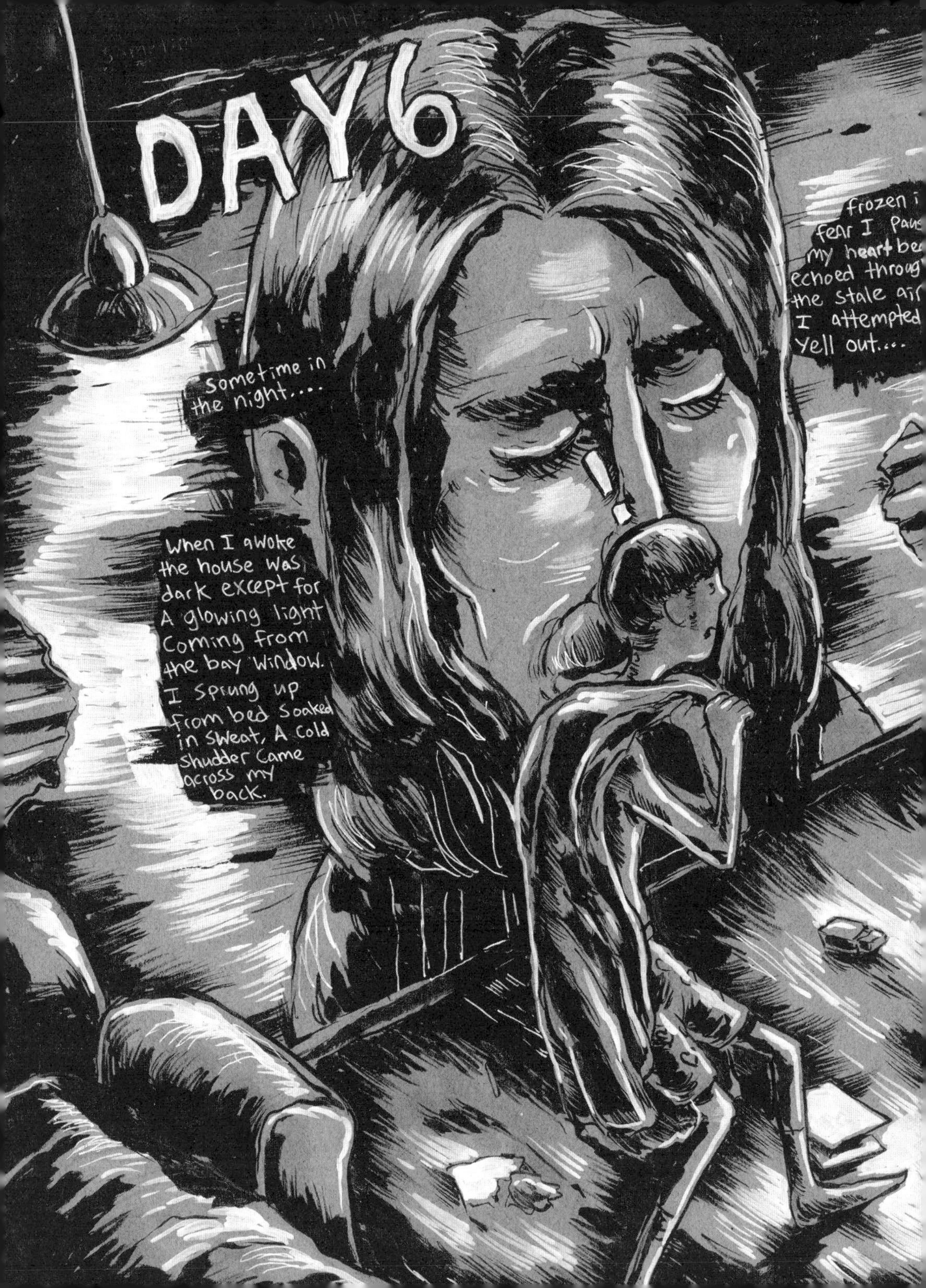
DAY 6
Sometime in the night....
When I awoke the house was dark except for A glowing light Coming from the bay window. I sprung up from bed Soaked in Sweat, A cold shudder Came across my back.
frozen i fear I Paus my heart be echoed throug the stale air I attempted yell out....

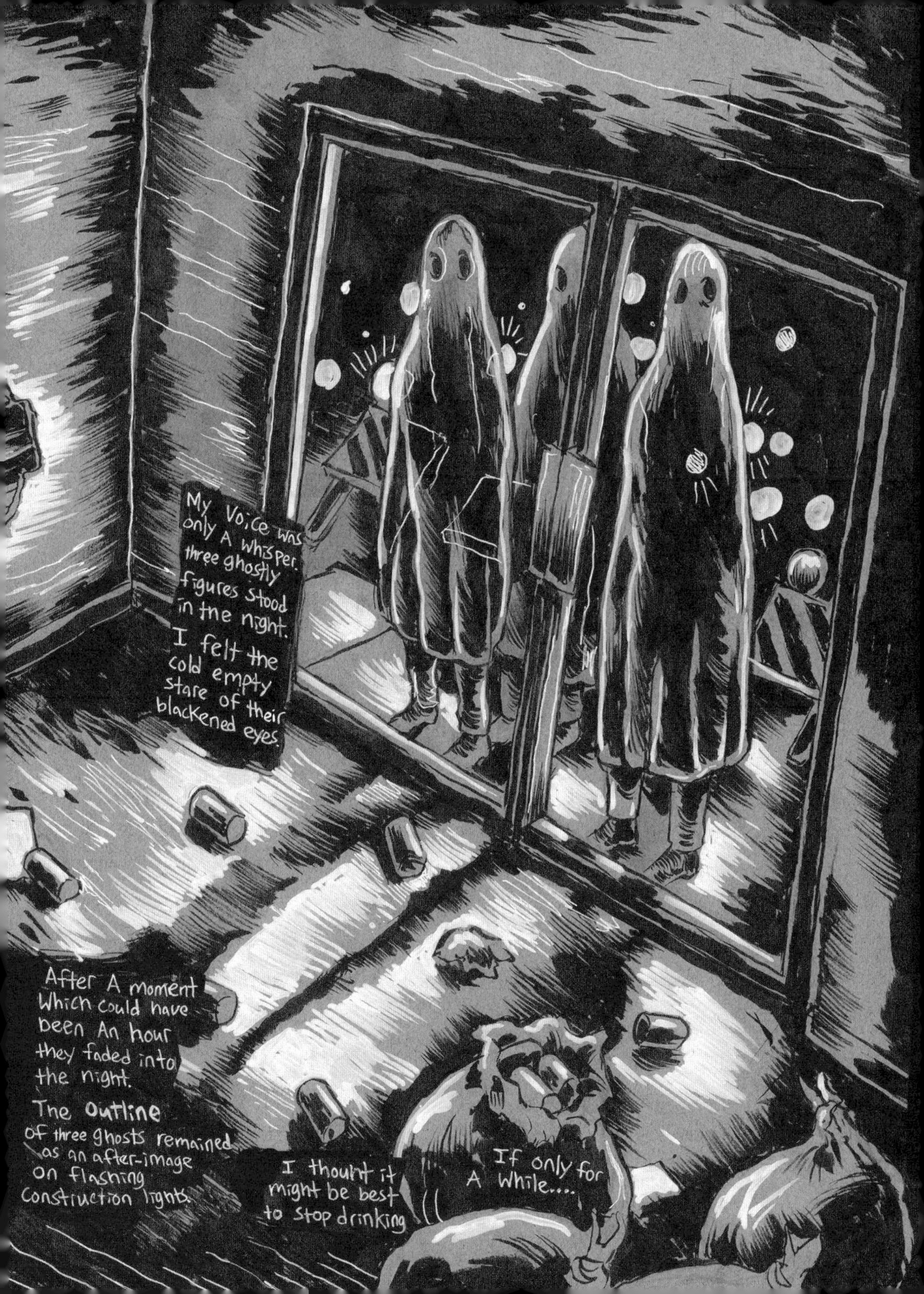
My Voice was only A whisper.
three ghostly figures stood in the night.
I felt the cold empty stare of their blackened eyes.
After A moment Which could have been An hour they faded into the night.
The Outline of three ghosts remained as an after-image on flashing construction lights.
I thouht it might be best to stop drinking
If only for A While....

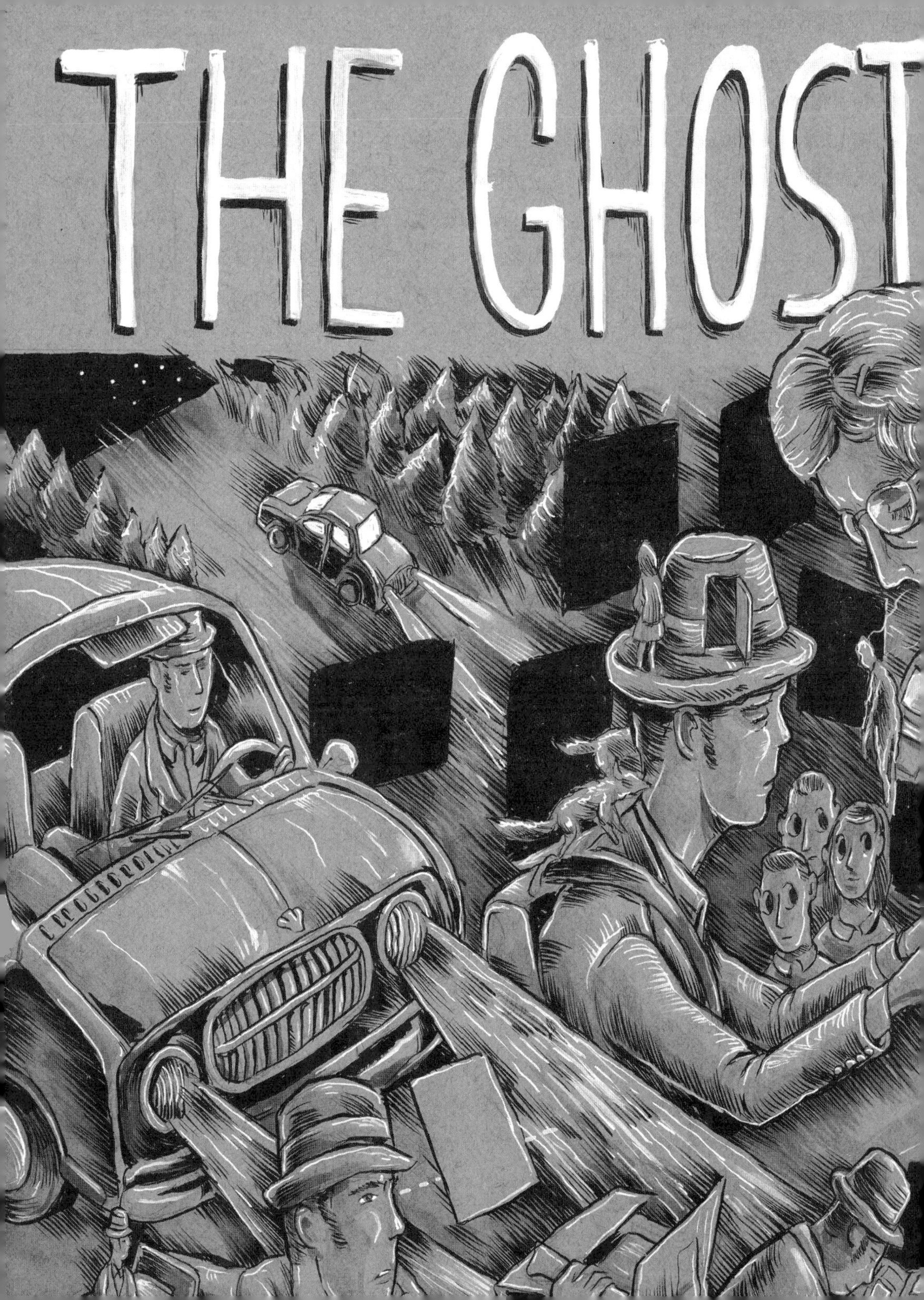
THE GHOST

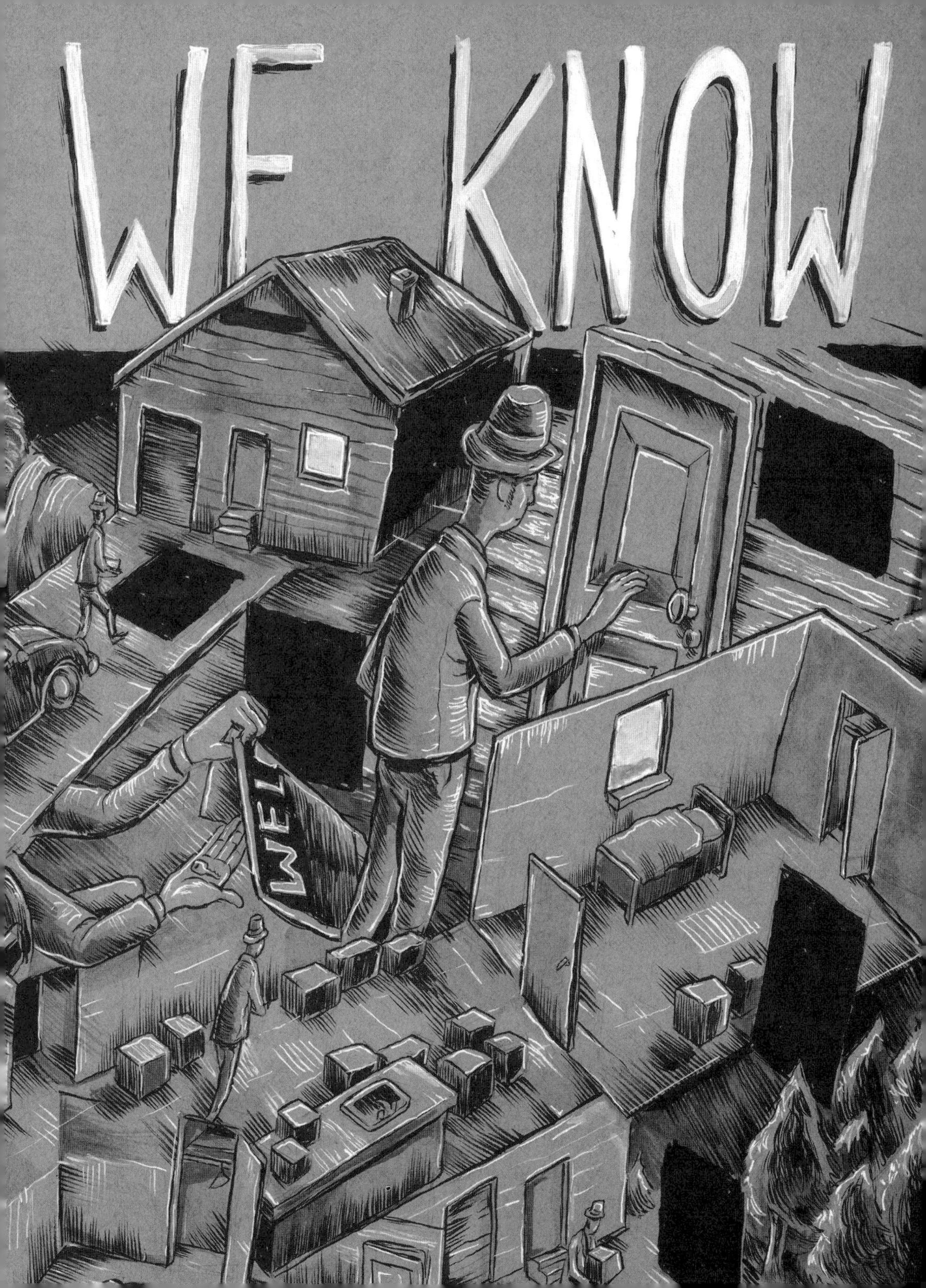
WE KNOW
WELL

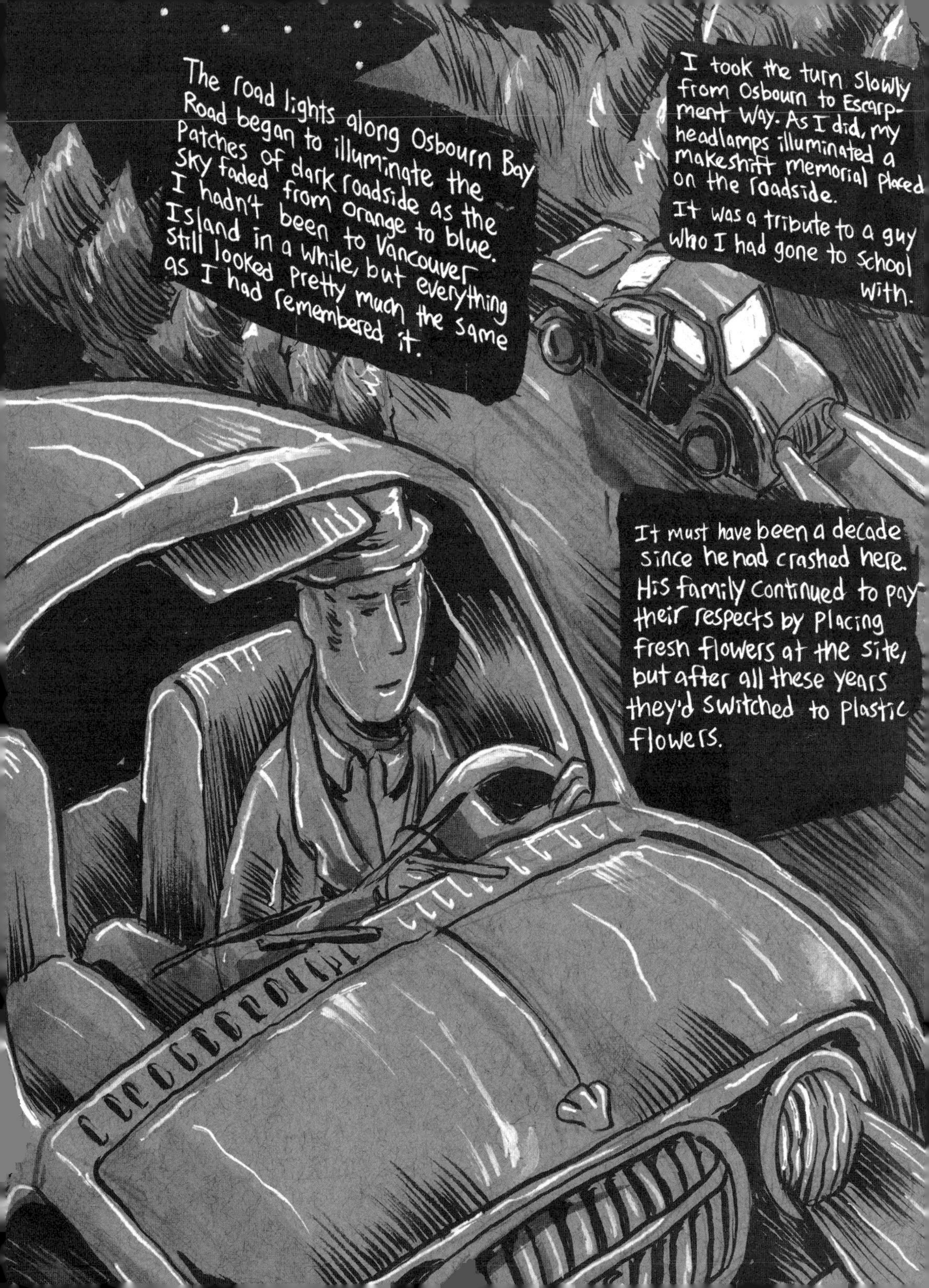
The road lights along Osbourn Bay Road began to illuminate the Patches of dark roadside as the Sky faded from orange to blue. I hadn't been to Vancouver Island in a while, but everything still looked Pretty much the same as I had remembered it.
I took the turn slowly from Osbourn to Escarpment Way. As I did, my headlamps illuminated a makeshift memorial placed on the roadside.
It was a tribute to a guy who I had gone to school with.
It must have been a decade since he had crashed here. His family continued to pay their respects by placing fresh flowers at the site, but after all these years they'd switched to plastic flowers.

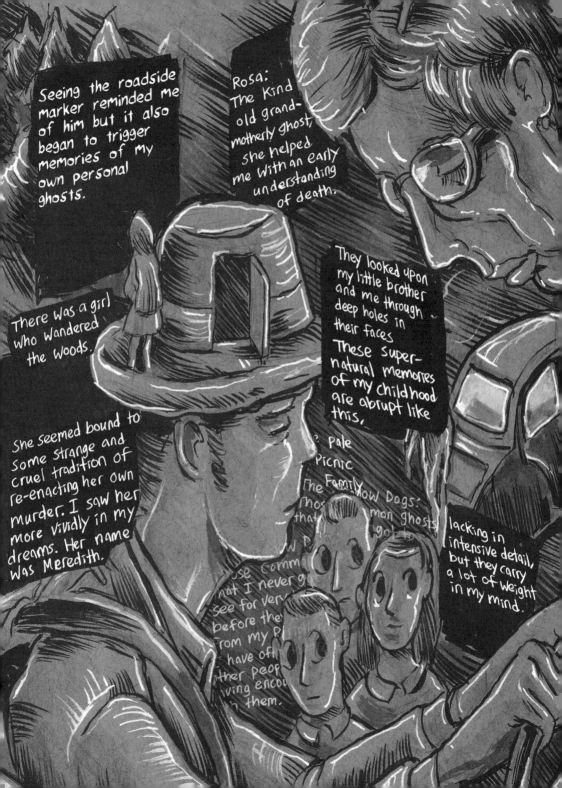

Seeing the roadside marker reminded me of him but it also began to trigger memories of my own personal ghosts.

Rosa: The kind old grand-motherly ghost, she helped me with an early understanding of death.

There was a girl who wandered the woods.

They looked upon my little brother and me through deep holes in their faces. These super-natural memories of my childhood are abrupt like this.

She seemed bound to some strange and cruel tradition of re-enacting her own murder. I saw her more vividly in my dreams. Her name was Meredith.

Pale Picnic Family Yellow Dogs: The most common ghosts that I got

lacking in intensive detail, but they carry a lot of weight in my mind.

those commo that I never g see for very before they from my p have of ther peop ving encou them.

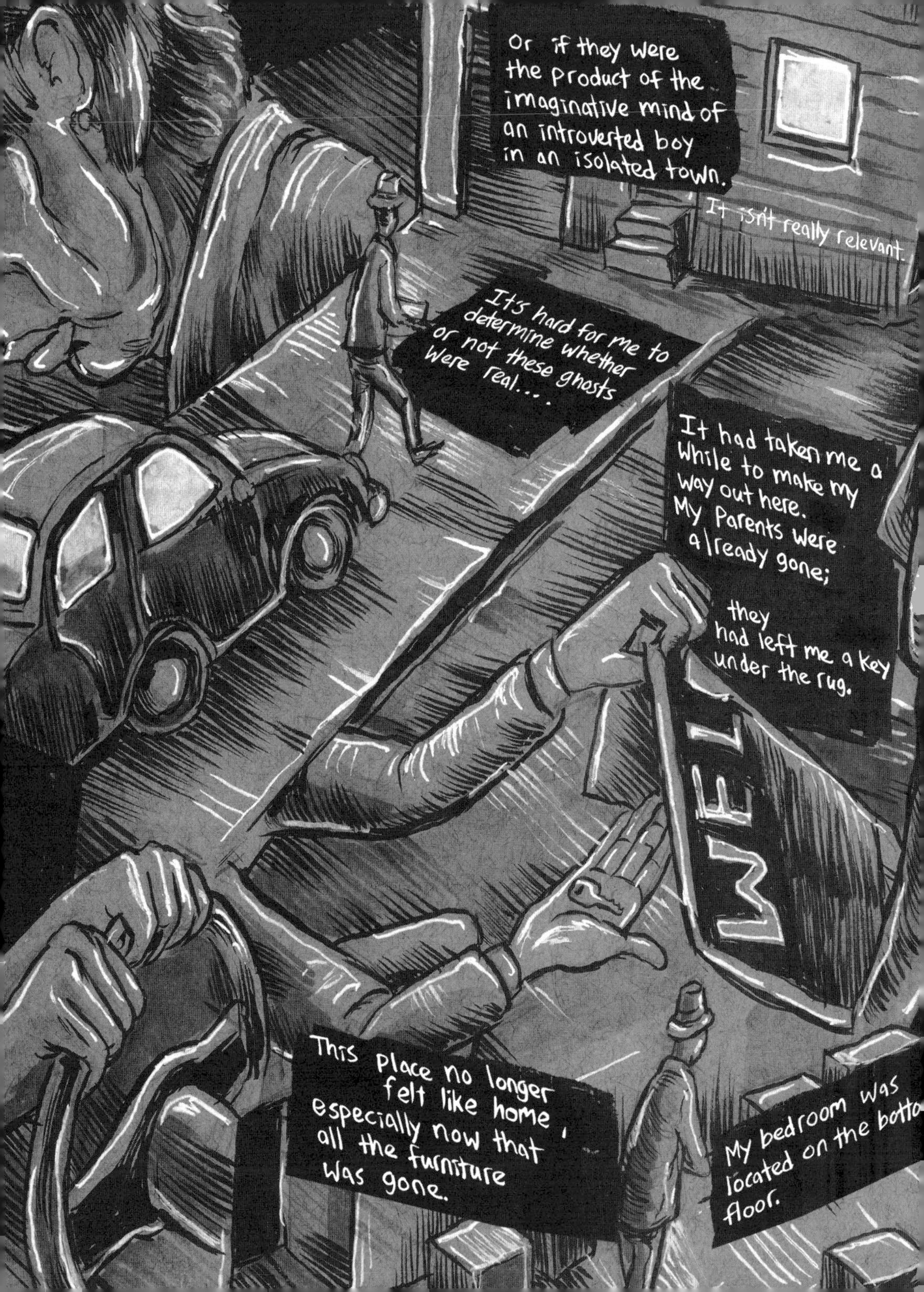
Or if they were the product of the imaginative mind of an introverted boy in an isolated town.
It isn't really relevant.
It's hard for me to determine whether or not these ghosts were real....
It had taken me a while to make my way out here. My parents were already gone;
they had left me a key under the rug.
WEL
This place no longer felt like home, especially now that all the furniture was gone.
My bedroom was located on the botto floor.

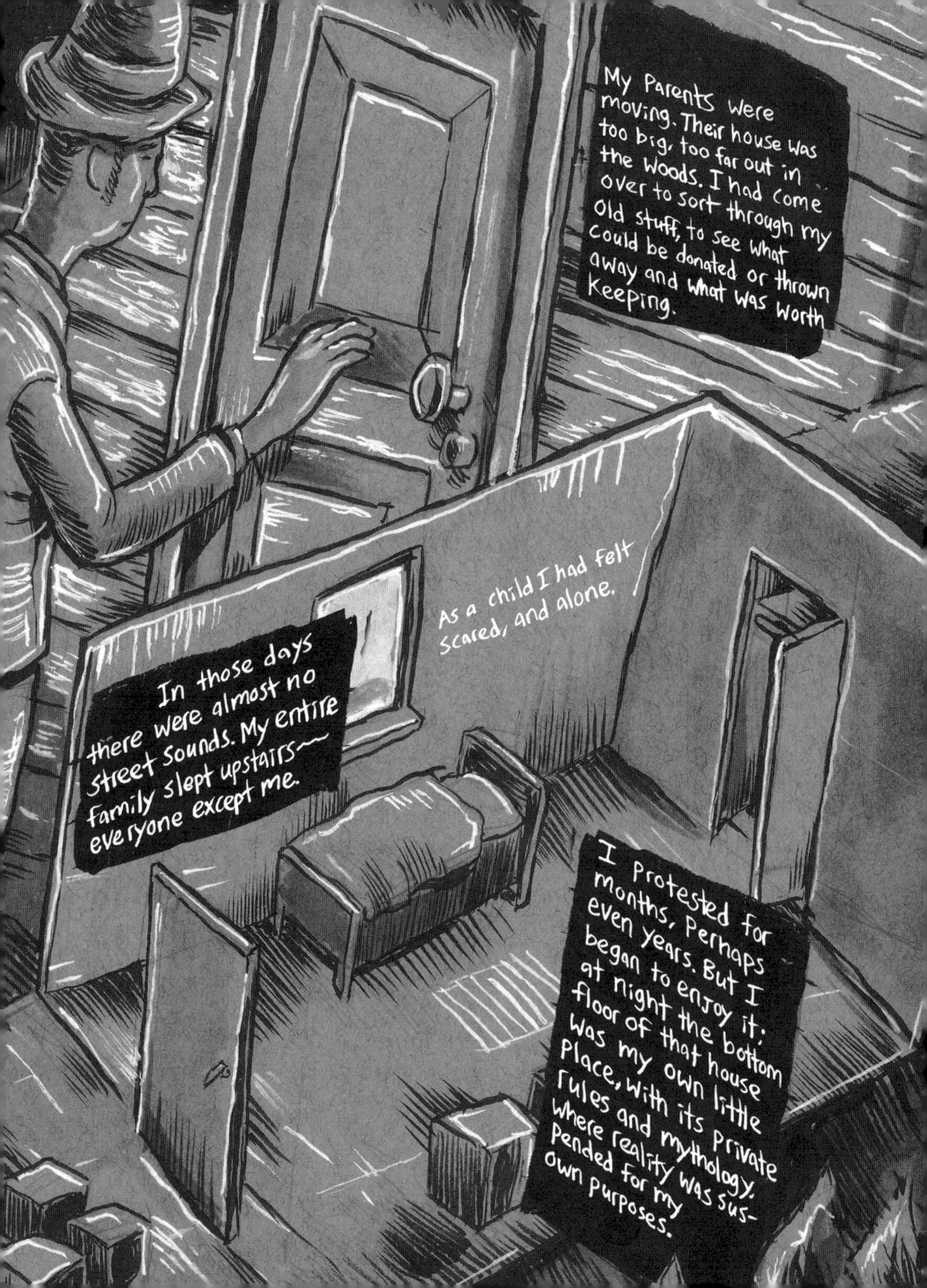
My Parents were moving. Their house was too big, too far out in the woods. I had come over to sort through my old stuff, to see what could be donated or thrown away and what was worth keeping.
As a child I had felt scared, and alone.
In those days there were almost no street sounds. My entire family slept upstairs— everyone except me.
I Protested for months, Perhaps even years. But I began to enjoy it: at night the bottom floor of that house was my own little Place, with its private rules and mythology, where reality was suspended for my own purposes.

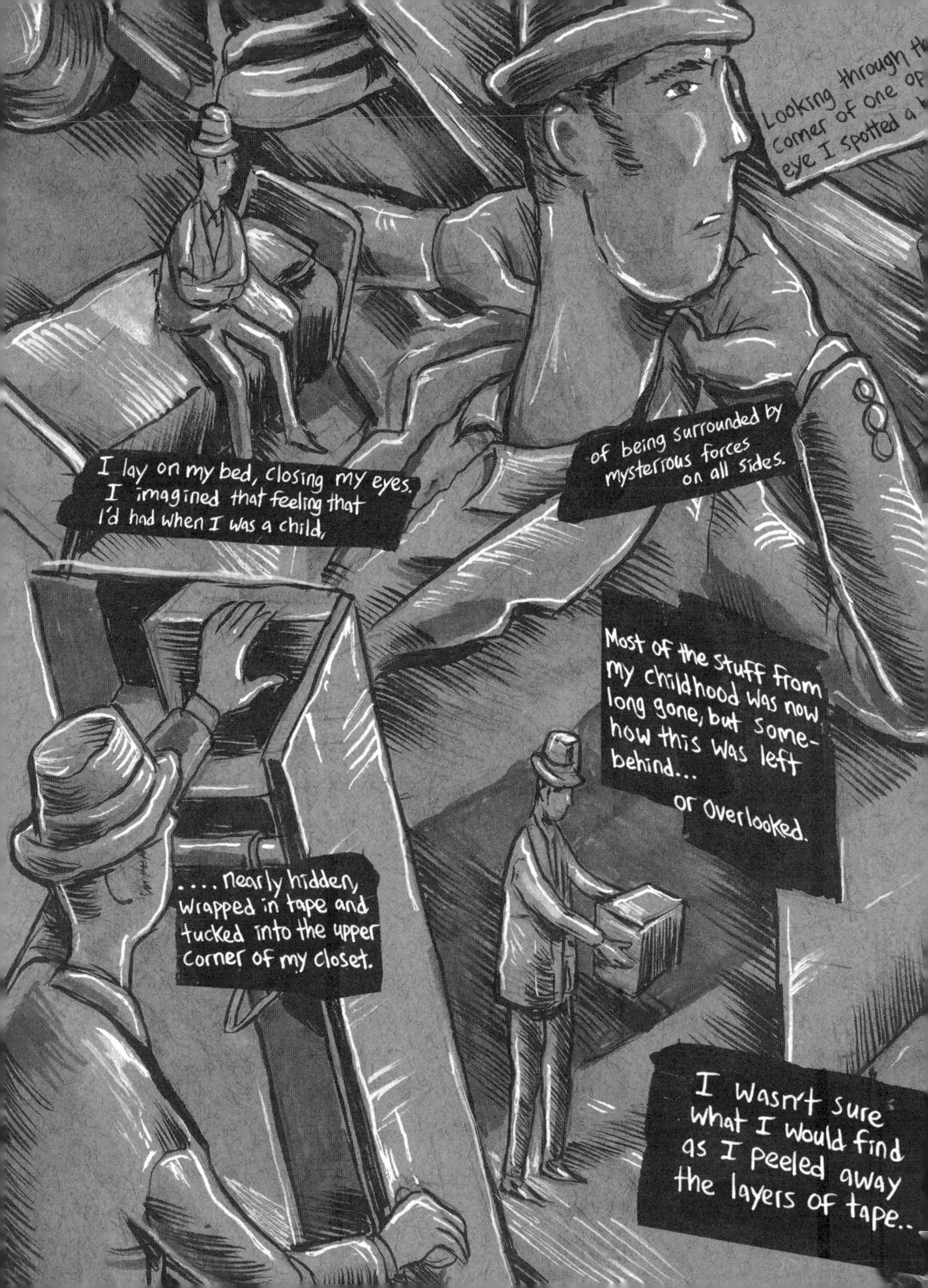
Looking through th
corner of one op
eye I spotted a
I lay on my bed, closing my eyes. I imagined that feeling that I'd had when I was a child,
of being surrounded by mysterious forces on all sides.
Most of the stuff from my childhood was now long gone, but some-how this was left behind... or Overlooked.
....nearly hidden, wrapped in tape and tucked into the upper corner of my closet.
I wasn't sure what I would find as I peeled away the layers of tape..

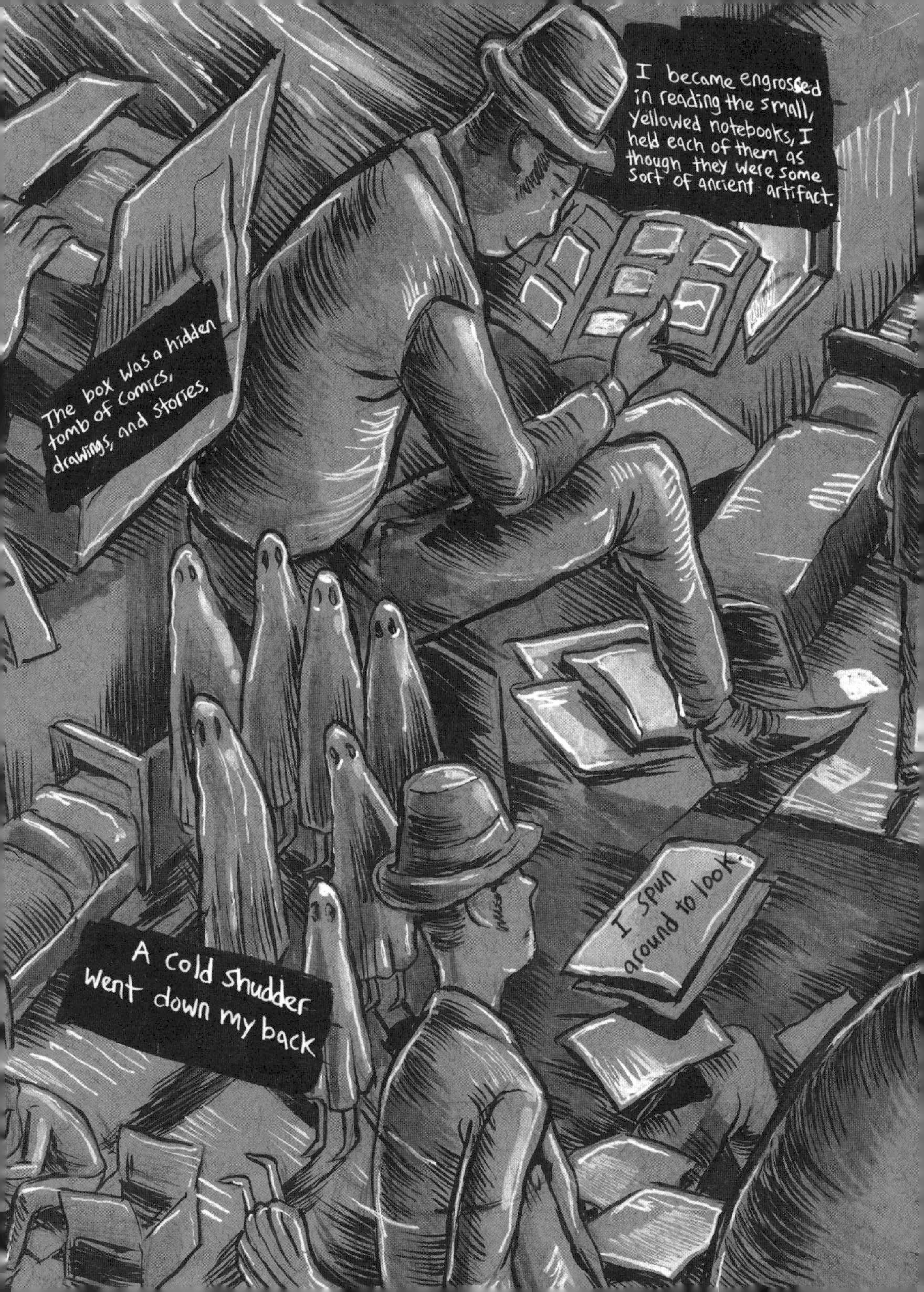
I became engrossed in reading the small, yellowed notebooks, I held each of them as though they were some sort of ancient artifact.
The box was a hidden tomb of comics, drawings, and stories.
I spun around to look.
A cold shudder went down my back

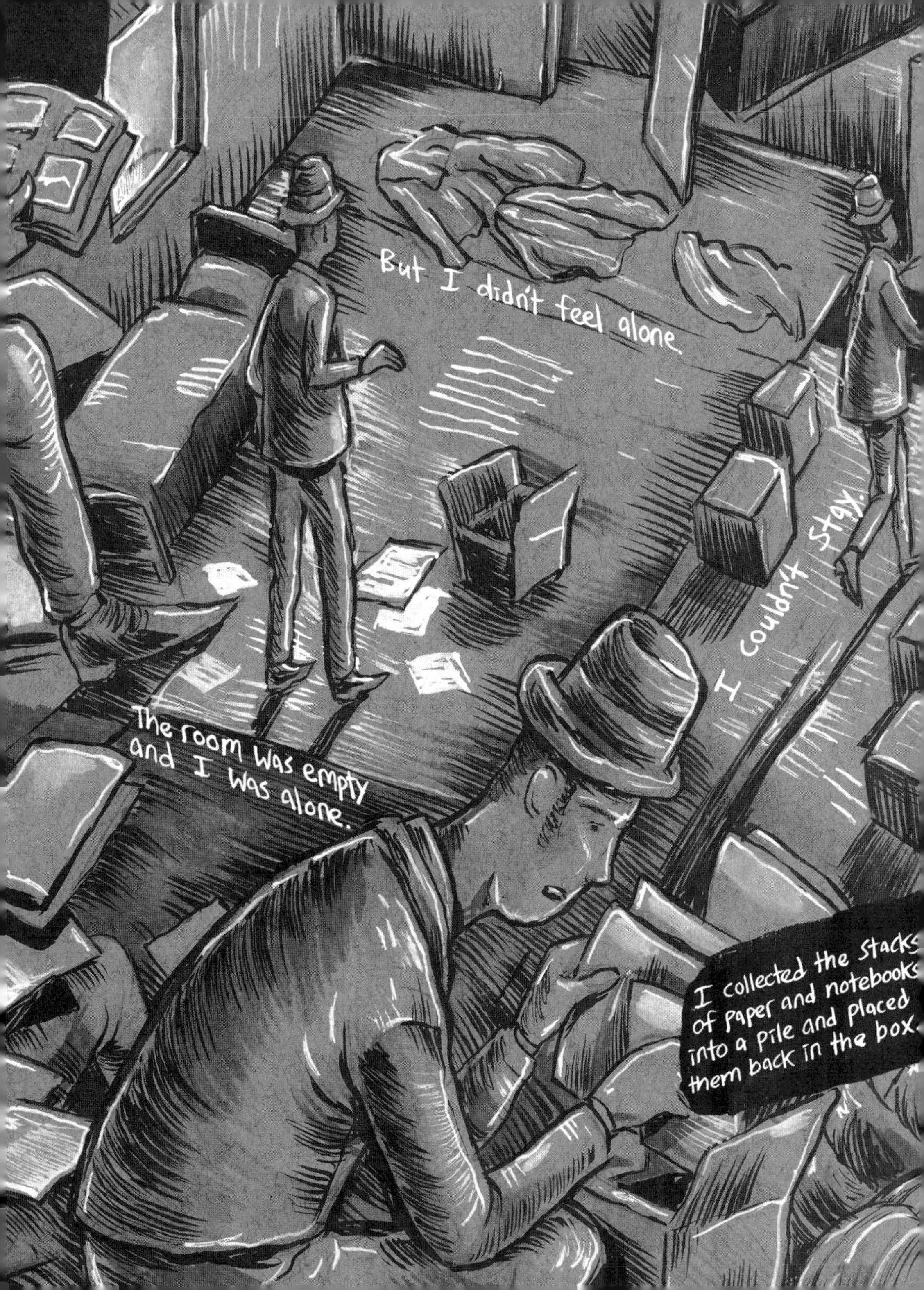
But I didn't feel alone.
I couldn't stay.
The room was empty and I was alone.
I collected the stacks of paper and notebooks into a pile and placed them back in the box.

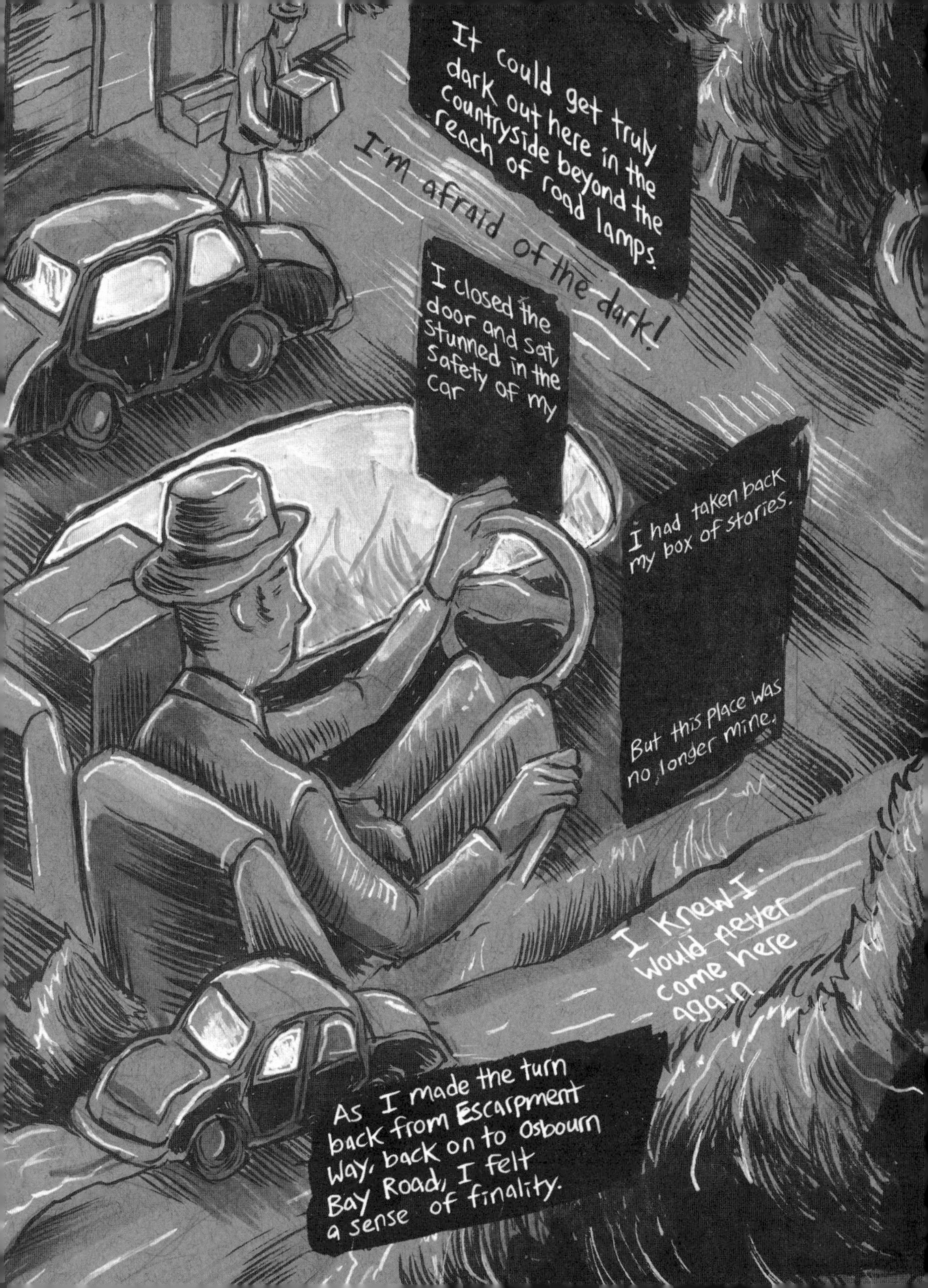
It could get truly dark out here in the countryside beyond the reach of road lamps.
I'm afraid of the dark!
I closed the door and sat, stunned in the safety of my car
I had taken back my box of stories.
But this place was no longer mine.
I knew I would never come here again.
As I made the turn back from Escarpment Way, back on to Osbourn Bay Road, I felt a sense of finality.

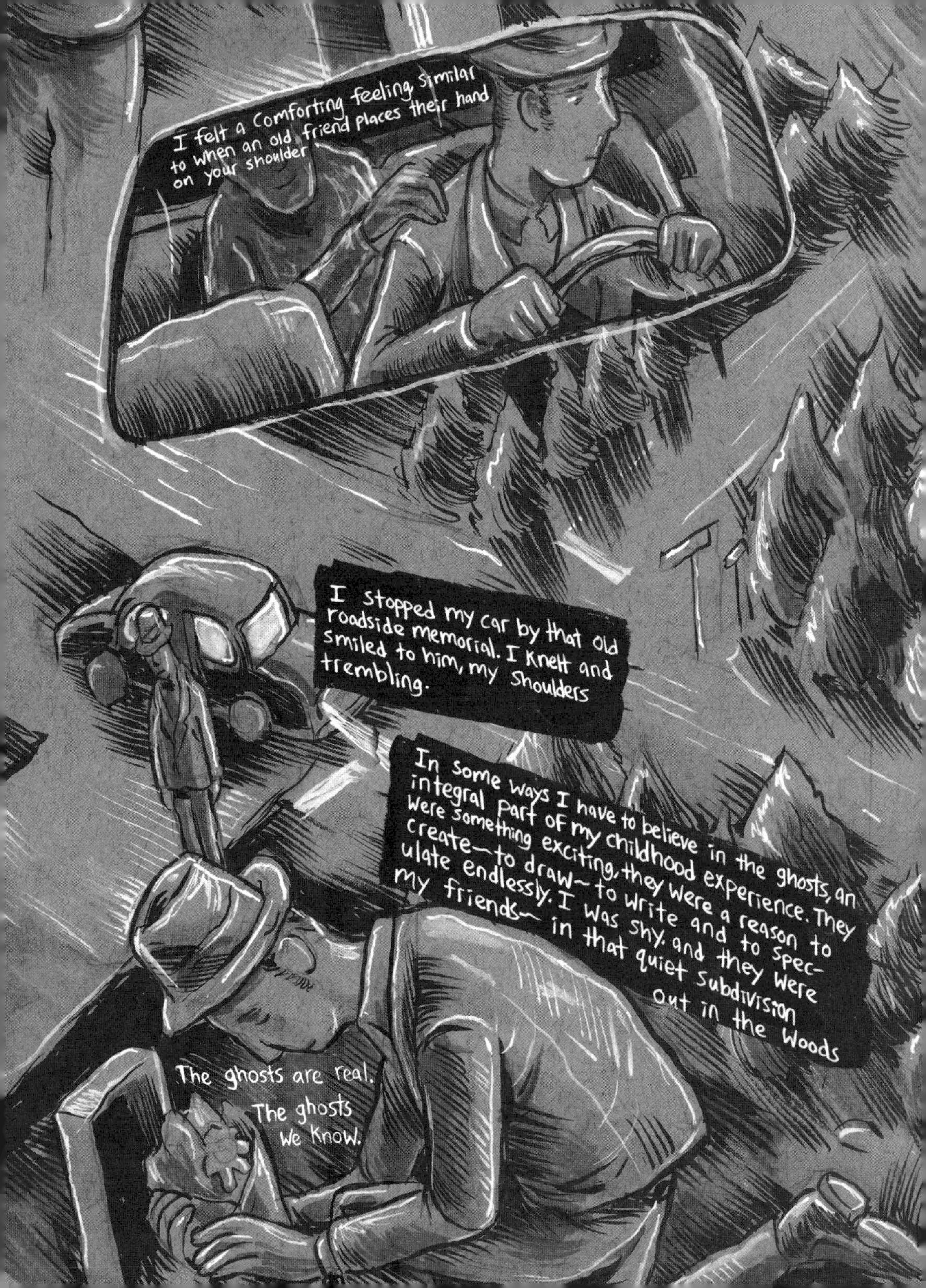
I felt a comforting feeling similar to when an old friend places their hand on your shoulder
I stopped my car by that old roadside memorial. I knelt and smiled to him, my shoulders trembling.
In some ways I have to believe in the ghosts, an integral part of my childhood experience. They were something exciting, they were a reason to create~ to draw~ to write and to speculate endlessly. I was shy. and they were my friends~ in that quiet subdivision out in the woods
The ghosts are real.
The ghosts we know.

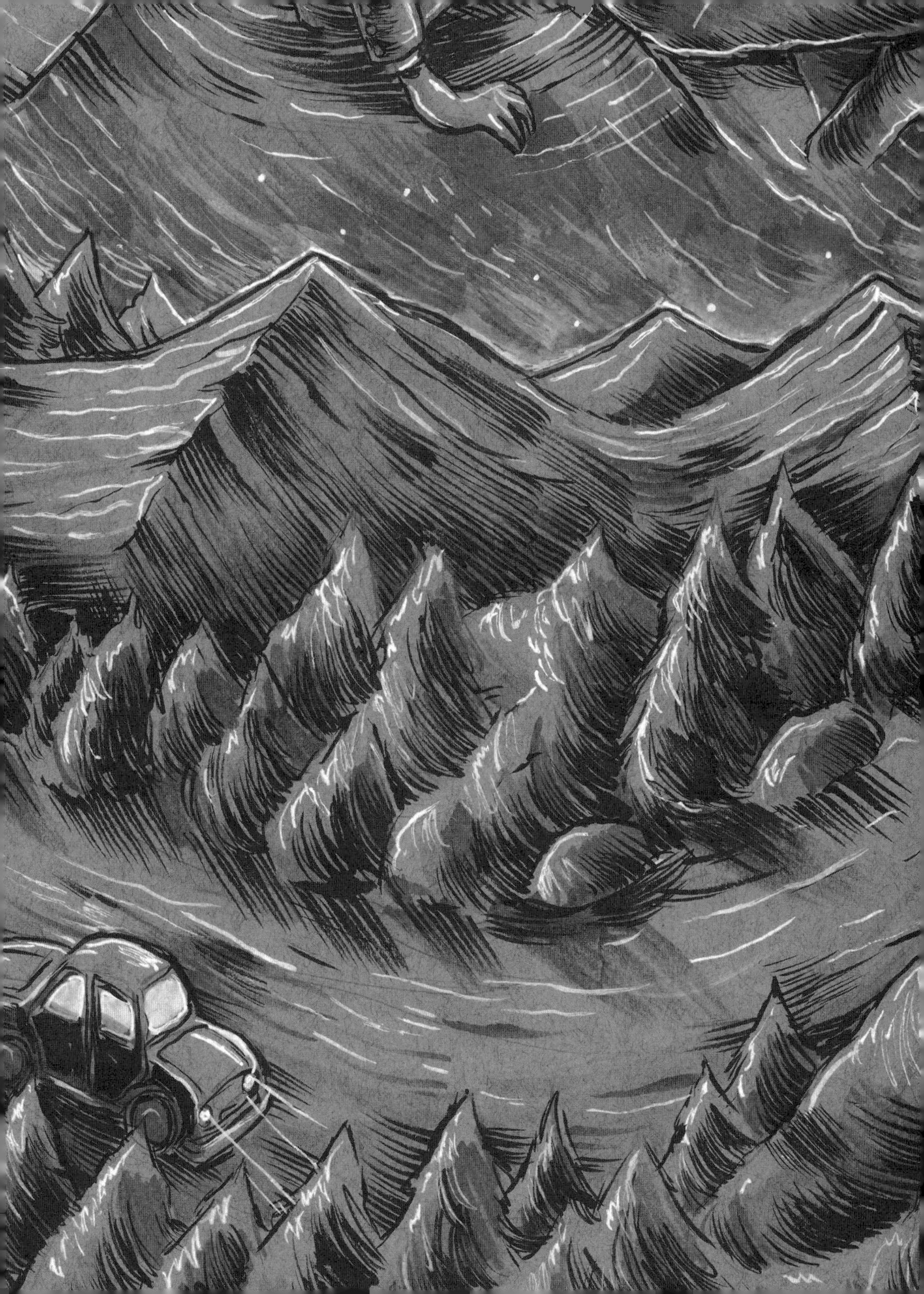

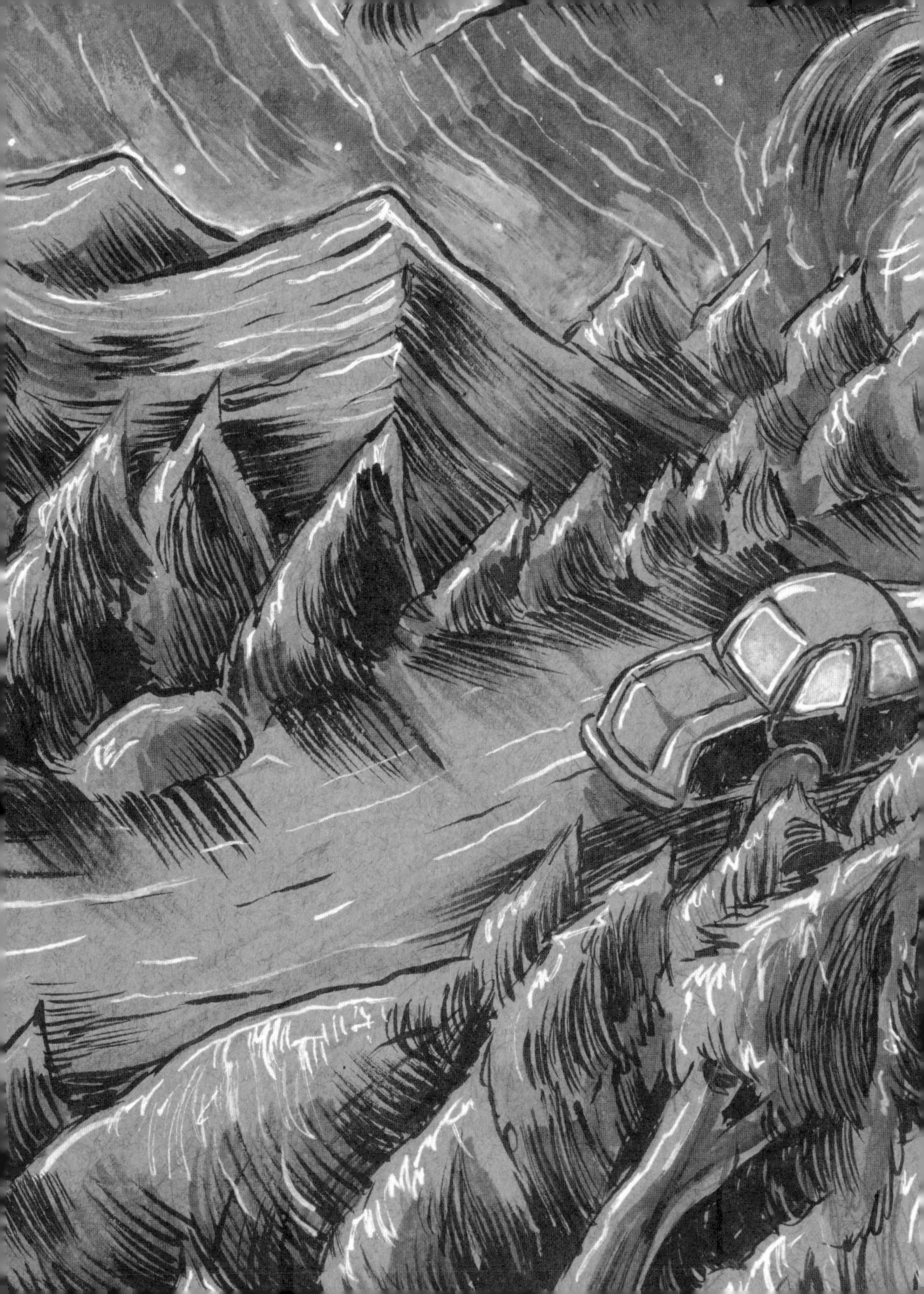

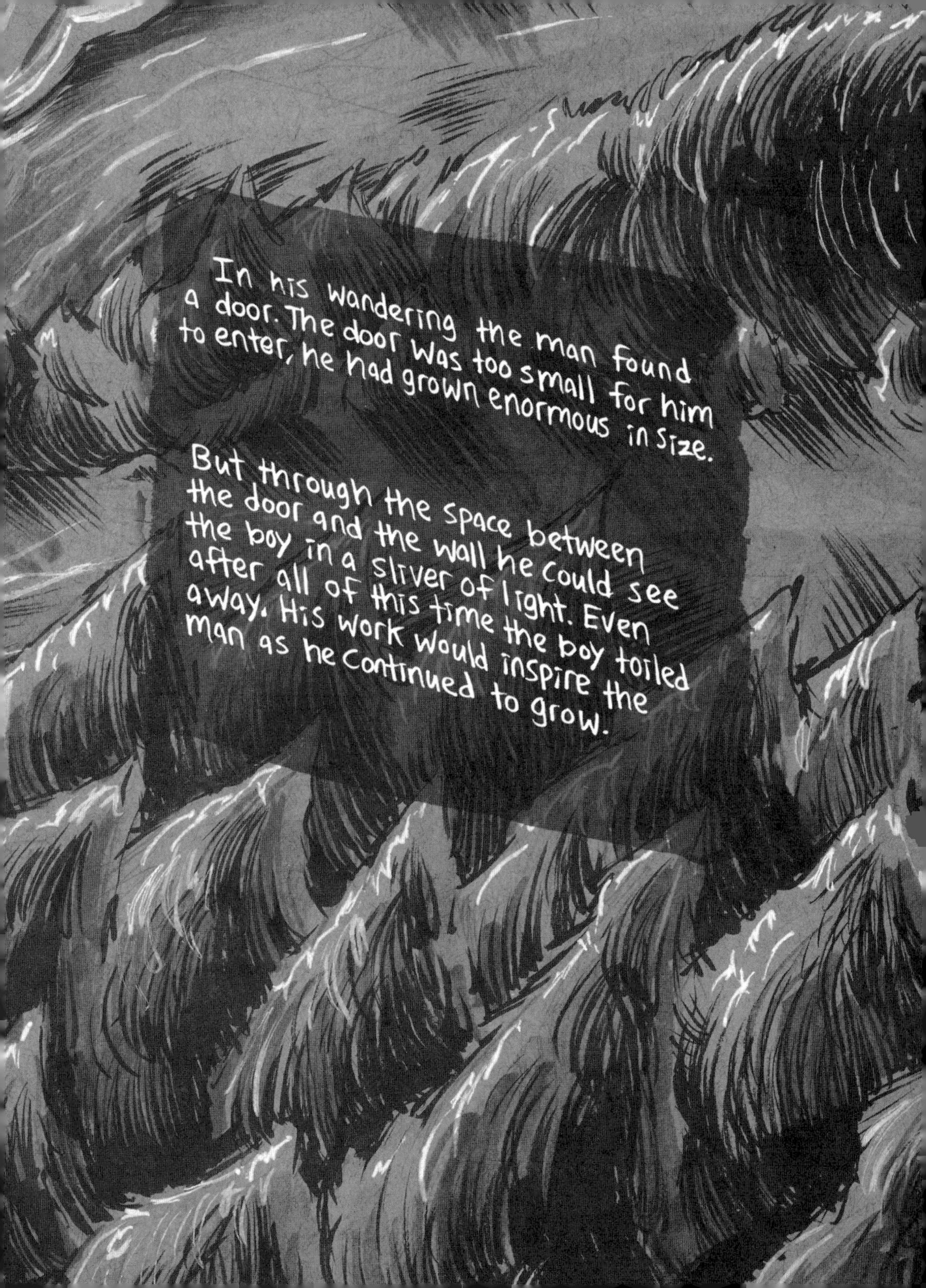
In his wandering the man found a door. The door was too small for him to enter, he had grown enormous in size.
But through the space between the door and the wall he could see the boy in a sliver of light. Even after all of this time the boy toiled away. His work would inspire the man as he continued to grow.

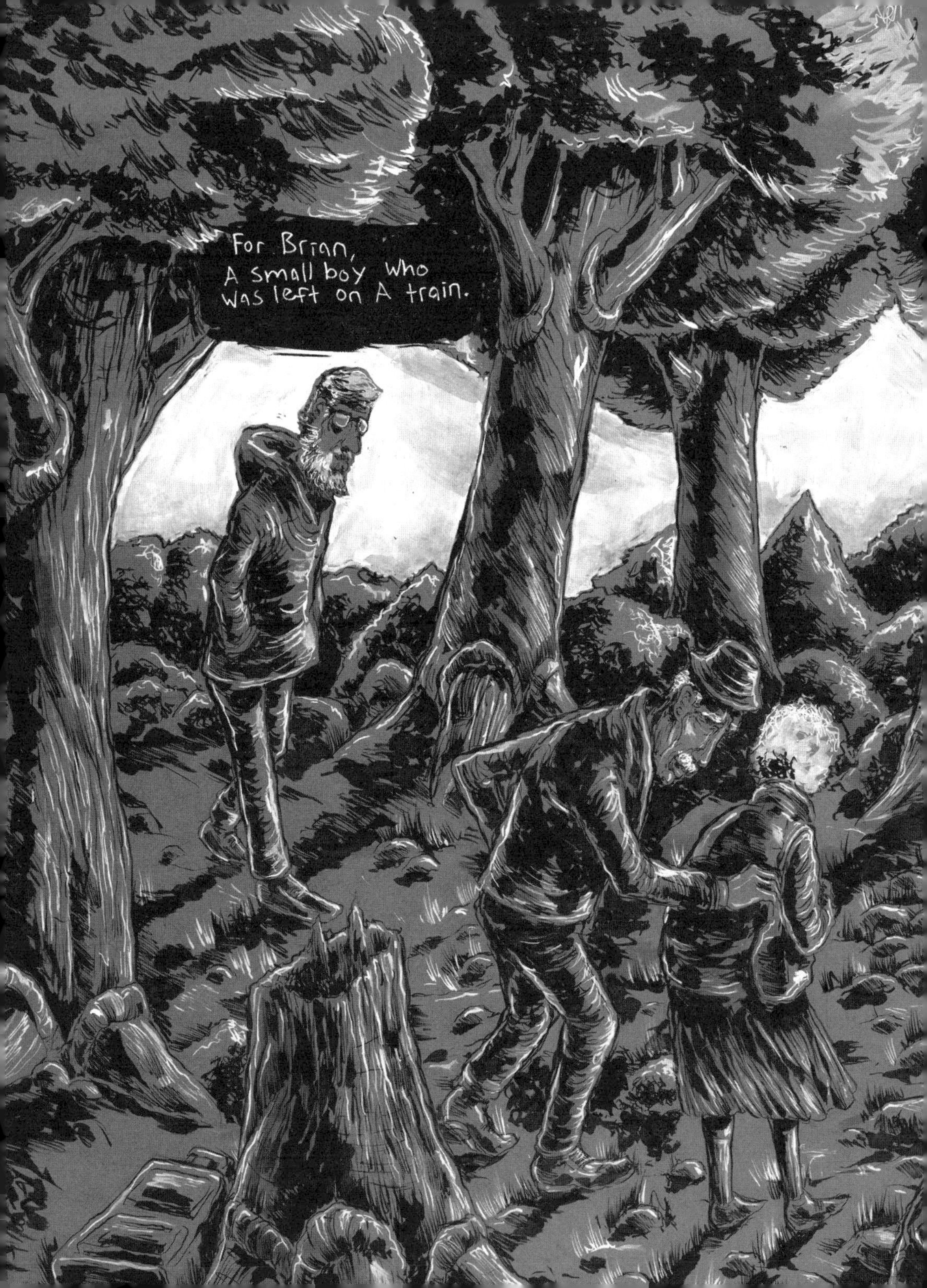
For Brian,
A small boy who
was left on A train.

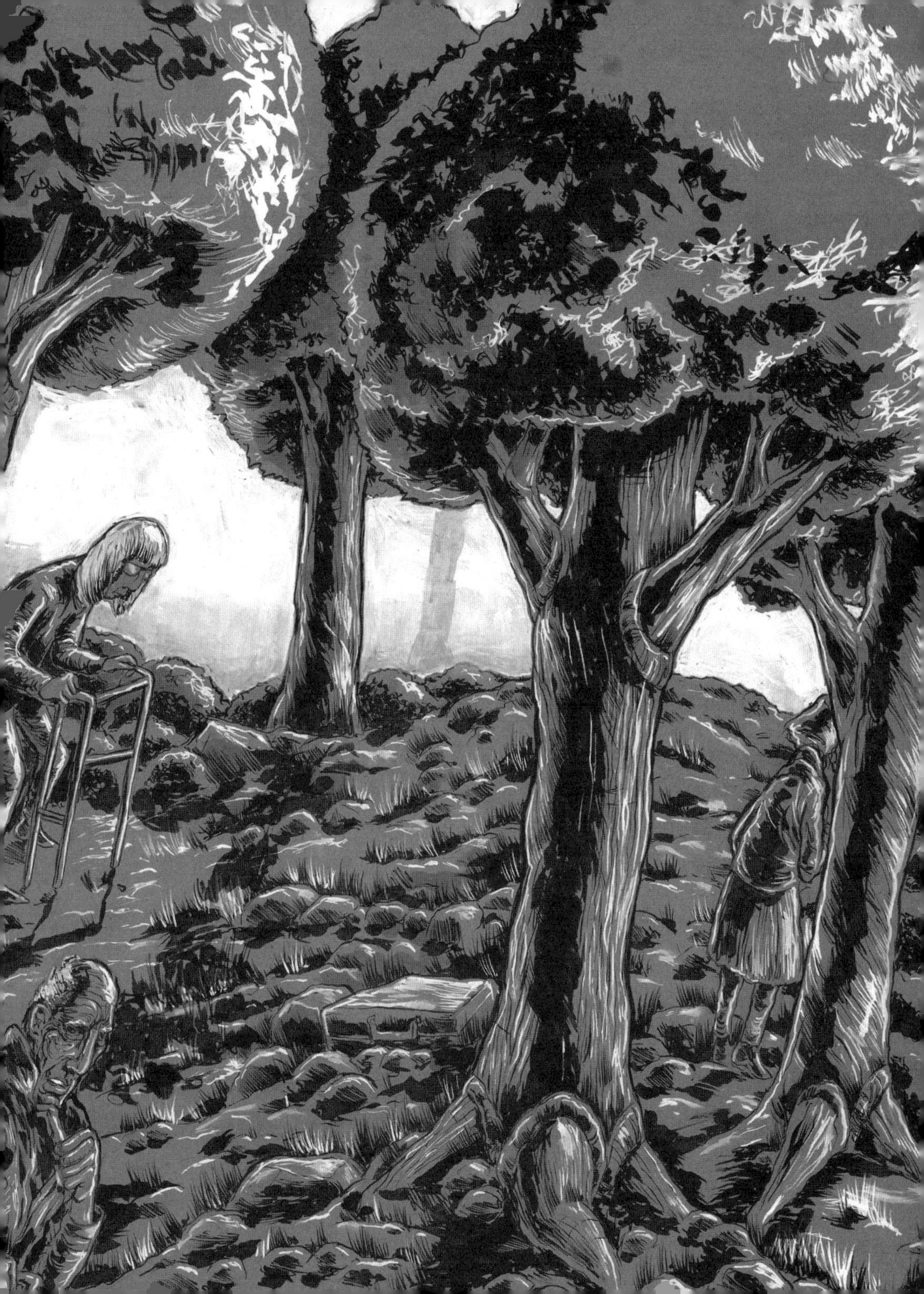

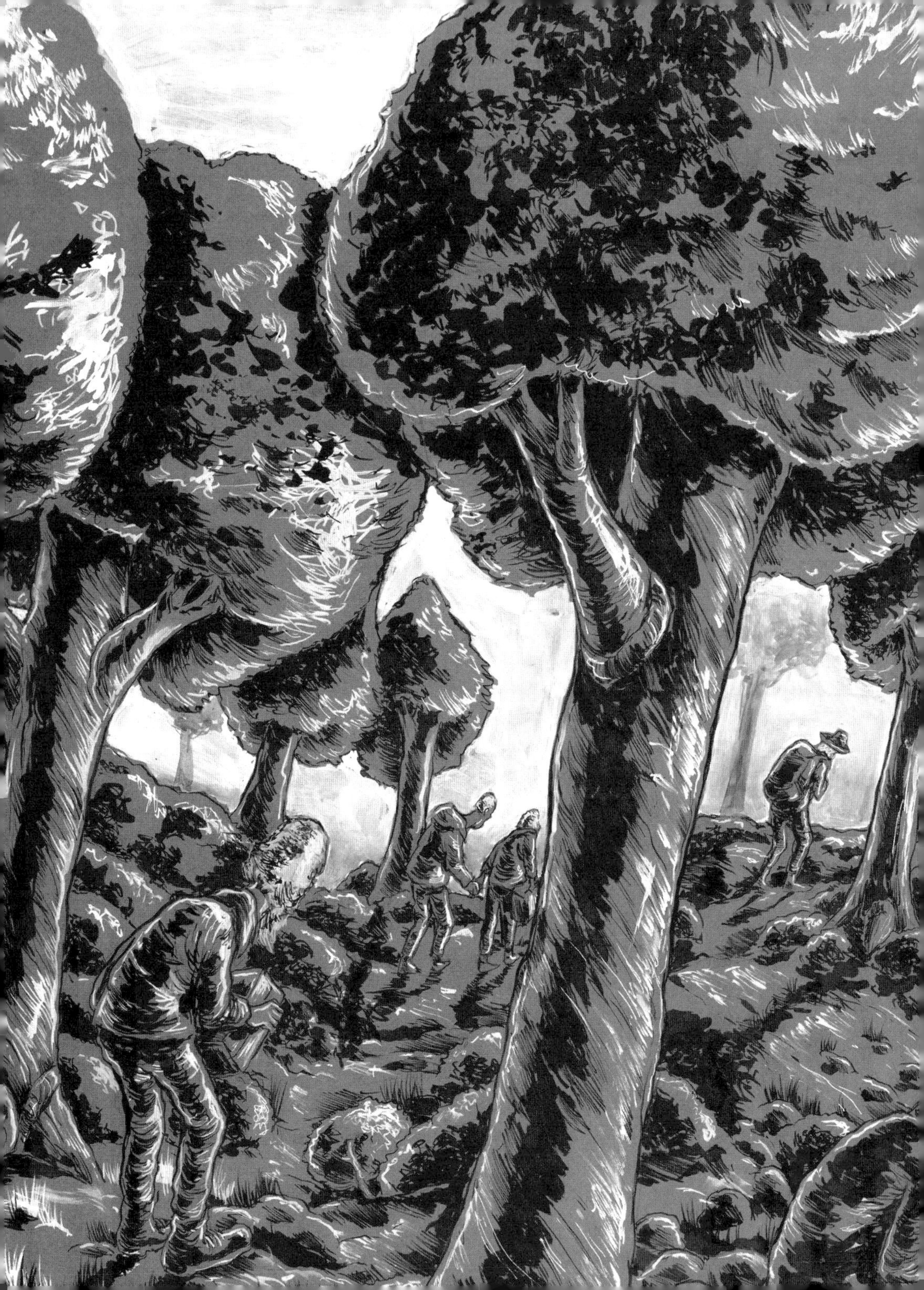

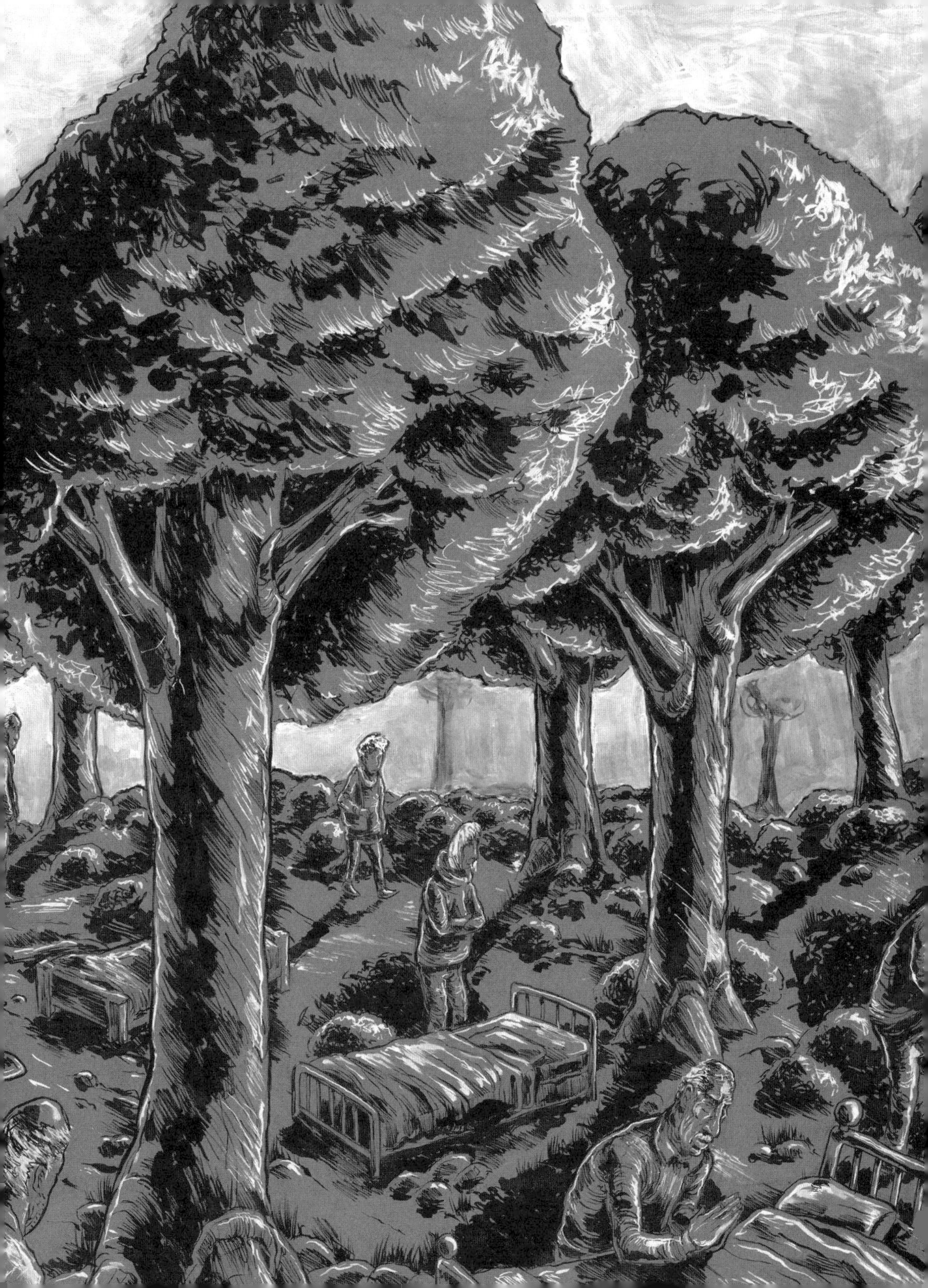

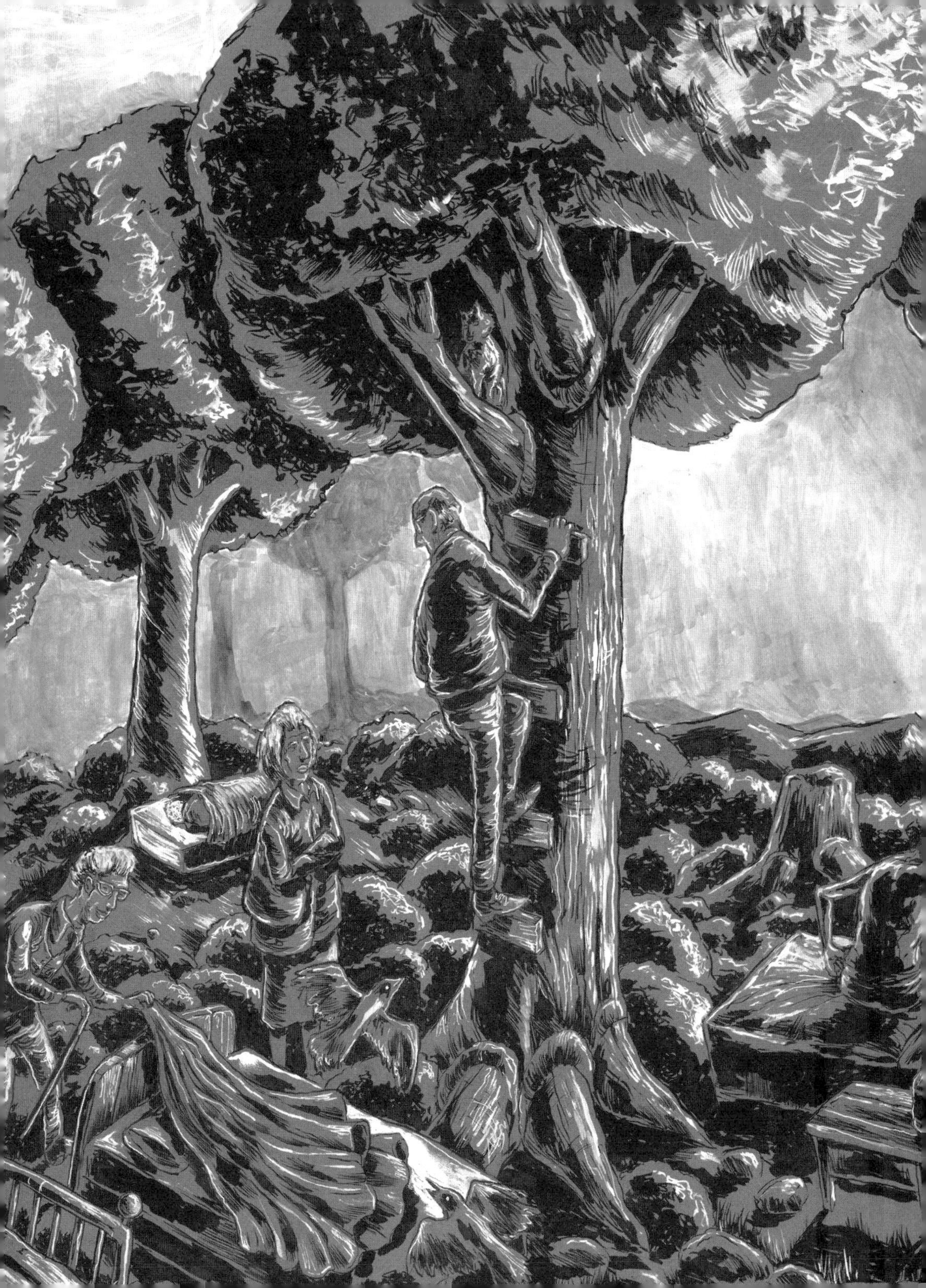

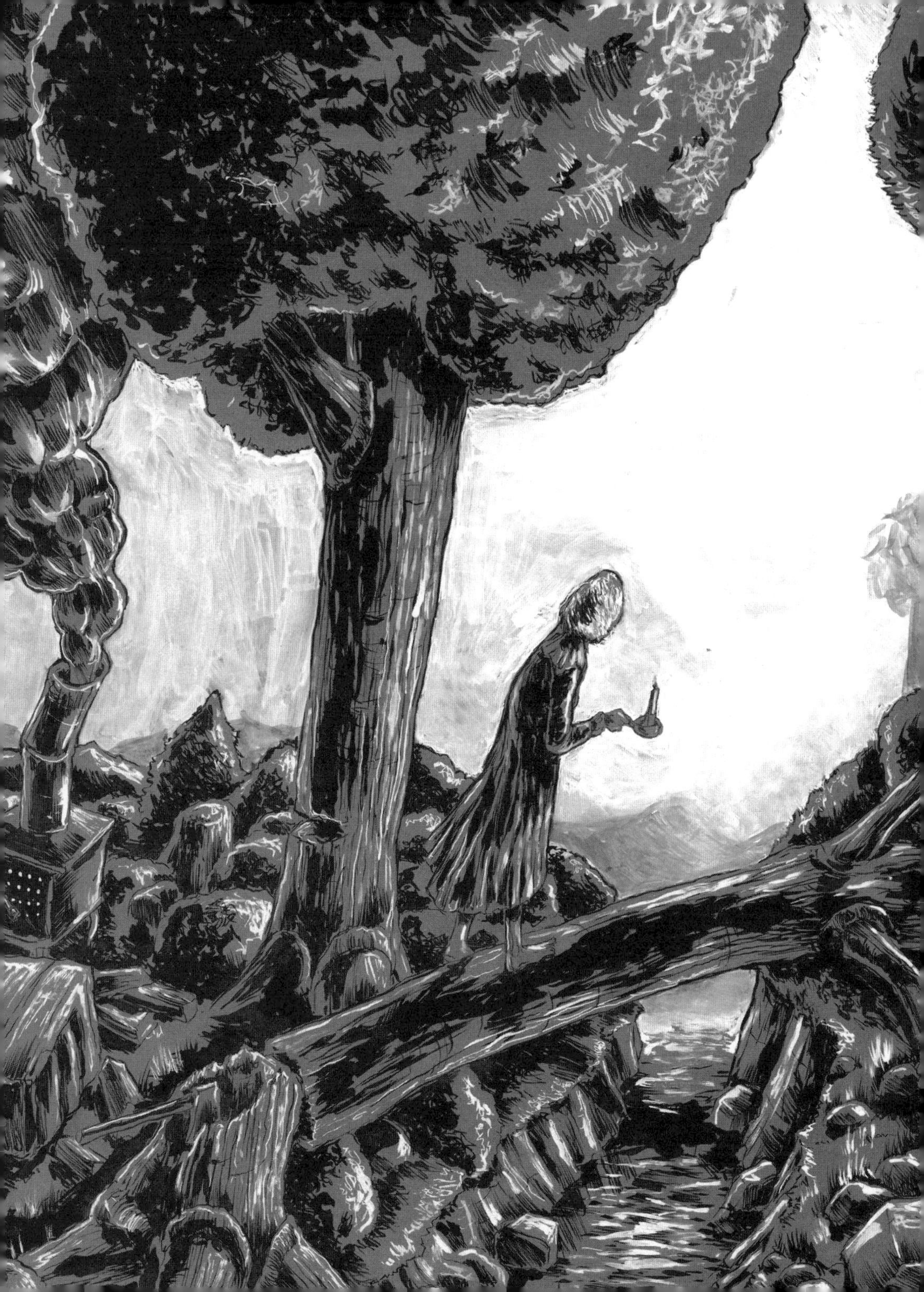

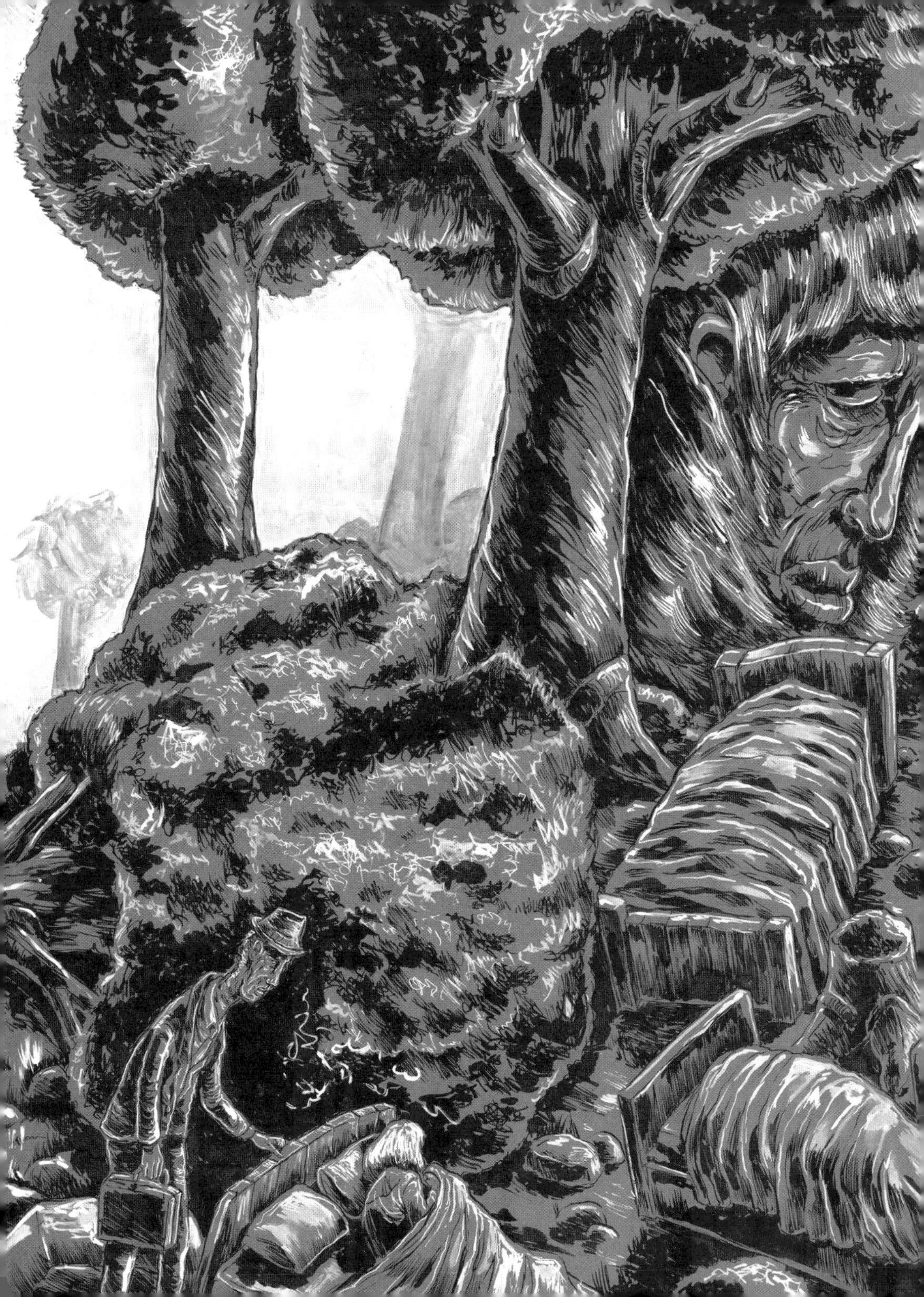

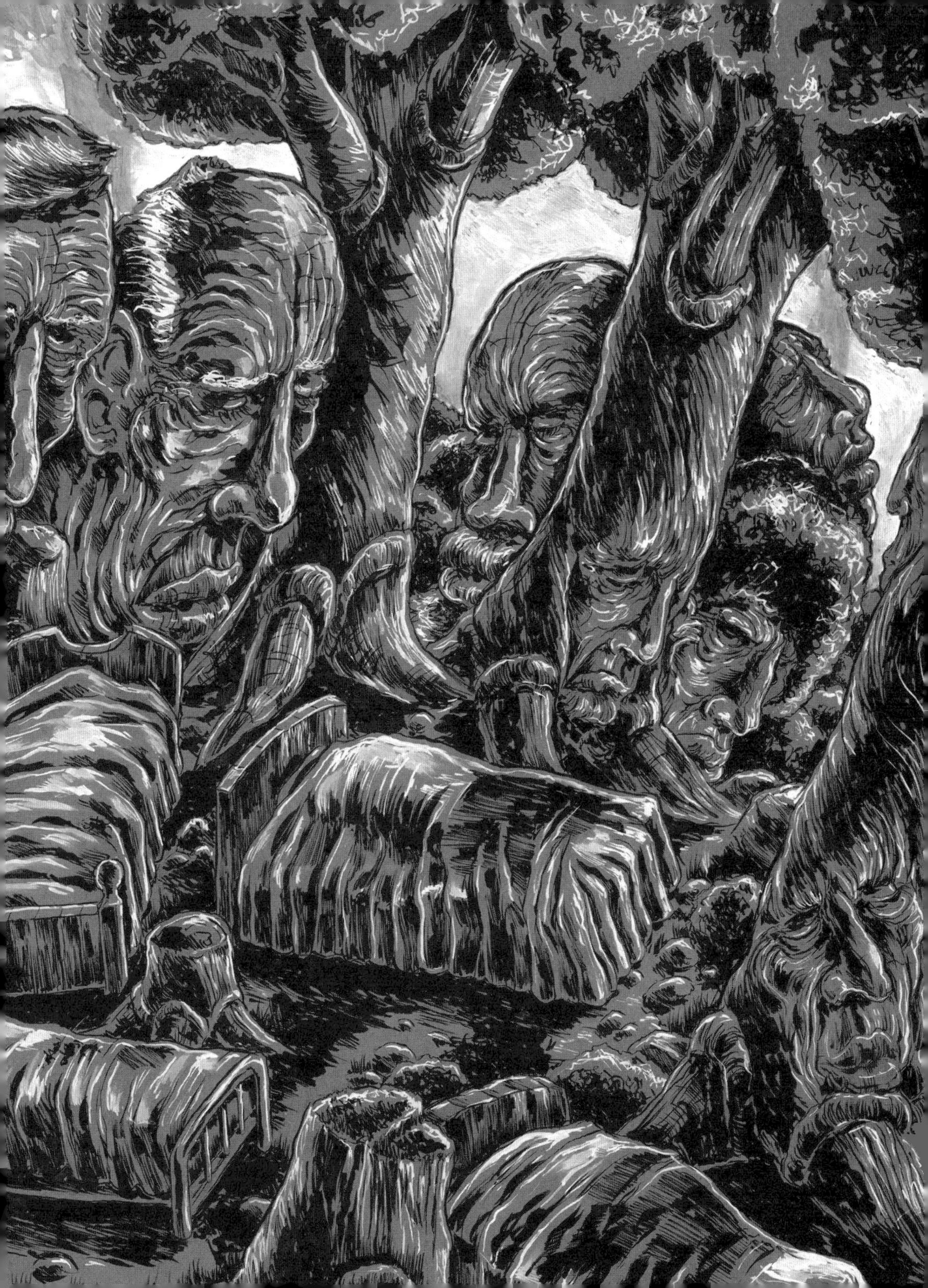

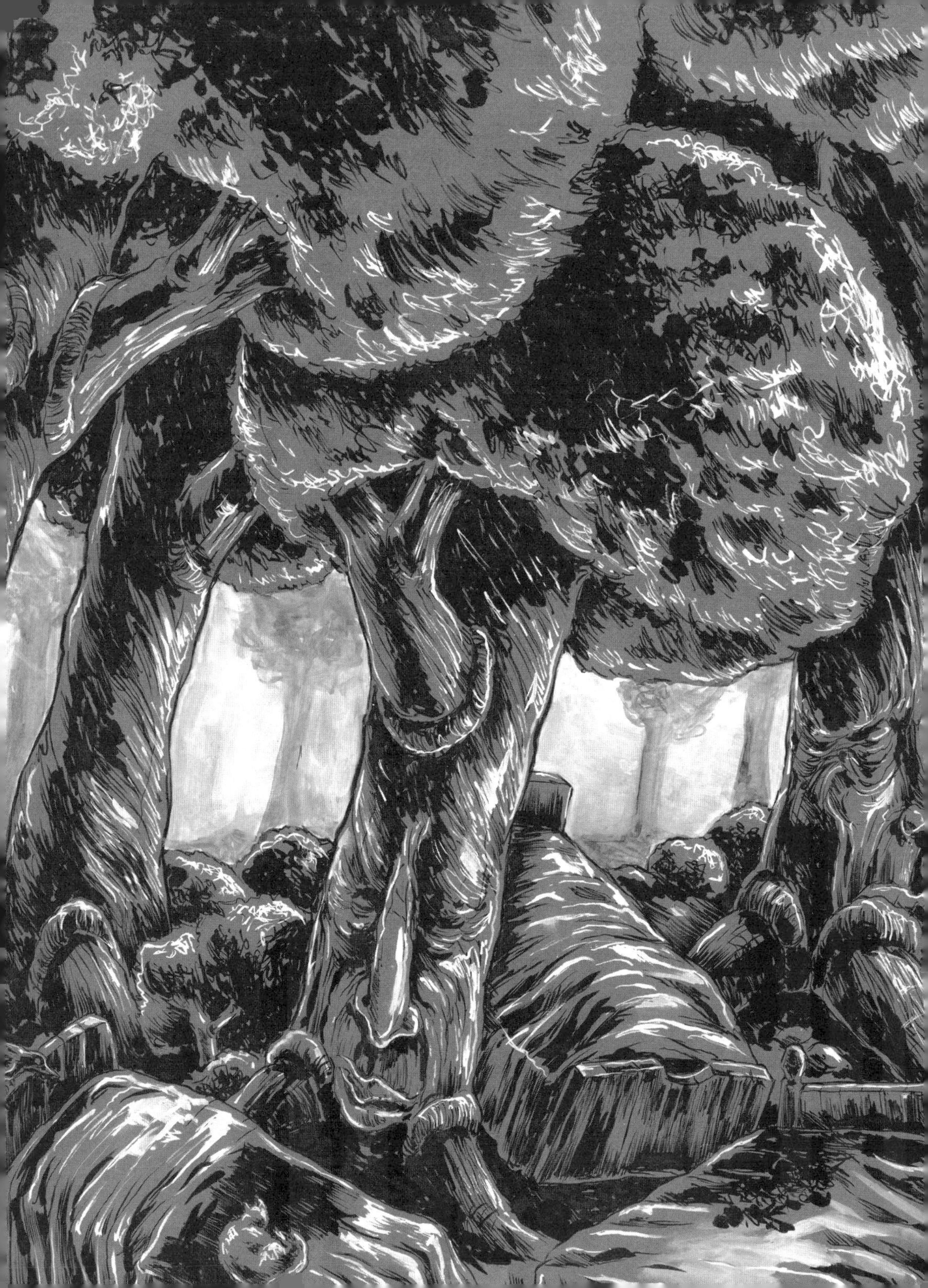

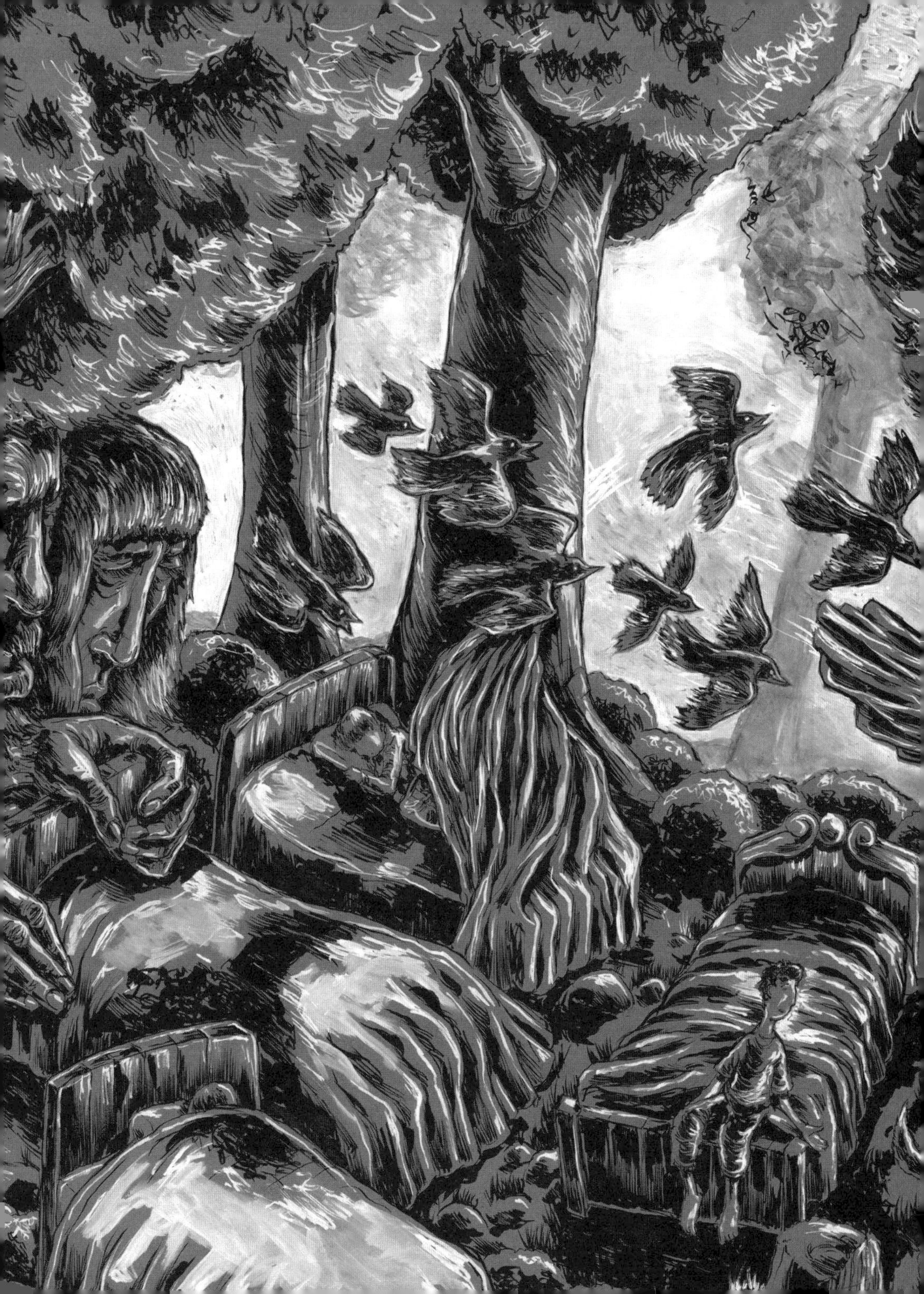

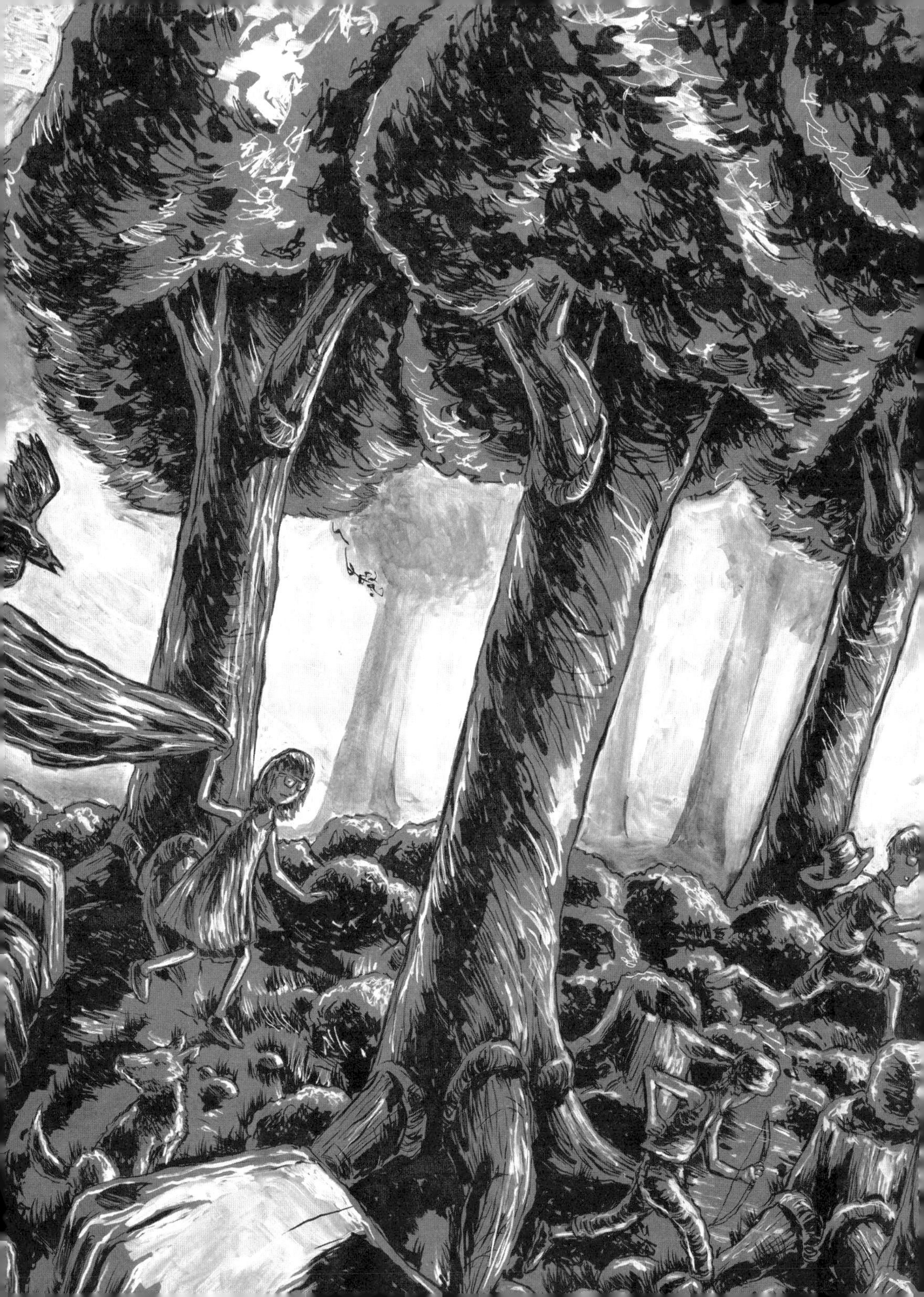

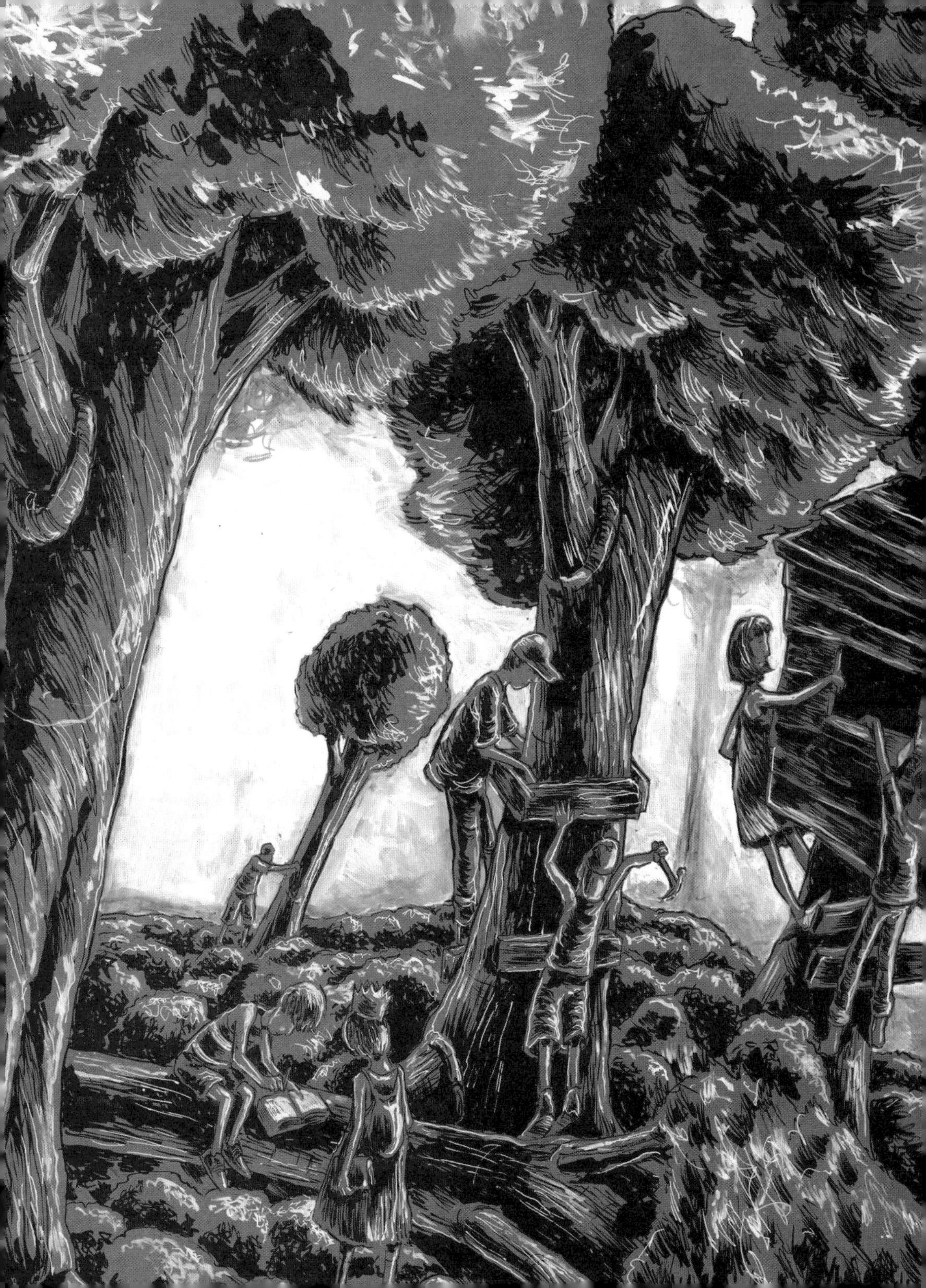

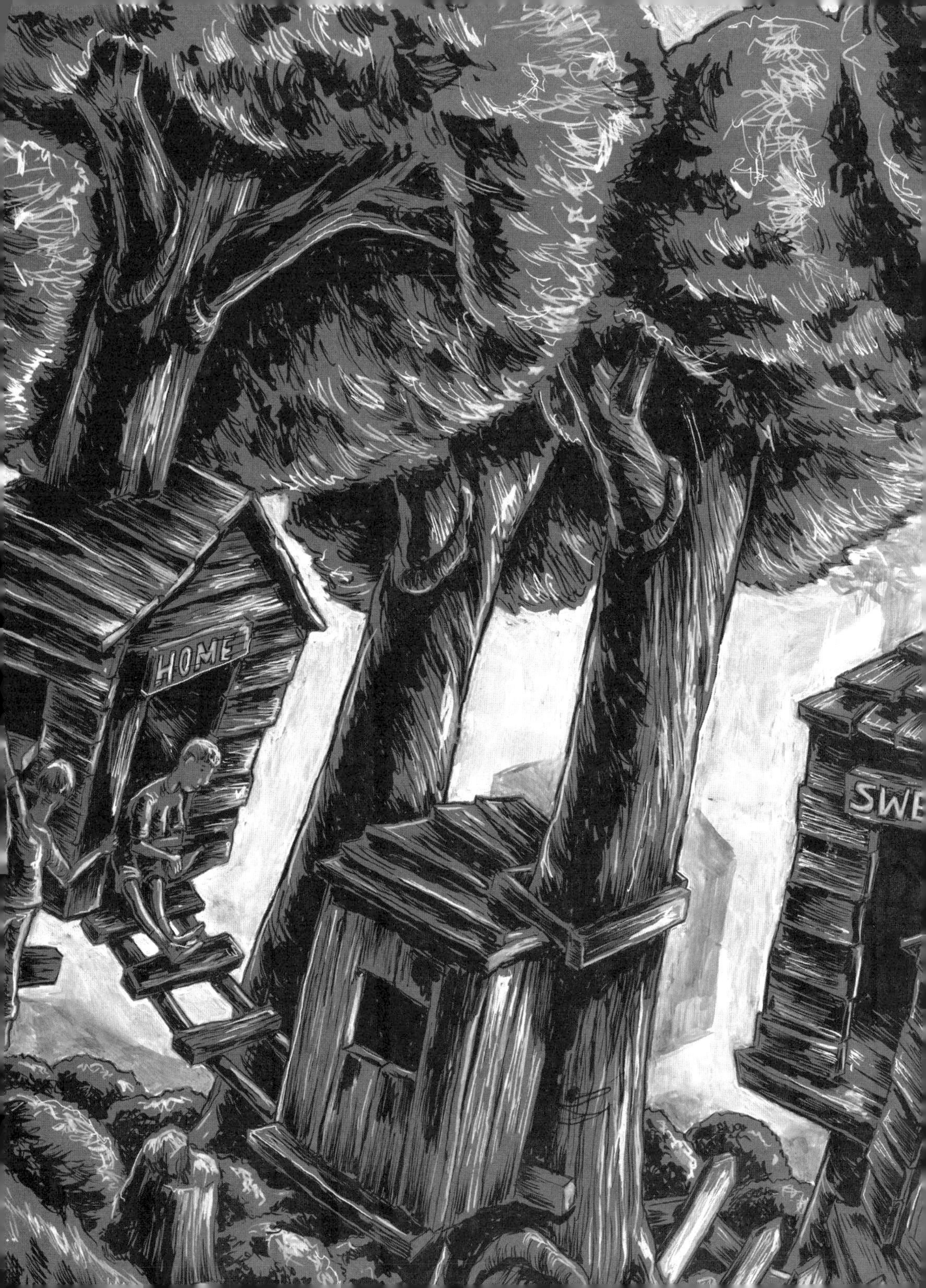
HOME
SWE

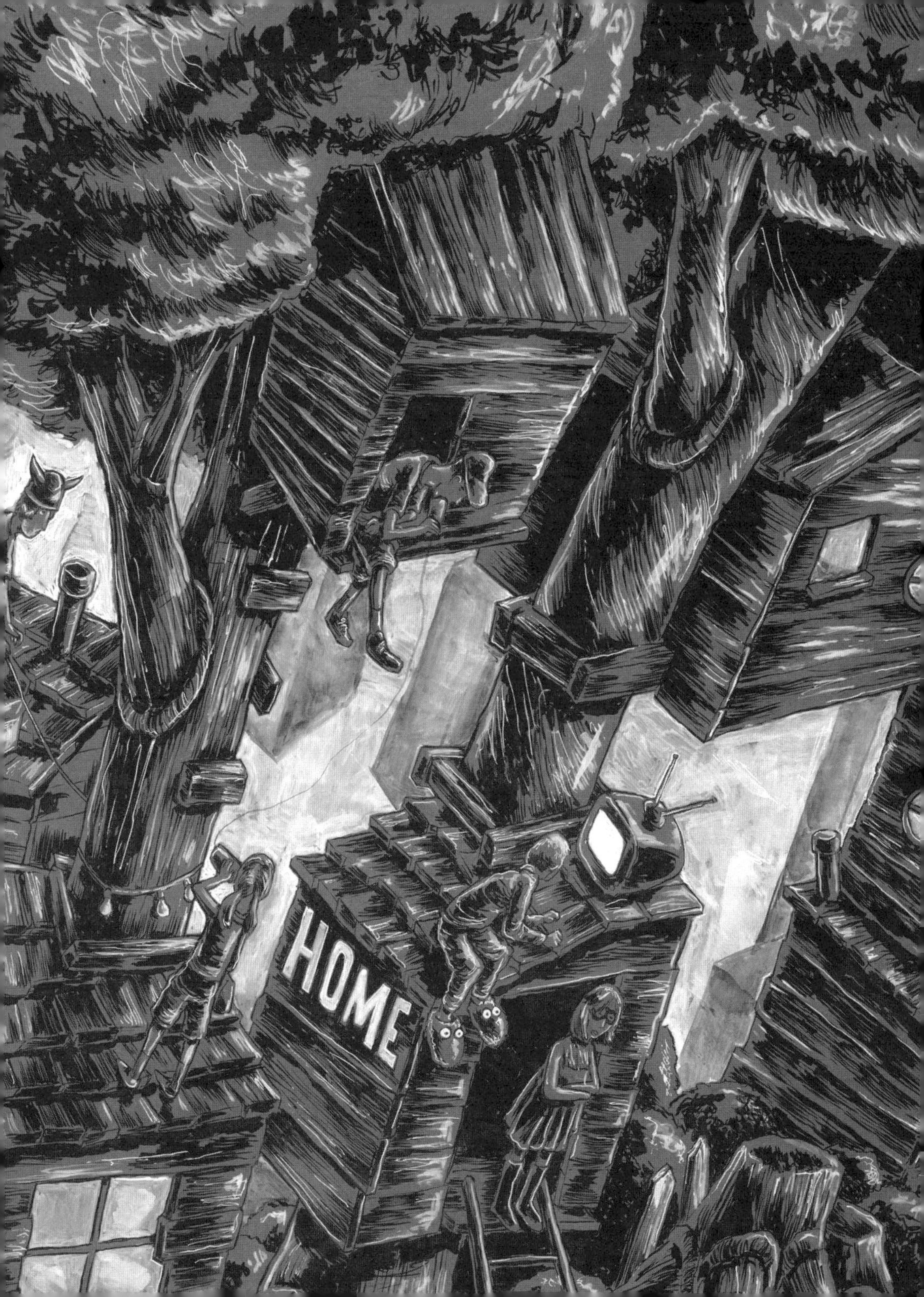
HOME

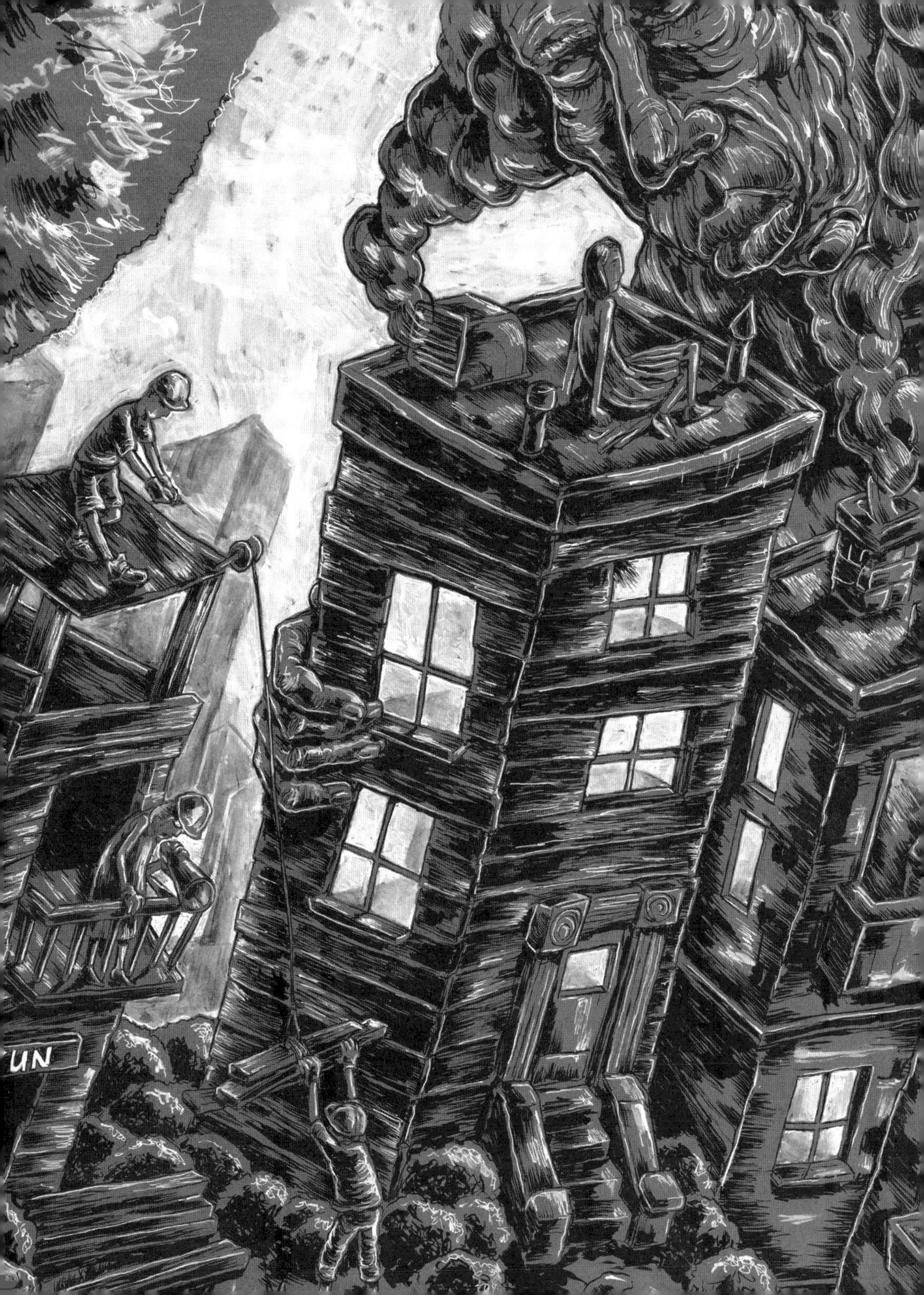
UN

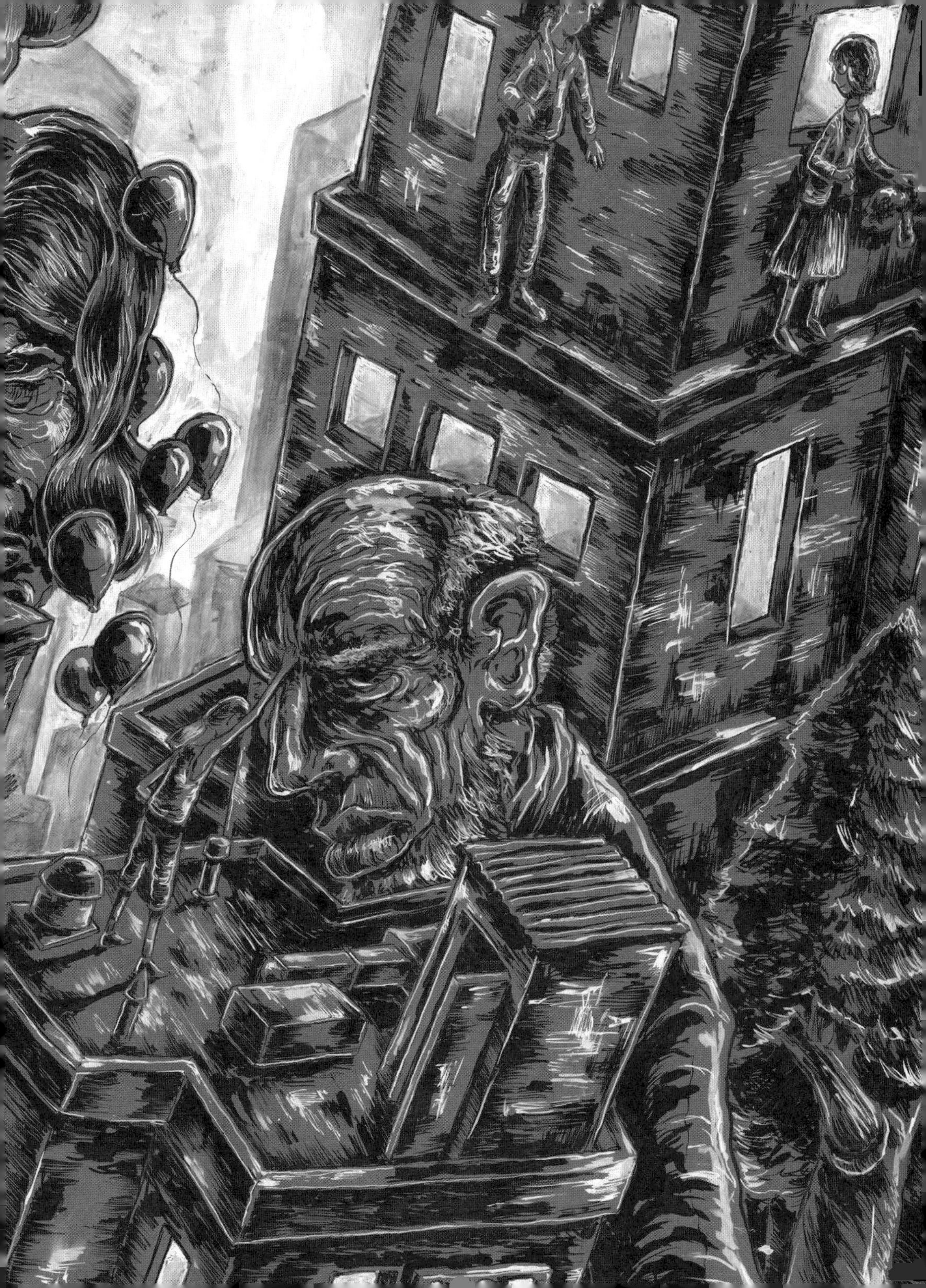

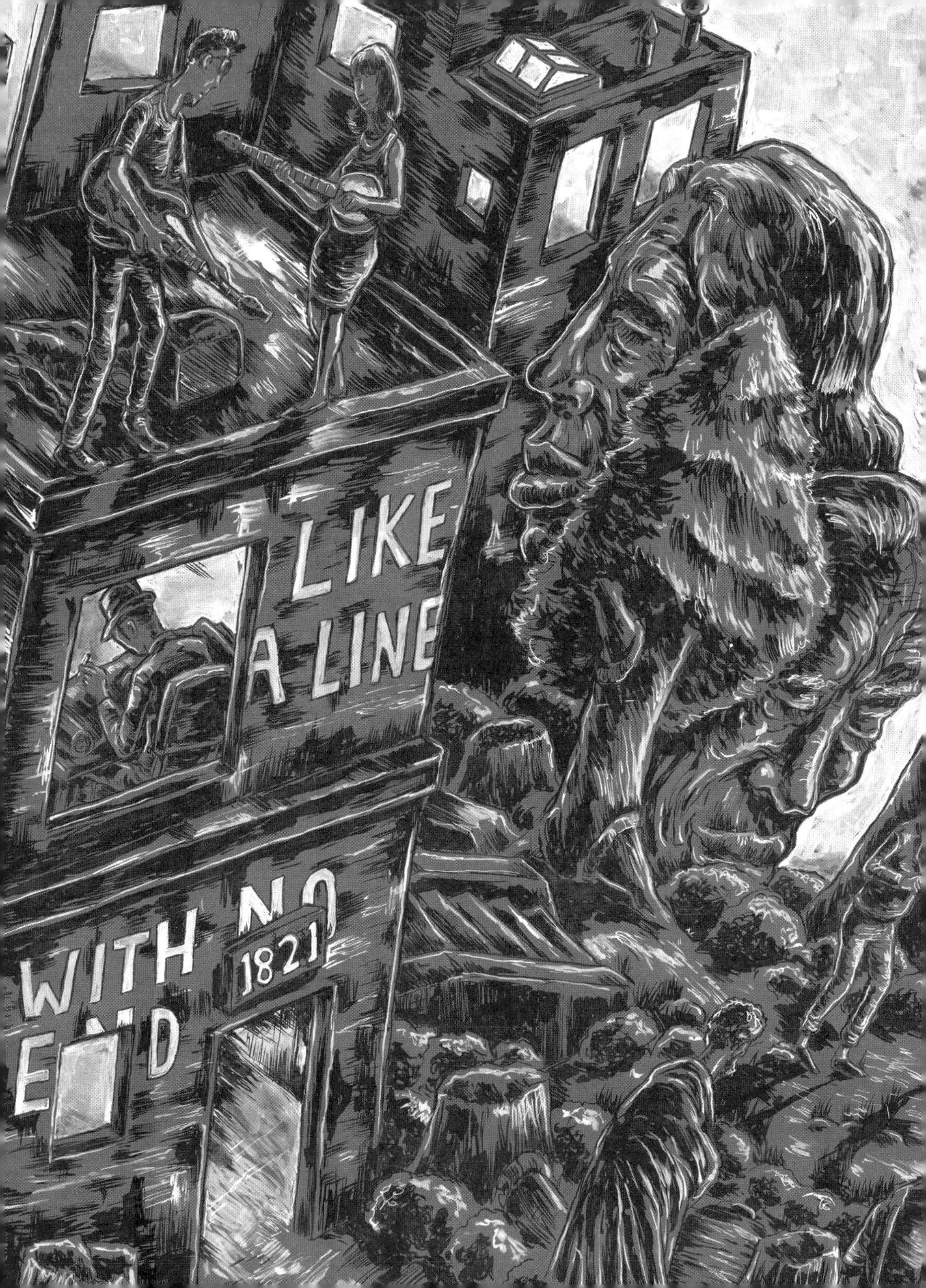

LIKE
A LINE
WITH NO
END
1821

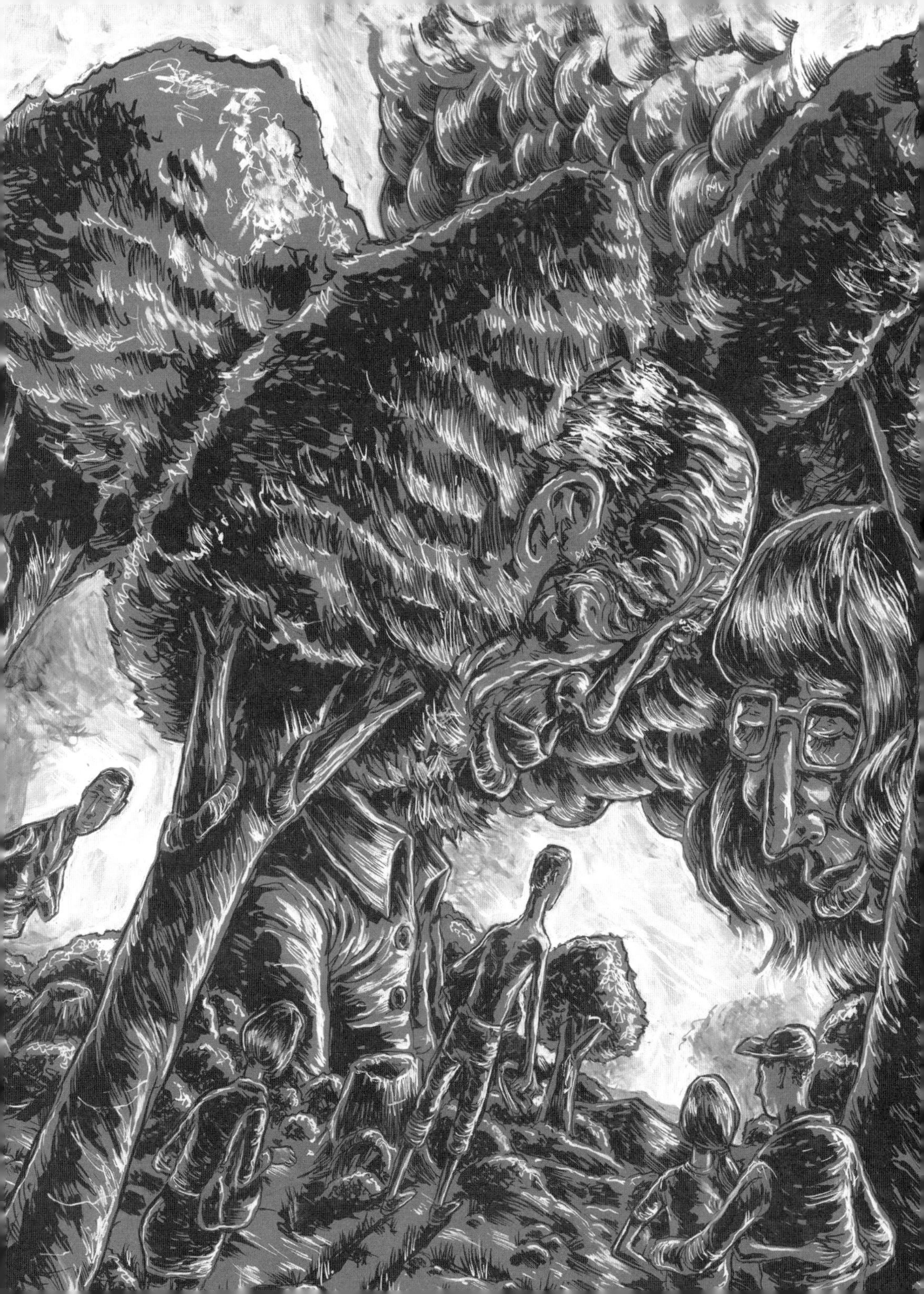

Thanks to Andy Brown,
Priscilla, and my family.